Corporate Bankruptcy in Sudan Law

Abdelrahman Maudawi Abdelrahim Alhadi

Title: **Corporate Bankruptcy in Sudan Law**

ISBN: 979-8-89966-487-8

Author: Abdelrahman Maudawi Abdelrahim Alhadi

Cover image: www.pixabay.com

Publisher: Generis Publishing
Online orders: www.generis-publishing.com
Contact email: info@generis-publishing.com

Generis
PUBLISHING

Author:

Dr. Abdelrahman Mudawi Abdelrahim Alhadi

Corporate Bankruptcy in Sudan Law – Alhadi

Blurb:

This book provides a comprehensive analysis of the legal provisions governing corporate bankruptcy in Sudanese law. It offers a comparative study of international best practices and explores potential reforms to enhance the Sudanese legal framework.

About the Author:

Dr. Abdulrahman Mudawi Abdulrahim Alhadi is a leading expert in corporate law and bankruptcy. He holds a PhD in Law from [University Name] and has extensive experience advising businesses and government agencies on legal matters.

Contents

Dedication

I dedicate this study to the memory of my beloved parents, may Allah envelop them in His vast mercy and grant them the highest place in Paradise. To my gracious wife and dear children, I ask Allah to grant them success and guidance, and to make this humble effort an ongoing charity (ṣadaqah jāriyah) for all of us.

Truly, He is the best of those who are hoped for, and to Him is the rightful path.

Acknowledgment

I extend my highest thanks and appreciation to the University of Gezira, represented by the Faculty of Postgraduate Studies – Department of Private Law, for the support and facilities that greatly contributed to the completion of this study.

I express special gratitude to my esteemed academic supervisors, Professor Jawda Mohamed Ibrahim Al-Nour and Dr. Ali Hussein Al-Gilani, whose commendable efforts in supervising this scholarly work were invaluable. I ask Allah to make their knowledge beneficial to the country and its people, and to reward them abundantly for their guidance, meticulous review, and dedication to refining this research to its intended outcome.

I also express my sincere thanks and appreciation to all my distinguished professors during my undergraduate studies at the University of Neelain and my master's studies at Omdurman Islamic University.

Moreover, I gratefully acknowledge the administrative and academic staff of the University of Gezira, and all those who provided moral support throughout this academic journey.

Abstract

Bankruptcy is regarded as one of the most significant legal mechanisms aimed at balancing the rights of creditors with the protection of defaulting debtors. This is achieved through organized legal procedures that ensure a fair distribution of the bankrupt's assets.

Accordingly, this study seeks to examine the legal provisions governing corporate bankruptcy under Sudanese law. It clarifies the concept and types of bankruptcy and distinguishes between personal and corporate bankruptcy. The study further explores the reasons behind the increasing number of bankruptcy claims, the legal impact of bankruptcy declaration in the context of criminal proceedings against the bankrupt, and the relevant legal controls. It also highlights the legislative framework of bankruptcy in Sudan.

Adopting a descriptive, analytical, and comparative methodology, the study reveals that the Sudanese Companies Act, prior to amendment, was not compliant with Islamic Sharia, allowing the inclusion of interest-bearing financial instruments such as stocks and bonds. Moreover, it did not adequately reflect Sudan's socio-economic needs, nor did it provide clear mechanisms for resolving disputes between shareholders and creditors, leading to persistent ambiguities in some provisions.

The amended law still lacks provisions to prevent bankrupt individuals from leaving the country before settling their financial obligations. It also fails to clearly distinguish between bankruptcy due to force majeure and fraudulent bankruptcy. Current bankruptcy procedures are slow and bureaucratically complex, undermining market stability and investor confidence in the Sudanese legal system.

The study recommends amending the Sudanese Bankruptcy Act of 1929 to align it with modern legal and economic developments. It advocates for simplified procedures to expedite bankruptcy resolutions, thereby contributing to market stability and protecting creditors' rights. Additionally, the state must enforce stringent controls over asset liquidation and ensure that available funds are allocated to debt settlement, preventing the diversion of assets before bankruptcy declaration. Policies for financially rehabilitating bankrupt individuals—such as allowing them to restart post-debt settlement—should also be adopted to foster positive reintegration into the economy.

Introduction

Praise be to Allah, Lord of the Worlds, the Most Gracious, the Most Merciful. May peace and blessings be upon the noblest of prophets and messengers, our Master Muhammad, and upon his family and companions.

Bankruptcy constitutes one of the most significant legal frameworks aimed at balancing the rights of creditors with the protection of financially distressed debtors. This is achieved through structured legal procedures that ensure the equitable distribution of the bankrupt's assets. The system is primarily applicable to traders, whether individuals or corporate entities, who become unable to meet their outstanding financial obligations. In Sudan, bankruptcy cases are governed by specific laws and regulations, whereby bankruptcy is declared pursuant to a judicial decision issued by the competent court, based on a petition submitted by the debtor, a creditor, or a relevant regulatory authority.

Sudanese law classifies companies under the Companies Act of 1925 into several categories: public companies, private companies, partnerships, private concession companies, and companies with national and foreign capital (joint ventures). Although the declaration of bankruptcy serves to safeguard the financial and commercial system, it also entails serious legal consequences, such as the loss of commercial capacity or legal liability in certain cases.

On another note, corporate bankruptcy differs fundamentally from a state's inability to fulfill its financial obligations (State Default). The latter arises when a sovereign fails to meet its financial commitments to international creditors, a situation referred to as Sovereign Default. Although sovereign default does not entail the same legal ramifications faced by individuals or corporations, it significantly impacts the state's credit rating and undermines the confidence of global financial institutions. This, in turn, limits its ability to attract foreign investment and may, in some cases, result in the imposition of financial or political conditions that constrain its economic sovereignty.

Accordingly, this research aims to examine the legal provisions governing corporate bankruptcy in Sudan by analyzing the relevant laws and legislation, while also conducting a comparative study with other legal systems. The research will focus on the effectiveness of these legal frameworks in creating a fair and balanced legal environment for both creditors and bankrupt entities. It will also address the challenges encountered in the implementation of such laws and explore the necessity of legal reforms that align with modern economic and legislative developments.

Significance of the Study

Given the pivotal role that bankruptcy law plays in ensuring a balance between the rights of creditors and the stability of economic activity, this study endeavors to shed light on the legal rules regulating corporate bankruptcy in Sudan and assess their alignment with practical realities and recent legislative developments. The importance of the subject is manifested in the following aspects:

1. The scarcity of legal studies addressing corporate bankruptcy in Sudan, where the issue remains underexplored—particularly considering the continued enforcement of the Bankruptcy Act of 1929, which no longer reflects current economic developments.
2. The noticeable increase in bankruptcy declarations and liquidation proceedings—whether involving individuals or corporate entities—with a recent surge in voluntary and judicial liquidations under the Companies Act of 1925. This trend necessitates a thorough legal examination.
3. The direct legal impact of bankruptcy and liquidation proceedings on creditors' rights, as such actions affect the procedures for debt recovery based on cheques, promissory notes, or bills of exchange. This highlights the need for a detailed analysis of the legislation governing these matters.
4. **Distinction Between Individual and Corporate Bankruptcy:** Individuals are subject to the Bankruptcy Act of 1925, while corporate bankruptcies are governed by the Companies Act of 1929, particularly Articles 148 and onwards. Furthermore, Article 92 of the Bankruptcy Act of 1929 explicitly prohibits the initiation of bankruptcy proceedings against companies registered under the Companies Act. This legal limitation warrants a detailed examination of its implications and legal consequences.
5. **Analysis of the Legal Effects of Company Liquidation:** An in-depth analysis is required of the legal consequences of corporate liquidation under the procedures prescribed by the Companies Act of 1925 (Articles 155–193). This aims to clarify the legal framework governing liquidation following a judicial ruling.
6. **Differentiation Between Liquidation Due to Insolvency and Bankruptcy Proceedings:**
   There exists a fundamental distinction between liquidation initiated due to insolvency and formal bankruptcy proceedings, in terms of both legal framework and resulting implications. Hence, it is imperative to identify the essential differences between the two.

7. **Assessment of the Legal and Economic Impact of Bankruptcy:** A comprehensive evaluation is necessary regarding the economic and legal effects of bankruptcy on the bankrupt company, its creditors, and other liable parties. This analysis will contribute to assessing the effectiveness of the existing legal frameworks in protecting rights and ensuring fairness among the involved parties.
8. **Identification of Legal Gaps in Sudanese Bankruptcy Law:** This study aims to uncover deficiencies in the current Sudanese bankruptcy legislation and offer proposals for reform to align it with modern economic and legal developments. Such reforms are vital to establishing a more equitable and stable legal environment.
9. **Analysis of Procedural Stages of Bankruptcy:** A detailed examination will be conducted on the procedural stages of bankruptcy as stipulated in Sudanese legislation, particularly the Bankruptcy Act of 1929 and the Civil Procedure Act of 1986, to evaluate their adequacy in safeguarding the rights of both creditors and debtors.

Research Problem

Commercial transactions—especially within the corporate sector—have undergone substantial developments, complicating the legal framework governing them. With companies now recognized as separate legal entities possessing independent financial liability distinct from that of their partners, the personal assets of shareholders are shielded beyond their capital contributions. This evolution has given rise to several legal challenges, particularly concerning bankruptcy and liquidation procedures and their respective consequences.

In light of the rising number of bankruptcy declarations—whether genuine or as a means of evading financial obligations—a series of pressing legal questions emerge, necessitating thorough research and analysis. These include:

1. What are the underlying reasons behind the recent surge in bankruptcy filings?
2. Does the declaration of bankruptcy halt criminal proceedings against the bankrupt party, and what are the legal conditions governing this?
3. To what extent is the bankruptcy regime being exploited by companies as a mechanism to evade criminal liability?
4. What is the legal distinction between cessation of payment and refusal to fulfill financial obligations, and what are the legal consequences of each?
5. Is a bankrupt trader or company permitted to resume commercial activity after bankruptcy has been declared, and what legal restrictions apply in this regard?

This study seeks to offer a rigorous legal analysis addressing these questions by reviewing the legislative framework governing bankruptcy in Sudan and comparing it with other legal systems. The objective is to identify legislative shortcomings and assess the impact of the current legal framework on the broader legal and economic environment.

Previous Studies

A review of the available literature on *bankruptcy in Sudanese law* reveals that, while these studies have addressed the topic comprehensively, most have predominantly focused on corporate provisions without giving due attention to certain fundamental aspects—particularly the Companies Act of 2015. The following are the most notable related studies:

1. **Ilham Saleh Ahmed Ibrahim**, *"The Bankruptcy System in Sudanese Law (A Comparative Study)"*
   This study examined the bankruptcy system in Sudan in comparison with other legal systems. However, it did not offer a detailed analysis of the 2015 Sudanese Companies Act.
2. **Zubeida Abdelhadi Atim Mohamed Ahmed El-Neel**, *"Bankruptcy Declaration and Its Legal Effects in Sudanese and Egyptian Law (A Comparative Study)"* – University of Al-Neelain
   The study presented a comparative view between Sudanese and Egyptian laws regarding the effects of a bankruptcy ruling, but it lacked a focused analysis of the 2015 Companies Act.
3. **Maha Abdelrahman Al-Mubarak Abu Shama**, *"Bankruptcy and Insolvency in Jurisprudence and Judiciary"*
   A partial thesis submitted for a master's degree, which focused on the distinctions between bankruptcy and insolvency but did not explore the specific legal implications of bankruptcy for companies.
4. **Ibtisam Al-Sayed Hassan**, *"Bankruptcy in Law Compared with Islamic Jurisprudence"* – University of Khartoum, 1999
   This study presented a comparison between Sudanese bankruptcy law and Islamic jurisprudence but did not examine the Companies Act of 2015.
5. **Shawqi Adam Abdullah Sabeel**, *"The Effects of Bankruptcy Declaration in Jurisprudence and Law (A Comparative Study)"* – University of Al-Neelain, 2017

The study concentrated on the legal and jurisprudential effects of bankruptcy declaration but fell short of sufficiently addressing bankruptcy within the corporate framework

Points of Distinction Between the Current Study and Previous Studies

1. Legal Modernization:

This study distinguishes itself by focusing on the 2015 Companies Act, which has not been addressed in detail in the previous literature.

2. Detailed Impact on Companies:

The present research emphasizes the legal consequences of bankruptcy on companies, while many earlier studies focused primarily on individuals or general aspects.

3. Research Contribution:

Unlike studies limited to comparisons with Egyptian law or Islamic jurisprudence, this research offers a critical analysis of the deficiencies within the Sudanese bankruptcy system and proposes legal reforms.

In conclusion, this study aims to provide a substantial contribution to the interpretation and application of bankruptcy law in Sudan. It particularly highlights the provisions of the 2015 Companies Act and assesses its effects on companies and creditors. The study aspires to enhance legal understanding and promote a more equitable and stable legislative environment.

Conclusion

This section presents the key findings and recommendations of the study.

Key Findings:

- The Bankruptcy Act excludes companies from its provisions, as company liquidation is governed by the Companies Act.
- The legal system relies on a civil bankruptcy model that does not distinguish between merchant and non-merchant debtors, enumerating the causes of bankruptcy declaration exhaustively.
- The law identifies specific acts as bankruptcy crimes and grants civil courts broad authority in adjudicating such matters.
- Procedures tend to be prolonged to facilitate potential settlements between debtor and creditors prior to the declaration of bankruptcy.

Chapter One: The Concept, Types, Essential Elements, Legal Personality, and Dissolution of a Company

Section One: The Concept of a Company in Islamic Jurisprudence and Law

Subsection One: Definition of a Company—Linguistic, Juristic, and Legal Perspective

First: Linguistic and Terminological Definition

According to *Taj al-'Arus*, the Arabic term *sharika* (company or partnership) is derived from the verb *sharika*—meaning "to share or associate." It appears in three phonetic forms: *sharika* (with a fatḥa), *shirka* (with a kasra), and *sharaka* (with a sukun on the rā'). The core meaning revolves around *intermingling* and *joint participation*. It may refer to the blending of ownership, shared activity, or a mutual undertaking between two or more parties.

The term is used in the Qur'an in several contexts denoting shared ownership or mutual involvement. For example:

- **"But if there are more than two, they shall share in a third."** (Surah Al-Nisa: 12)
- **"And share with them in wealth and children."** (Surah Al-Isra: 64)
- **"And let him share with me in my task."** (Surah Taha: 32)
- And also in the sense of "mixing":
  "Verily, many partners oppress one another." (Surah Sad: 24), where *khulata'* refers to partners.

Hence, from a linguistic standpoint, *sharika* implies a condition of plurality and joint ownership or effort in a shared matter.

Second: The Concept of a Company in Islamic Jurisprudence

In Islamic jurisprudence (*fiqh*), a *contract of partnership ('aqd al-sharika)* is defined as an agreement between two or more individuals to combine their capital or labor in pursuit of a common objective, primarily profit generation.

As defined by Ibn Qudamah:

"Partnership is an agreement between two or more parties to pool their assets for a common financial gain."

The classification of partnerships in Islamic jurisprudence depends on the nature of the contribution by the partners and the type of ownership involved. The principal types include:

1. Partnership of Capital (Sharikat al-Amwāl):

Where each partner contributes funds, which are collectively invested for profit.

2. Partnership of Labor (Sharikat al-Abdān):

Partners contribute labor or services instead of capital and share profits accordingly.

3. Partnership of Reputation or Credit (Sharikat al-Wujūh):

Established on mutual trust, this type involves partners relying on their reputation to engage in commercial transactions on credit, sharing profits without initial capital.

4. Silent Partnership (Sharikat al-Muḍārabah):

Involves one partner (rab al-mal) providing the capital, while the other (muḍārib) contributes effort or expertise. Profits are distributed as per agreement.

Third: Classification by Ownership and Nature of the Contract

Islamic jurisprudence further categorizes partnerships as follows:

A. Partnership by Permission (Sharikat al-Ibāḥa):

This refers to commonly accessible resources, which the public may utilize equally, such as water, pasture, or fire. As per the hadith:

"The Muslims are partners in three things: water, pasture, and fire." These become private property only upon lawful possession, as illustrated by the hadith:
"Whoever takes possession of something no one has possessed before has a stronger claim to it."

B. Partnership by Ownership (Sharikat al-Milk):

This can arise:

- **Voluntarily:** Through mutual agreement (e.g., co-purchase).
- **Involuntarily:** By operation of law (e.g., inheritance or wills), without a prior act of the parties.

C. Partnership by Contract (Sharikat al-'Aqd):

A formal agreement concluded between two or more parties to collaborate commercially, which is the most common type in modern transactions.

Conclusion of the Subsection:

Islamic jurisprudence provides a comprehensive and nuanced understanding of partnerships, differentiating them based on the nature of the contribution, source of ownership, and form of agreement. This framework not only encompasses financial dimensions but also considers social and ethical contexts, thereby offering a flexible legal structure responsive to both historical and contemporary commercial realities.

Continuing Subsection One: The Concept of a Company in Islamic Jurisprudence and Law

Partnerships based on labor and mutual trust—such as *Sharikat al-Abdan* (partnership of bodies/labor) and *Sharikat al-Wujuh* (partnership of reputation)—demonstrate the flexibility of Islamic jurisprudence in its conceptualization of partnership. This juristic flexibility makes the Islamic concept of partnership more comprehensive than many modern legal conceptions, which tend to focus primarily on financial and commercial dimensions.

The researcher notes that the traditional Islamic classification of partnerships into *Sharikat al-Ibaha* (partnership of common utility), *Sharikat al-Milk* (co-ownership), and *Sharikat al-'Aqd* (contractual partnership) reflects a profound understanding of property in Islamic law. Islamic jurists carefully distinguish between public, shared, and private ownership, assigning distinct legal rulings to each.

For instance, *Sharikat al-Ibaha* reflects the principle of collective benefit from natural resources such as water, pasture, and fire—resources whose use may not be monopolized, as emphasized in various Prophetic traditions. This classification underscores the social and ethical dimension of Islamic legislation, emphasizing communal access and equitable distribution of resources.

On the other hand, *Sharikat al-Milk* refers to co-ownership of property that may arise either voluntarily, through deliberate acts (such as joint acquisition), or involuntarily, such as through inheritance. This reflects Islamic law's nuanced approach to ownership, which seeks to strike a balance between individual and collective interests.

Sharikat al-'Aqd, or contractual partnership, most closely resembles the modern concept of commercial companies. It is based on the mutual consent of parties to establish a legal relationship governed by reciprocal obligations. However, the researcher observes that, despite offering detailed legal rulings regarding partnerships, Islamic jurisprudence did not develop organizational structures comparable to modern joint-stock companies. Traditional Islamic partnerships remained largely within the framework of personal or general partnerships.

In light of these distinctions, the researcher highlights the need for contemporary studies that bridge classical juristic principles with modern corporate legal frameworks. Such studies are essential in addressing the realities of corporate governance in the Muslim world, especially in jurisdictions with codified commercial laws—such as Sudan's Companies Act of 2015.

This research aims to provide a comparative analysis between classical Islamic rulings and contemporary legal regulations, exploring the extent to which modern legal frameworks align with Islamic principles in the governance and management of companies.

Definition of a Company in Islamic Jurisprudence

From a terminological perspective, some jurists did not provide a comprehensive definition of *sharika* (company) in its general sense. Rather, the majority referred to it as a specific type of contract, even when no actual intermingling of assets occurred—since the contract itself constitutes the cause of such mixing. Given the diversity in types and legal rulings, juristic definitions vary by school of thought:

Maliki Definition:

The Malikis define partnership as:

"Authorization for two individuals to transact jointly on their own behalf—i.e., each partner grants the other the right to dispose of jointly owned property while retaining their own rights of disposition."

They also describe it as:

"The stabilization of a proprietary interest between two or more owners in a valuable item."

This implies the establishment of joint ownership in something of monetary value between two or more persons, where each partner has the right to manage the asset as an owner. The Maliki definition further states:

"That which is created by choice between two or more persons through commingling of property to obtain profit—and may also arise involuntarily, such as through inheritance."

This inclusive definition encompasses both voluntary partnerships (contractual) and involuntary ones (ownership-based), thus covering all categories of partnership.

Hanafi Definition:

The Hanafis define a partnership as:

"A contract between two or more persons involving the sharing of capital and profit."

This is considered the most precise definition, as it captures the legal nature of *sharika* as a contract. Other definitions focus more on the objectives or legal consequences of the partnership, such as:

"The mutual entitlement of two or more individuals to a single object."

This broader interpretation includes any form of joint interest in a subject matter—whether physical property, debt, reputation, labor, or otherwise—thus encompassing all categories of partnership under Islamic law.

Shafi'i Definition:

According to the Shafi'i school:

"Partnership is the mutual entitlement of two or more persons to a thing by way of joint ownership."

This definition also appears comprehensive, covering all types of partnerships. The phrase "mutual entitlement in one thing" includes various forms of co-ownership, such as inheritance, gift, bequest, or spoils of war. The inclusion of "a contract that entails such an arrangement" brings into scope the different contractual partnerships, including *'Inan*, *Mufawada*, *Wujuh*, *Abdan*, *Amwal*, and *Mudharaba*, regardless of their legal validity according to each school.

Thus, these definitions demonstrate that Islamic jurisprudence provides a holistic framework for understanding and regulating partnerships, addressing both voluntary and involuntary forms of ownership and collaboration.

Hanbali Definition of Partnership:

The Hanbali school defines partnership as:

"Union in entitlement or disposition."

This definition is comprehensive, encompassing all categories of partnership: *Sharikat al-Ibaha* (partnership of usage), *Sharikat al-Milk* (co-ownership), and *Sharikat al-'Aqd* (contractual partnership). The "union in entitlement" includes entitlement to the corpus (*'ayn*) of an object—whether through permissible use (*ibaha*), gift, inheritance, purchase, spoils of war, or bequest—and makes no distinction between whether the partners jointly own the property, its usufruct, or one without the other. The definition also covers more nuanced scenarios, such as joint liability in cases like defamation: for instance, if two persons jointly own a slave and the slave is insulted by another person, the punishment is applied as if one entity is offended.

Moreover, "union in disposition" encompasses all forms of contractual partnerships, including partnerships in capital (*Sharikat al-Amwal*), reputation (*Sharikat al-Wujuh*), labor (*Sharikat al-Abdan*), or a combination of capital and labor—as in *Mudharabah* (trust-based investment partnership).

Discussion and Analysis of Definitions:

Despite the apparent inclusivity of the aforementioned juristic definitions, upon close examination, they reveal certain limitations in capturing the overarching essence and comprehensive conceptualization of partnership.

For example, the Hanbalis emphasize contractual partnerships in their definition, highlighting the permissibility of the partners' actions under the contract without addressing how the partnership itself is constituted.

The Shafi'i jurists, by contrast, focus on the establishment of joint rights resulting from the contract, without giving due attention to the mechanisms of transaction, investment, or profit-seeking. Their framework treats co-ownership (*Sharikat al-Milk*) as the foundational type, with contractual partnerships (*Sharikat al-'Aqd*) as a derivative form. Furthermore, according to their view, explicit permission is required for transactions involving company assets—mere statements such as "we have formed a partnership" are insufficient, as they may be interpreted as descriptive rather than constitutive.

Both the Hanafi and Maliki schools based their definitions on juristic consequences and legal presumptions rather than providing a precise, universal conceptualization. Many of their jurists elaborated on the types and classifications of partnerships without offering a general, comprehensive definition.

In light of the above, the researcher observes that the multiplicity of definitions reflects the diversity of juristic perspectives concerning partnership. Nonetheless, the Hanafi definition is regarded as the most comprehensive and precise. They define a partnership as:

"Union in entitlement or disposition."

This definition is notable for encompassing all forms of partnerships, as it includes:

- **Union in entitlement** (*ijtima' fi al-istihqaq*), which applies to *Sharikat al-Milk* (co-ownership).
- **Union in disposition** (*ijtima' fi al-tasarruf*), which applies to *Sharikat al-'Aqd*, wherein two or more parties agree to jointly manage and profit from an investment. Such partnerships are categorized as:
  - **Capital-based partnerships** (*Sharikat al-Amwal*): sharing both capital and profit.
  - **Mudharabah (Qirad)**: a profit-sharing contract where one party provides capital and the other contributes labor or expertise.
  - Sometimes, such arrangements may be referred to more generally as "mu'amalat" (financial dealings).

Legal Foundations for the Legitimacy of Partnerships in Islamic Law:

The legitimacy of partnership is established through evidence from the Qur'an, Sunnah, scholarly consensus (*ijma'*), and reason (*ma'qul*), according to the majority of jurists.

From the Qur'an:

Allah Almighty says:

"He sets forth for you a parable from your own selves: Do you have among those whom your right hands possess any partners in what We have provided for you, such that you are equal therein, fearing them as you fear one another?" **(Surah Ar-Rum: 28)**

This verse presents a rhetorical parable illustrating the irrationality of associating partners with Allah by highlighting how people would not accept such partnership in their own wealth. The verse implies that just as people reject sharing their wealth with their servants as equals, it is even more inconceivable to attribute partners to Allah in His dominion.

Some scholars interpret this verse as a fundamental textual basis (*asl*) for the permissibility of partnerships among human beings. They argue that it demonstrates the human need for cooperation and shared ownership due to mutual dependence in managing wealth and economic resources. By contrast, Allah—the Eternal, Self-Sufficient—transcends any need for partnership, which presupposes mutual support.

Thus, if such partnerships are rejected between a servant and his master in matters of ownership, it is even more inappropriate to posit any form of partnership with Allah in His actions or attributes. The theological message here implies that partnership necessarily involves need and collaboration—attributes that are incompatible with divine perfection. However, for humans, who are inherently dependent on one another, partnership in wealth and commerce is a logical and necessary arrangement.

Evidences for the Legitimacy of Partnerships in Islamic Law

1. From the Qur'an:

- **Inheritance of *Kalalah*:**

Allah the Exalted says:

"And if a man or a woman leaves neither ascendants nor descendants but has a brother or a sister, then each one of them receives a sixth. But if they are more than two, they share a third..."

(Surah An-Nisa: 12)

This verse pertains to inheritance in the case of *kalalah*—a person who dies leaving neither parents nor children. If the deceased leaves siblings from the mother, each receives a sixth. If they are more than two, they equally share one-third. This establishes the concept of **co-ownership in inheritance** (*sharikat al-milk fil-irth*) among maternal siblings, as they are described as *partners in one-third*, signifying joint entitlement and equal distribution.

- **Mixing with Orphans**:

Allah Almighty says:

"They ask you about the orphans. Say: Improvement for them is best; and if you mix your affairs with theirs, then they are your brothers. And Allah knows the corrupter from the reformer."

(Surah Al-Baqarah: 220)

This verse permits **mixing with orphans**, which may include joint consumption and management of food and property. Some jurists infer from this that **joint participation (partnership)** in food and resources is permissible, especially when motivated by care, kinship, or shared religious duty. The verse reflects the principle of ease and mercy in financial dealings, particularly where vulnerability exists.

- **Story of the Partners in the Time of Prophet David (Dāwūd):** Allah says:

"Indeed, many partners wrong one another, except those who believe and do righteous deeds – and few are they."

(Surah Ṣād: 24)

The term *khulata'* in this verse refers to **partners in ownership or enterprise**. Though the verse recounts a situation from the time of Prophet David (peace be upon him), many jurists who accept *Shar'u man qablana* (the laws of previous prophets) as binding unless abrogated, cite this as supporting evidence for the **legitimacy and historical continuity of partnerships**. The verse not only affirms the existence of partnerships but also recognizes the ethical challenges they may entail, emphasizing justice and righteousness among partners.

2. From the Sunnah:

- **Divine Statement (Hadith Qudsi):**

"Allah says: I am the third of two partners as long as one does not betray the other. If one of them betrays his partner, I depart from between them." (Narrated by Abu Huraira)

This hadith affirms the **permissibility of partnership** and highlights the **spiritual dimension** of honesty and trust in such relationships. It suggests divine support and blessing in partnerships founded upon integrity, while warning that betrayal negates this divine presence. The hadith serves as both a **legal and moral foundation** for partnership contracts.

- **Partnership of the Prophet (peace be upon him) Before Prophethood:**

It is reported that **Al-Sā'ib al-Makhzūmī** said: "I was the partner of the Prophet (peace be upon him) before the Prophethood. On the Day of the Conquest (of Makkah), the Prophet said to me: *'Welcome, my brother and my partner. You used to never dispute nor deceive.'*"

This statement validates the **pre-Islamic practice of partnerships**, which was later confirmed by Islam without objection. It also reflects the Prophet's endorsement of ethical business conduct, further legitimizing partnerships as a socially accepted and religiously sanctioned form of transaction.

3. Scholarly Consensus and Rational Justification:

- **Consensus (*Ijmā'*):**

Muslim jurists have reached a consensus on the **general permissibility of partnerships**, though they may differ regarding specific types or contractual forms.

- **Rational Justification (*Ma'qūl*):**

Partnerships are founded on rational principles that promote cooperation and mutual assistance in achieving shared economic goals. Islam encourages social solidarity and ease in transactions, as reflected in the Qur'anic verse:

"He has not placed upon you in the religion any hardship."

(Surah Al-Hajj: 78)

And:

"Allah intends for you ease and does not intend for you hardship."

(Surah Al-Baqarah: 185)

And in the saying of the Prophet (peace be upon him):

"The religion most beloved to Allah is the easy and tolerant one (al-ḥanīfiyya al-samḥā')."

In line with this holistic vision, Islamic law recognizes various **contracts and financial dealings** that serve human needs, such as **sales, leases, partnerships, and *muḍārabah*** (profit-sharing investment). These contracts facilitate lawful earnings and reflect a practical application of divine guidance in economic life.

Researcher's Perspective:

Based on the evidence from the Qur'an, Sunnah, and juristic consensus, the researcher affirms that **partnerships in Islam are not only permitted but encouraged**, as they reflect the values of cooperation (*ta'āwun*) and social solidarity (*takāful*). Islam views partnership as a **practical instrument** for wealth development, enabling joint investment of capital and labor for mutual benefit.

The researcher argues that **Islamic partnership law aligns with the objectives of Sharī'ah (Maqāṣid al-Sharī'ah)**—particularly in preserving and developing wealth (*ḥifẓ al-māl*). This is evident in Allah's command:

"And cooperate in righteousness and piety..."

(Surah Al-Mā'idah: 2)

Partnerships thus offer a legitimate and effective means to invest wealth, create jobs, and stabilize the Islamic economy.

Moreover, partnerships promote **economic inclusion**, allowing individuals with limited capital or expertise to participate in large-scale ventures. This supports **wealth redistribution** and reduces concentration of resources in the hands of a few. It also **prevents hoarding** of wealth by encouraging its productive use through investment.

The researcher further opines that **partnership with non-Muslims is permissible**, provided they do not unilaterally manage the business in ways that contravene Islamic law—such as engaging in *ribā* (usury), fraud, or trade in prohibited items (e.g., alcohol, pork). This reflects the **flexibility and openness** of Islamic economic law, which accommodates cross-cultural collaboration within a framework of ethical constraints.

In conclusion, the researcher sees the Islamic concept of partnership as a dynamic and comprehensive model that not only drives economic development but also fulfills higher Sharī'ah objectives. It fosters collaboration, productivity, and equitable distribution, making it a cornerstone of a just and prosperous society.

Section Two: Capital Companies in Islamic Jurisprudence

The concept of capital companies in Islamic jurisprudence is based on an agreement between two or more persons to jointly invest money and engage in trade, where they agree to buy and sell goods together or leave the type of commercial activity open without specifying it, with the condition of sharing profits according to a specified agreement. One party may initiate the partnership offer, which the other may accept verbally or by action.

Capital companies are divided into two main types:

1. **Shirka al-'Inan (Partnership of Effort and Capital)**
2. **Shirka al-Mufawada (Partnership of Negotiation/Agreement)**

Shirka al-'Inan (Partnership of Effort and Capital):

This is when two men contribute their money to work in it and share the profit between them. It is called 'Inan because they are equal in money and management, like two horsemen who equalize their reins and ride together; their reins ('inān) are equal. It is also said that it comes from each partner "leaning" ('anna) to share with the other. Another explanation is that it is derived from *al-mu'ānana* (opposition), where one opposes the other with equal money and effort — each partner opposes the other with his capital and actions.

This type of company is unanimously considered permissible by scholars and is the most common form among people. In Shirka al-'Inan, equality in capital or management is not required. One partner's capital may be greater than the other's, and one may be responsible for the management while the other is not. They may share profits equally or unequally, based on the agreement they make. However, losses are borne only in proportion to the capital invested, according to the principle:
"Profit is according to what is stipulated, and loss is according to the amount of the two capitals."

Conditions for the Validity of Shirka al-'Inan according to the Hanafis:

1. **The subject of the contract must be capable of agency:**

Since the rule of partnership is the shared benefit derived from trade, and the benefit is only truly shared if each partner is an agent (wakil) for the other over half the capital and principal. Therefore, each partner is an agent for the other by virtue of the partnership contract. The partnership is invalid in transactions that do not allow agency, such as gathering firewood, hunting, and fishing, where ownership remains with the person who physically performs the act.

2. **Profit must be a known proportion:**

Each partner's share of the profit must be a known ratio, such as one-fifth or one-tenth. If the profit share is unknown, the partnership is void because the subject matter of the contract (the profit) must be definite; uncertainty invalidates the contract.

3. **Profit must be a common undivided share, not a fixed amount:**

If a fixed profit amount is specified, like ten or one hundred, the partnership is invalid. The contract requires that profit be shared in a way that reflects the actual result, and assigning a fixed sum could lead to one partner receiving all the profit even if it's less than that, which contradicts the nature of the partnership contract. These three conditions apply to all contract-based partnerships.

4. **The capital must be present and in kind at the time of purchase:**

The capital cannot be a debt or absent money, because the purpose of the partnership is profit through trade, which requires a present capital. Profit depends on managing actual capital, and managing absent money is impossible. Also, a debtor may fail to pay, and a partner may be unable to bring absent capital.

For example, if one person gives another 1,000 dirhams and says, "Go buy and sell with the same amount, and we will share the profit equally," and the other does so and provides proof, the partnership is valid. What matters is the presence of the capital at the time of purchase, not at the time of the contract, as the partnership takes effect at the purchase.

Mixing the capitals is not required because the partnership includes agency. Whatever is valid for agency is valid for partnership. Agency is permissible over two capitals before mixing, so the same applies to partnership. Scholars say that what is lost before mixing belongs solely to its owner since the partnership is not complete until purchase; what is lost before that does not count. But if loss occurs after purchase by one partner, it is shared between the capitals since the contract is complete.

5. **Capital must be in absolute money — which is not specified by individual units — such as dirhams and dinars:**

Examples of dinars include current circulating coins. The partnership of 'Inan is not valid with commodities (goods and merchandise) because:

a. First, partnerships in commodities cause uncertainty in profit division, since capital is the value of goods, not the actual goods, and value is uncertain, depending on estimate and opinion, leading to disputes in division. This uncertainty does not exist in coins because the capital is the coins themselves.
b. Second, it leads to profit from something not guaranteed, and the Prophet Muhammad ﷺ forbade earning profit from what is not guaranteed (narrated by al-Tirmidhi).

The Shafi'i Conditions for Shirka al-'Inan (Capital Partnership):

1. **There must be a formula (expression) indicating permission for each to act on behalf of the other:**

   It is not sufficient to merely say "we partnered" because that could be interpreted as merely reporting the existence of a partnership rather than granting permission to act. Therefore, each partner may only act with respect to their own share. However, a second view among the Shafi'is is that it suffices if the meaning is understood by custom (urf).

2. **Both contracting parties must be qualified for agency (wakala):**

   Since each acts over their own money with ownership and over the other's money by permission, each is both principal and agent.

3. **The capital must be of fungible items (mithliyyah),** such as dirhams, dinars, barley, wheat, iron, and the like.

   The partnership is invalid if the capital is of non-fungible items (mutaqawwim) like clothing or similar goods. The reason fungible items other than currency are valid is that when mixed with others of the same kind, the distinction disappears and they become like coins. The invalidity of non-fungible items is because they are distinct individual items, which cannot be mixed, and thus one partner's capital might be lost or diminished without the ability to divide it.

4. **Mixing of the two capitals so they cannot be distinguished:**

   This mixing must occur before the contract; if it happens after or even in the same session, the partnership is invalid.

5. **Profit and loss must be proportional to the capitals,** whether the partners share equally in work or not, because profit is the fruit of the capitals. For example, if they jointly own a tree or a sheep that produces offspring, profit and loss share according to capital invested.

The Hanbali Conditions for Shirka al-'Inan:

1. Both contracting parties must be qualified for agency (wakala), as Shirka al-'Inan is based on agency and trust; each entrusts their money to the other and authorizes them to act.

2. Each must authorize the other to act; if the permission is general to all trades, the partner may act in all; if it is limited to a specific kind or place, the partner may act only within that limit.
3. Capital must be dirhams and dinars, because these are the values of things and the prices of sales. Therefore, the capital cannot be:

a) Commercial goods (ʿurūḍ at-tijāra), because partnerships over goods either involve the goods themselves or their values or prices.

b) Partnership in livestock (naqra'n) is invalid because their value fluctuates, so their ruling is like goods.

c) Partnership in spoilt money (malūs) is invalid; its value fluctuates. Exception: very minor forgery for benefit is allowed.

4. Capital must be known; it is not permissible for the capital to be unknown or arbitrary because it must be referred to when settling accounts.
5. Capital must be present; it cannot be absent money or debt because it cannot be acted upon immediately, which is the purpose of the partnership.

The Maliki Conditions for Shirka al-'Inan:

1. Both partners must be qualified for agency and trusteeship, meaning they are free, adult, and sane.
2. There must be an indication of partnership by word or deed known customarily, such as both saying "we partnered," or one saying and the other remaining silent, or one saying "partner with me" and the other consenting.
3. If one's capital is gold or silver, the other's must be the same; partnership between gold and paper money is invalid. They must also agree on exchange, weight, and quality because the partnership combines sales and agency.
4. Each must authorize the other to act freely, such as placing the capital in a shop or with their agent.
5. Profit for each must be proportional to their capital; differing profit shares with equal capital is invalid.

Conclusion from the above:

The Shafi'i school (may God have mercy on him) invalidates such contracts where each partner stipulates a fixed profit from his own capital, arguing that the term partnership applies only to the mixing of capitals, and profits are branches thereof. Partners cannot share in profits unless they share in capital. Stipulating a fixed profit for each from their own capital amounts to *gharar* (excessive uncertainty), which is impermissible.

On the other hand, Malik, Abu Hanifa, and Ahmad permit and validate this type of partnership. Their evidence is that the partnership of negotiation (Mufawada) combines types of partnerships (Inan, Ju'uh), so if each type is valid separately, their combination is also valid, and people have practiced it for ages without objection.

Context on Islamic Banking:

Islamic banks began in the 1970s with limited jurisprudential foundations, facing challenges including mimicking conventional systems and focusing heavily on Murabaha (cost-plus financing), which closely resembles interest-bearing loans. While easy and low-risk, this model does not support the real economy as partnerships like Musharaka (profit-sharing) and Mudaraba (entrepreneurial partnerships) do, which foster economic development without negative effects like inflation or unemployment, and help create jobs and increase demand for investment goods.

A major problem faced was the absence of clear criteria to evaluate the working capital provider or the entrepreneur partner, adding to challenges.

To improve Islamic banking applications, the rulings of Shirka al-'Inan can be used practically by Islamic banks, relying more on Musharaka and Mudaraba. The following operational procedures are used in some banks:

1. **Request for partnership financing:**

The client applies for partnership financing to import permissible goods.

2. **Credit study:**

The bank studies the request, and if the data are positive, the bank approves it.

3. **Signing a partnership agreement in ownership of goods:**

An agreement is concluded allowing both parties to share ownership of the goods.

4. **Opening a Participation Account:**

A participation account is opened in which the shares of the bank and the client are deposited. Typically, the bank's share constitutes 99%, while the client's share is 1%.

5. **Opening the Letter of Credit:**

The bank opens a documentary letter of credit encompassing all the specifications of the goods, including delivery and insurance conditions in accordance with international customs, while ensuring compliance with Islamic Sharia provisions.

This type of arrangement promotes productive financing and is based on a genuine partnership between the bank and the client, thereby contributing to the development of the real economy while mitigating potential financial risks.

The researcher's perspective in this regard emphasizes the importance of activating Islamic financing tools based on participation (Musharaka) and profit-sharing (Mudaraba), especially within Islamic banks. The researcher observes that, at their inception, Islamic banks were influenced by conventional financing systems, which led to their concentration on Murabaha (cost-plus financing). Although Murabaha facilitated the practical application of Islamic banking and initially reduced risks, the researcher argues that it does not serve the real economy. Rather, it may contribute to inflation and unemployment due to the lack of financing for productive or developmental projects.

Accordingly, the researcher contends that Islamic financial partnerships, such as Musharaka and Mudaraba, more effectively support the economy because they create employment opportunities, increase demand for investment goods, and help reduce the poverty gap through the integration of capital, labor, and expertise.

Regarding banking practice, the researcher asserts the necessity for Islamic banks to expand their reliance on Musharaka and Mudaraba instead of predominantly depending on Murabaha. The researcher also highlights the absence of a clear criterion for client evaluation within the frameworks of Musharaka and Mudaraba, an issue Islamic banks should address. Correcting this deficiency would contribute to establishing a more transparent Islamic banking system with genuine economic benefits.

In conclusion, the researcher believes that applying the provisions of the **Shirkah al-'Inan** (joint ownership partnership) in Islamic banks can substantially contribute to achieving economic and developmental objectives in Islamic countries. This is achieved through reliance on financial tools that foster economic growth, realize integration between capital and labor, and contribute to reforming the Islamic financial system in a manner that serves the interests of society as a whole.

The letter of credit is forwarded to the correspondent bank, which in turn debits the amount on the maturity date in favor of the beneficiary through the beneficiary's bank.

6. **Receipt of Goods Subject to Participation:**

Upon arrival of the goods, typically by land shipment, the goods are delivered to the partner's warehouse, where the bank's share is held in trust and may not be disposed of. The bank inspects the goods and signs an inspection report regarding the goods covered by the letter of credit.

7. **Settlement of Participation:**

The bank settles the participation by selling its share to the client either via Murabaha (cost-plus sale) or by leasing its share to the client through a lease ending with ownership transfer (Ijarah Muntahia Bittamleek), if the subject of participation is leaseable (i.e., the client benefits from the goods while the ownership remains intact).

8. **Disposition by the Partner:**

If the partner (client) disposes of the bank's share by transferring ownership through sale or if the goods perish, the letter of credit converts to a sight credit, and the client bears the obligation to pay the supplier, sometimes compensating the bank.

9. **Non-Ownership-Transferring Disposition:**

If the client's disposition does not transfer ownership, such as installing doors or windows, the participation continues and is settled by selling the bank's share to the client.

Accordingly, diminishing Musharaka (participation) may include, as noted above:
a) Selling the bank's share to the client at the end of the term or in successive installments based on a promise.

b) Leasing the bank's share to the client by lease ending with ownership transfer, whether ownership transfer occurs gradually or in a lump sum at the end of the contract.

Second: Diminishing Musharaka in the Ownership of an Asset with Operational Income with Financial Leasing or Production Participation:

- In this scenario, the financing bank partners with the client in owning an asset that generates operational income, with the bank's ownership share diminishing over time according to a mutually agreed schedule. The contract may take one of two forms:
- The first form: The bank leases its share to the client through a lease ending with ownership transfer, which is considered an Ijarah al-Musha' (joint lease) and is permissible according to most jurists. The lessee's rental payments include the usufruct fee of the bank's share and payments that extinguish the bank's ownership of the leased asset. The rental amount may be fixed or variable according to a benchmark index regulated by Ijarah rules. The provisions of Ijarah apply to this contract, and there is no necessary correlation between the rent and the operational income generated by the lessee. The promise of ownership transfer may be at nominal or market value, which does not constitute a guarantee of capital as this is a ownership partnership (Shirkah Milk) rather than a contractual partnership (Shirkah 'Aqd).
- The second form: The bank and its partner (the client) enter a production partnership whereby the bank contributes its joint ownership share of the asset, and the partner works on it. The income generated is divided between them according to their agreement. This arrangement combines two types of partnerships:
  - Ownership partnership, where the bank and client jointly own an asset;
  - Contractual partnership, where the bank contributes its share for the client to work upon, with income shared accordingly.

3. Shirkah al-Mufawadah (Equal Partnership):

Linguistically, "Mufawadah" means equality and partnership; it is an interaction derived from delegation, whereby each partner entrusts their share to the other. It is said, "Their property is in mutual trust between them" when they are partners in it.

This type of partnership is named "Mufawadah" due to equality in capital, profit, and authority to act. Al-Hidayah states: "It is a general partnership in all trades, where each partner delegates the company's affairs to the other absolutely." It is also said to be a form of delegation, where each partner authorizes the other to act on their behalf at all times, whether present or absent.

The Maliki school defines it as: "Each partner delegates the other to manage their property both in presence and absence, across all types of assets." The Shafi'i school defines it as: "A contract wherein partners jointly engage in labor and capital, and each guarantees the other's obligations whether by compulsion, sale, or suretyship."

Mudaraba is considered a type of partnership where the parties share profits but not capital, as the capital is contributed by one party, and the other provides labor. It resembles Ijarah (leasing) since the worker is entitled to a share of the profit as compensation for labor.

Technically, it is a contract where each partner delegates authority to the other in both presence and absence, obliging each to be bound by the acts of the other. It involves two or more parties agreeing to share labor under the condition that they are equal in capital, management, and debt (joint liability). Each partner acts as surety for the other in obligations related to purchase and sale. They are jointly and severally liable concerning the rights and duties of their commerce. Each partner acts as an agent for the other regarding rights due, and as a guarantor regarding obligations owed.

It is narrated by Abu Nu'aim and others that the Prophet Muhammad (peace be upon him) engaged in Mudaraba with Khadijah (may Allah be pleased with her) when he was twenty-five, traveling to the Levant with her capital before marriage, accompanied by her servant Maysarah, and gained considerable profit, from which he was entitled to a share. This practice was common and continued after his prophethood, which he endorsed. It is also reported that he said: "Three transactions bring blessing: deferred sale, partnership (Mudaraba), and mixing barley with flour for household use, not for sale."

Hakim ibn Hizam, companion of the Prophet, narrated that he used to condition on the partner that the capital not be invested in perishable assets such as "wet livers," nor used to purchase animals prone to loss, nor transported by sea or stored in flood-prone areas; failure to observe this rendered the partner liable for the capital.

According to the Hanafi school, it is a partnership where all partners share equally in capital and profit, with each working independently on their partner's capital. Their capitals, suitable to constitute the partnership capital, are equal. This partnership is called Shirkah al-Mufawadah, sharing the same conditions of equality in capital, profit, and authority to act as Shirkah al-'Inan (joint ownership partnership), hence the name Mufawadah—each partner delegates the other to manage all trade capital.

Accordingly, the researcher holds that this type of partnership (Sharikat al-Mufawadah) requires the joint participation of the partners in all their rights, including monetary inheritance, found treasure (rukaz), lost property (luqta), as well as their obligations such as debts arising from trade, loans, guarantees, usurpation, value of damaged property, and fines related to animals or clothing, among other financial liabilities, according to the views of Abu Hanifa and Muhammad.

In other words, the Mufawadah partnership is established on the basis of sharing whatever each partner owns of property that is valid to be capital for the partnership—namely, present cash—with all partners equal in profit and capital. Each partner must actively manage their partner's capital independently according to their judgment. If one partner alone owns capital suitable to be the partnership's capital, such as cash, this does not constitute a Mufawadah partnership even if called so, due to the absence of equality in capital. However, if one partner owns a chattel or a debt owed by a person, or immovable property, this does not affect the validity of the partnership, as such property cannot serve as valid partnership capital; this is comparable to a partner's ownership of a wife. Thus, if a partner becomes entitled to money from inheritance or similar, the partnership is voided if the money is cash (silver or gold) and is actually received. However, if the partner receives goods or immovable property, the Mufawadah partnership remains valid.

The Hanafi and Zaydi schools permit this partnership based on the Prophet's (peace be upon him) saying: "When you negotiate, make the negotiation excellent," and "Negotiate, for it is a source of greater blessing," as well as due to the fact that people have dealt with it through all ages without objection. Although there is some uncertainty in this partnership—namely, it involves agency in the purchase of unknown goods and guarantees on unknown persons—this uncertainty is tolerable because such contracts are valid when made incidentally rather than intentionally, as in the case of Mudarabah, which involves agency in purchasing unknown goods.

The Maliki school also permits the Mufawadah partnership but with a different meaning than that of the Hanafis: namely, the partnership is established so that each partner has absolute independent authority to manage the capital—whether present or absent—through buying, selling, lending, borrowing, leasing, hiring, guaranteeing, appointing agents, and all other acts required in trade. Each partner is bound by whatever their partner does. The partnership applies only to the capital contributed to the partnership, excluding any separate property owned individually by each partner. If the partnership is made with the stipulation that no partner may independently dispose of the capital without the consent of the others, then this is called "Sharikah 'Unnan" (joint management partnership) by the Malikis. On this basis, there is no disagreement among the jurists about the concept of Mufawadah partnership according to the Malikis.

From the foregoing, the researcher derives the following conclusions:

- **Legitimacy of Partnership in Islam:** It is clear from Islamic texts and the Prophetic tradition that Islam recognizes the system of partnerships, whether through Mufawadah or other types, to achieve the economic interests of individuals and society.
- **Foundation of Mufawadah Partnership:** The Mufawadah partnership is grounded on the principle of delegation and equality among partners in capital, management, and profit, making it a distinct model of partnership that requires complete trust among parties.
- **Differences Among Schools in Definition and Scope:** Despite general consensus on the permissibility of Mufawadah partnership, there are differences among the schools regarding its details. The Hanafis extend its scope to include shared responsibility for all rights and obligations, while the Malikis restrict it to independent management of the capital within agreed limits.
- **Flexibility of Islamic Contract Law:** The jurisprudential variations reflect the flexibility of Islamic law in sanctioning financial transactions according to human needs and economic requirements, adapting legal rulings to changing circumstances without compromising foundational principles.
- **Role of Partnerships in Economic Development:** Islamic jurisprudence underscores the importance of partnerships in wealth growth and social solidarity, allowing for pooling of capital and investment, thereby strengthening the Islamic economy and achieving financial justice.
- **Realization of Cooperation and Solidarity:** Mufawadah and other partnerships in Islam embody the principle of cooperation and mutual

support, promoting a collective interest that transcends personal profit toward societal development.

- **Necessity of Regulating Transactions According to Sharia:** Although Mufawadah partnership permits freedom of management for each partner, jurists emphasize adherence to Sharia provisions and avoidance of prohibited transactions such as usury (riba), fraud, and dealings in forbidden items, highlighting the need to regulate economic activity according to Islamic ethical standards.

Section Three: Contractual Partnerships in Islamic Jurisprudence

Linguistic Meaning of Contract:

The term "contract" in the language has several meanings. It is said to mean a covenant or pledge; its plural is "covenants." For example, it is said: "I entrusted so-and-so with such and such," meaning I obligated him to that. "Mu'aqadah" means an agreement or treaty. "Aaqadah" means he made a covenant with him, and "ta'aqadu al-qawm" means the people made a pact. It is also said: "I tied the rope with a knot," meaning it was fastened. It is further said to mean documentation and confirmation, as in "I took the oath firmly." It can also mean tightening or making something firm, such as the "knot of marriage" or others. Additionally, it is said to mean what a person binds himself to, like "I believed thus and thus," meaning I contracted with my heart and conscience.

The summary of these statements is that, linguistically, a contract implies the linking or binding of two things and the commitment to something, whether by action or abstention, by one or both parties. This can be physical, like tying a rope, or abstract, as it is used in what people bind themselves to in dealings.

Technical (Terminological) Meaning of Contract:

Allah Almighty says:

"O you who have believed, fulfill [all] contracts."

Ibn Abbas stated that this means fulfilling what Allah has permitted, prohibited, ordained, and set limits on in all matters. Zaid ibn Aslam said contracts are six: the covenant with Allah, the covenant of alliance, the partnership contract, the sales contract, the marriage contract, and the oath contract. Al-Hasan said it means the return of a debt, necessitating fulfillment of contracts of sales, leases, marriages, and all that the name "contracts" encompasses.

Al-Zajjaj said it means to fulfill the covenant of Allah upon you and the covenant among yourselves. The Prophet Muhammad, peace be upon him, said: *"Muslims are bound by their conditions except a condition that permits what is forbidden or forbids what is permitted."*

Accordingly, contracts include what Allah has obligated His servants regarding religious duties and rulings, and what people make among themselves of trusts, transactions, and similar matters that require fulfillment. The command is generally interpreted as a recommendation or obligation, and includes avoiding the prohibited and disliked, due to the comprehensiveness of the term, which is a plural form with definite article, making it more comprehensive and fulfilling in meaning.

Jurisprudential Definition of Contract:

Jurists define it as the linkage of the offer from one contracting party to the acceptance of the other in a way that is confirmed by the subject of the contract. Thus, in Islamic law, a contract includes all lawful transactions, whether in financial dealings or others, such as marriage contracts, exchange contracts like sales and leasing, donation contracts like gifts and wills, those that start as donations and end in reciprocal transactions such as loans, guarantees, cancellations such as endowments and debt forgiveness, authorizations like agency and partnership, and restrictions such as agent dismissal and placing a minor under guardianship.

Based on the above, it can be said that contracts necessary for commercial and corporate transactions can be developed within Islamic jurisprudence as long as they do not conflict with the principles and rules established by Sharia.

Definition of Contractual Partnership:

Hanafi jurists defined it as a contract between partners sharing in capital and profit. From this definition, it is understood that a contractual partnership is realized by the mutual consent and expression of the partners' will, such as one saying to the other, "I share you in this or general trade," and the other accepts. Since partnership is a contract, it must be indicated by its essential element or what substitutes for speech, like a gesture or writing, which results in the legal effect of establishing the partnership between two or more persons in money or its equivalent.

The Hanbalis defined a contractual partnership as "a union in disposal," meaning the gathering of two or more persons in the act of disposing due to the commingling of partners' funds. Accordingly, the Hanbalis defined the contractual partnership by the effect of the contract, which is the permissibility of partners to dispose of the partnership's funds.

Section Three: Contractual Companies in Islamic Jurisprudence

Definition of Contractual Partnership According to the Shafi'i School:

The Shafi'i scholars defined a contractual partnership as the establishment of a right for two or more individuals on a shared basis. Alternatively, it is a contract that results in such a relationship. Accordingly, the Shafi'is consider ownership-based partnership (Shirkah al-Milk) as the foundation, and the contractual partnership is built upon it. Thus, in their view, what matters in any contract is the intent associated with the specific name of the contract, regardless of the elements used to form it.

Definition According to the Maliki School:

The Maliki jurists defined a contractual partnership as: each of the partners authorizing the other to act with his wealth or body on their joint behalf. This definition implies that each partner works for himself and his co-partner in the other's wealth. This is the essence of the authorization mentioned in the definition. Therefore, neither of them is permitted to act solely for their own benefit, as this would render it an agency (wakālah), not a partnership. Nor is it permissible for either partner to prevent the other from working with him in his share of the wealth, as this would negate the meaning of partnership.

Definition by Contemporary Jurists:

Modern jurists have defined a contractual partnership as: an agreement between two or more individuals to work for profit using money, labor, or reputation, where profit and loss are shared between them according to a legitimate agreement.

It has also been defined as: a contract between two or more individuals to share in capital and its profit, or in the profit alone without sharing capital, or in the wages of labor, or in buying and selling without there being capital jointly invested.

The researcher views the latter definition as the most comprehensive expression of the contractual concept of partnership, as it covers all its types—based on capital, labor, reputation, or mudarabah—and thus is the most inclusive in Islamic jurisprudence.

Essential Elements (Arkan) of Partnership Contracts

According to the majority of jurists, the essential elements of a partnership contract are:

- The offer and acceptance (contractual expression),
- The contracting parties,
- The subject matter of the contract (or its object).

Some Shafi'i scholars added "work" as an element. However, in the Hanafi school, partnership has only one essential element: the contract expression (offer and acceptance).

1. Contractual Expression (Offer and Acceptance)

The formation of a partnership contract, like all other contracts, requires the expression of mutual intent—what is referred to as the "contractual expression."

- The **contractual expression** is: “What is issued by the contracting parties indicating their internal intent to establish and conclude the partnership contract.”

According to jurists:

- **Offer (Ijaab):** What is issued by the party transferring ownership, even if said second.
- **Acceptance (Qabool):** What is issued by the recipient of ownership, even if said first.

The Hanafi view differs, stating:

- The **offer** is the statement issued first by either party.
- The **acceptance** is the statement issued second.

The basis of the disagreement between the Hanafis and the majority is whether the classification is based on who holds ownership (the majority’s view) or on the order of speech (Hanafi view).

Forms of Expressing Will to Establish a Partnership Contract

The intent to create a partnership contract can be expressed through:

- Verbal declaration,
- Writing,
- Actions,
- Gestures.

There is scholarly disagreement on some of these forms, but the preponderant opinion is that **custom ('urf)** is the determining factor. Whatever is considered by custom as an indication of intent to establish a partnership contract is legally valid. Al-Dardir said:

"A partnership becomes binding by what custom deems indicative of it."

2. The Contracting Parties

A contracting party is: "The one who concludes the contract, from whom the offer or acceptance is issued."

To do this, a person must have **full legal capacity to perform contracts** on his own behalf.

Full legal capacity is established for a rational person starting from puberty and sound judgment, which validates all of his transactions—whether beneficial or harmful—and is legally recognized.

Thus, agency becomes valid for the partners. Al-Dardir states:

"Partnership is only valid for those who can authorize and be authorized—that is, one who has the legal capacity to appoint or be appointed—namely, a free, adult, sane person."

Most jurists discussed the following key matters regarding the contracting parties:

- It is **permissible for a Muslim to partner with a non-Muslim**, according to most scholars, although it is disliked for fear the non-Muslim might engage in unlawful transactions—unless the Muslim handles the buying and selling exclusively.
- Scholars **differed in the case of Shirkah al-Mufawadah** (comprehensive partnership), which they require to include equality in religion.

They also **agree** that:

- A partnership must involve **more than one party**. It cannot be established unilaterally, in contrast to some secular laws (e.g., German and English law), which allow a single-person company, referred to as a "one-man company."

3. The Subject Matter (Object) of the Contract

The subject matter or object of the contract is:

"That which the contract is established upon, and in which the effects and rulings of the contract manifest."

The Object of the Contract (Ma'qood 'Alayh) in a Partnership

The object or subject matter of the contract in a partnership can be one of the following:

1. **Capital (Māl):**

This applies in **capital-based partnerships** (Shirkah al-Amwāl). Capital is divided by jurists into:

- **Cash (Māl Naqdī):** Refers to current circulating currency.
- **Tangible assets (Māl 'Aynī):** These are goods and merchandise.

Tangible assets are further divided into:

- **Standardized tangible assets (Mithlī):** These are items measured by volume or weight, such as wheat or barley.
- **Unique tangible assets (Qīmī):** These are items that vary in value individually, like livestock.

Jurists have differed regarding the validity of using certain types of assets in capital partnerships.

2. **Labor:**

This applies in **partnerships based on work** or **bodily effort** (Shirkah al-Abdān).

3. **Capital and Labor:**

This is the basis of the **Mudarabah partnership**, where one party provides the capital and the other provides the labor.

4. **Reputation and Guarantee (Wujāhāh and Dhamān):**

This applies in **Shirkah al-Wujūh (Partnership based on creditworthiness)**, according to those jurists who allow it.

Major Types of Contractual Partnerships in Islamic Jurisprudence

1. Shirkah al-Wujūh (Partnership Based on Reputation or Creditworthiness):

The word "Wajh" (face) **refers to prestige and social status. It is said, "So-and-so has wajh," meaning he is of high standing. A** "wajīh" **is a person respected in society. The Qur'an refers to this in:**

"O you who have believed, be not like those who abused Moses; then Allah cleared him of what they said. And he, in the sight of Allah, was honorable (wajīhan)." [Surah Al-Ahzab: 69]

This partnership is so named because people typically do not sell on credit to someone without capital unless he has a reputable status. It is as though the person buys using his reputation, then partners with another.

- The **Hanafis** also call it **Shirkah al-Mufallasīn** ("Partnership of the bankrupt").
- The **Malikis** define it as: *A reputable person selling on behalf of an unknown one in exchange for a share of the profit.*
- They also define **Shirkah al-Dhimam (Liability Partnership)** as: *An agreement between two parties to buy unspecified items without having capital on hand.*
- The **Shafi'is** define it as: *Two reputable people forming a partnership to buy on deferred payment terms, with the item owned jointly. Upon resale, the profit exceeding the purchase price is shared. It may also be where a reputable person buys on credit and assigns a lesser-known person to sell, and the profit is shared. Or a reputable man without capital partners with one who has capital, with one providing work and the other funds (without handing over the money), and the profit is shared.*

- The **Hanbalis** define it as: *Two people sharing the profit of what they purchase on credit using their good names (reputation).*

There is disagreement among jurists regarding the exact nature of **Shirkah al-Wujūh**, but they agree on the following:

- It involves partnership based on **liability and creditworthiness**, without capital or trade skills.
- The profit from items purchased on credit is shared.
- The **Malikis, Shafi'is, and Imamis** all recognize the case where a reputable person sells someone else's goods for a share of the profit as a valid example of this partnership.

The **Hanafis** define it as: *Two individuals, with no capital or labor, agree to jointly buy items on credit using their reputation, sell them, and share the profits equally or according to agreement.*

2. Shirkah al-Abdān (Partnership of Labor or Services):

Also known as:

- **Shirkah al-Ṣanā'i' (Craft Partnership)**
- **Shirkah al-Taqabbul (Undertaking Partnership)**

The various names stem from the nature of the capital:

- In **Shirkah al-A'māl**, the capital is labor.
- In **Shirkah al-Abdān**, the focus is bodily work.
- In **Shirkah al-Ṣanā'i'**, it is the craft or profession.
- In **Shirkah al-Taqabbul**, what one partner undertakes to do binds the other as well.

Definitions:

- **Shafi'i** definition: *Two or more people agree to share their earnings from their crafts equally or unequally, with the craft either being the same or different.*
- **Hanbali** definition: *A partnership where individuals work with their hands (as craftsmen) or earn from lawful means such as hunting, and share the proceeds.*

- **Maliki** definition: *Two or more craftsmen work together and share the wages based on the amount of work, provided the craft is the same or one partner's work complements the other's, and their efforts are equal or close.*

General Definition:

A partnership where two or more individuals agree to work jointly in a certain task or accept contracts, with the resulting earnings shared as per mutual agreement.

3. Shirkah al-Muḍārabah (Capital-Labor Partnership):

- The word **Muḍārabah** is derived from "ḍarb fī al-arḍ" (striking the earth), meaning **travel**, because trade typically involves travel. The Muḍārib (working partner) earns profit through effort and action.

The Qur'an says:

"And others travel through the land seeking of Allah's bounty." [Surah Al-Muzzammil: 20]

- The capital in this case is the act of traveling and engaging in trade.
- Muḍārabah is a term used by **Iraqis**, including the **Hanafis and Hanbalis**.
- It is also called **Qirāḍ** or **Muqāraḍah**, derived from **Qarḍ (cutting)**, because:

  - The capital owner allocates a portion of his wealth to the working partner.
  - He also allocates a portion of the **profit** to the worker.

- The term **Qirāḍ** is common among the **Hejazis**, and is used by the **Malikis, Shafi'is, and Ẓāhiris**.

Definition of *Muḍārabah* According to the Jurists:

Islamic jurists have provided various definitions of *muḍārabah* (silent partnership), many of which have not been free from critique or objection. This section outlines the definitions as given by the four major Islamic schools of jurisprudence, arranged chronologically according to their development.

1. Ḥanafī School

In *Takmila Fatḥ al-Qadīr*, *muḍārabah* is defined as:

"A contract of partnership consisting of capital from one party and labor from the other."

The author of *al-Nihāyah* stated:

"In Sharīʿah, *muḍārabah* is the act of entrusting someone with money to trade with, and the profit is shared between them according to what they have agreed upon."

Al-Mīrghānī added:

"*Muḍārabah* is a contract of partnership where one party provides capital and the other contributes labor."

He further elaborated that this implies a partnership in profit which arises from the capital of one and the labor of the other. Without both elements, there is no valid *muḍārabah*: if the entire profit is allocated to the capital provider, it becomes a *baiʿ al-biḍāʿah* (agency contract); if it is allocated to the laborer, it becomes a loan (*qarḍ*).

2. Mālikī School

In his *Mukhtaṣar*, Khalīl defines *qarāḍ* (synonymous with *muḍārabah*) as:

"Qarāḍ is an agency for trade with a specified sum of coined money, delivered to the agent, in exchange for a share in the profit, provided the capital and share are known."

The commentator explains:

Qarāḍ (from the root meaning 'to cut') is so named because the capital owner "cuts off" a portion of his capital for the agent to use in return for a share of the profit. The term 'agency' (*tawkīl*) signifies a specific mandate to trade using coined gold or silver (not in-kind goods or unminted metal), delivered by the owner to the agent, with a clearly defined shared percentage of profit from that capital—not a fixed amount.

3. Shāfiʿī School

The Shāfiʿī scholars offered multiple definitions, including:

- Imām al-Nawawī defined *muḍārabah* as:

"Entrusting someone with capital to trade, with the profit shared between the two."

- Zakariyyā al-Anṣārī stated:

"It is a contract that entails giving money to another to trade with, and the profit is divided between them."

4. Ḥanbalī School

The Ḥanbalīs also offered several definitions, which, like the others, are not immune from critique:

- *Kashshāf al-Qināʿ* defines it as:

"The handing over of a specific, known sum of money (or equivalent) to someone to trade with, in return for a known portion of the profit."

- Ibn Qudāmah states:

"Muḍārabah is when a person gives another some of his wealth to trade with, and the profit is shared between them."

Discussion of the Definitions:

- **Ḥanafīs**: While they rightly identify *muḍārabah* as a contract involving capital from one party and labor from another, they fail to address the specifics of profit distribution, the requirements for both contracting parties, and the qualifications of the capital.
- **Mālikīs**: Their definition outlines specific conditions necessary for a valid *muḍārabah*, but mistakenly identifies *muḍārabah* as being synonymous with the act of delivery, whereas it is in fact the contract itself—either prior to or simultaneous with the delivery of capital. It also wrongly implies that the agent is authorized to act before the contract is concluded, which is inaccurate, as agency (wakālah) is a result of the contract, not a precursor. Moreover, it does not clarify the required qualifications for either party.

- **Shāfiʿīs**: Although they do classify *muḍārabah* as a contract, they similarly omit the conditions required for the contracting parties and do not elaborate on profit-sharing.
- **Ḥanbalīs**: While they specify that the profit is to be shared according to mutual agreement, their definition fails to explicitly state the contractual nature of *muḍārabah* and does not address the necessary qualifications of the parties.

Comparative Conclusion:

All definitions reviewed lack a complete statement of the conditions required of both contracting parties. Furthermore, the Ḥanafī and Shāfiʿī definitions do not clearly outline the capital's requirements or the method of profit distribution. Only the Mālikī and Ḥanbalī definitions address the latter two aspects. Among all, only the Ḥanafī definition clearly identifies *muḍārabah* as a contract, while the rest fail to do so explicitly.

Thus, these definitions vary significantly in meaning and often omit essential elements that are key to understanding the true nature of *muḍārabah*.

The Researcher's Comprehensive Definition:

"Muḍārabah is a contract that entails the delivery of a specific, identified form of capital (or its equivalent), in terms of amount, type, and description, by a legally competent and discerning person with legal capacity (*jāʾiz al-taṣarruf*) to another person for the purpose of trade, in return for a clearly defined and proportionate share of the resulting profit."

Broader Analysis of "Company" (*Sharika*) in Islamic Jurisprudence:

Through an analytical study of the concept of partnership in Islamic jurisprudence, the researcher observes that Islamic scholars have offered nuanced and multi-faceted classifications of partnerships, based on the nature of each partner's contribution—whether capital, labor, or trust.

Hence, the jurisprudential definition of a *sharika* in Islam is not limited to a financial arrangement; rather, it encompasses social and ethical dimensions aimed at promoting justice and equity among individuals. A company in Islamic law is thus defined as:

"An agreement between two or more individuals to combine their capital or efforts toward a shared goal—namely, profit—while observing the core contractual elements: intention (*niyyah*), offer (*ījāb*), acceptance (*qabūl*), and lawfulness (*mashrūʿiyyah*)."

Based on this, the researcher categorizes partnerships into several types:

- **Capital-based companies** (*Sharikat al-Amwāl*)
- **Labor-based companies** (*Sharikat al-Abdān* or *Aʿmāl*)
- **Reputation-based companies** (*Sharikat al-Wujūh*)
- **Muḍārabah** (capital from one partner and labor from the other)

These classifications highlight how Islamic law offers flexibility in the division of roles, rights, and responsibilities among partners. For instance:

- In **capital companies**, the partnership is based mainly on monetary contributions.
- In **labor companies**, partners contribute their physical effort or skills.
- In **reputation companies**, trust and social standing form the basis of the agreement.

Jurisprudential Classifications Based on Social Impact:

The researcher notes that scholars have also categorized companies based on their societal role:

- **Companies of usufruct (*Sharikat al-Ibāḥah*)**: These involve shared access to natural resources, such as water, pastures, and fire, as reflected in the ḥadīth:

"Muslims are partners in three things: water, pasture, and fire."

This reflects the Islamic concept of public goods available to all without exclusivity, grounded in principles of social justice.

- **Ownership companies (*Sharikat al-Milk*)**: These arise either through intentional agreement (e.g., a partnership contract) or involuntarily (e.g., inheritance or bequest), showcasing the depth of Islamic jurisprudence in addressing ownership rights and shared obligations.

Final Note:

The researcher concludes that Islamic jurisprudence treats partnerships not merely as financial contracts but as structures rooted in moral values like trust, cooperation, and fairness. This stands in contrast to many modern legal systems, which often emphasize financial elements over ethical concerns.

Given this, there is an urgent need to develop contemporary legal studies that integrate Islamic jurisprudential principles with modern economic realities. In this context, the researcher believes that corporate law in the Islamic world—such as the **Sudanese Companies Act of 2015**—should incorporate Sharīʿah-based principles into modern legislative frameworks. This integration ensures a balanced legal system that upholds Islamic values while responding effectively to contemporary market challenges.

Thus, this study goes beyond simply examining Islamic partnership law; it seeks to critically compare it with modern legislation to identify gaps and opportunities for strengthening legal frameworks in a manner consistent with the objectives of Islamic law (*maqāṣid al-sharīʿah*), providing a comprehensive, just, and functional system for both individuals and society.

Chapter Two: The Legal Framework of Companies

Section One: The Emergence of Companies

The concept of forming companies is as ancient as humanity itself. Human nature is inherently inclined toward social interaction and cooperation to achieve mutual benefit. The idea of partnership began within households among siblings, extended to families and kinship groups, and gradually expanded over time to encompass broader cooperative endeavors. This evolution was driven by the ever-increasing human needs and demands, which often surpassed the capacity of individuals to fulfill on their own due to their physical and financial limitations. Consequently, early humans sought collaborative means with their peers, giving rise to the concept of companies as a mechanism to undertake major ventures, share expenses, and distribute both profits and losses among the partners.

This natural progression of the partnership concept reflects mankind's enduring need for collaboration and complementarity to fulfill economic and social objectives. The researcher notes that the Islamic concept of companies arose to institutionalize this innate human principle, offering a structured legal and ethical framework to govern such partnerships. This framework ensures fairness among partners and safeguards their respective rights.

The researcher observes that Islamic jurisprudence has developed various types of companies, such as **Shirket al-Ibahah (partnership by permissibility)**, **Shirket al-Milk (co-ownership)**, and **Shirket al-'Aqd (contractual partnership)**. These types demonstrate the flexibility of Islamic law in accommodating market and economic dynamics. Moreover, Islamic jurisprudence extended beyond mere financial contributions to include partnerships based on labor, expertise, and trust—such as **Shirket al-Abdan (partnership based on labor)** and **Shirket al-Wujooh (partnership based on reputation and creditworthiness)**. This distinguishes the Islamic system from modern economic systems that primarily emphasize capital contributions.

Based on this, the researcher contends that the company in Islam is not merely an economic tool but also a vehicle for achieving social solidarity and economic development. It contributes to equitable wealth distribution and enables individuals to utilize their financial and human resources in ways that align with the principles of Islamic Shariah.

From a historical legal perspective, one of the earliest codified laws—the **Code of Hammurabi**—contained provisions on partnerships, particularly in Articles 100 to 107. These articles defined a company as "a contract by which two or more persons agree to perform one or more acts with the intent of generating profit."

The Greek understanding of companies was largely confined to maritime trade and was based on the doctrine of high risk. However, the real evolution of the concept occurred in the second century BCE with the Romans, despite their economy being predominantly agricultural. The Romans categorized companies into two types: **companies of capital** and **companies engaging in specific types of trade**.

Among the Arabs, the concept of partnership was recognized in the form of **Khulataa' (co-owners)** or **Shurakaa' (partners)**. With the advent of Islam, the doctrine of partnership was clarified, classified into permissible and impermissible forms, and emphasized the importance of cooperation and solidarity for the benefit of both individuals and society. Throughout Islamic history—including the Ottoman era—numerous forms of companies were established. Notably, the **Majallat al-Ahkam al-'Adliyyah** (Ottoman Code of Civil Law) issued in 1305 AH (1887 AD) included rules on commercial partnerships.

In Europe, the modern concept of companies evolved during the **Middle Ages**, particularly in response to the Church's prohibition of usurious lending (riba). As a result, people sought alternative means to invest their wealth, leading to the formation of **capital-based companies** that pooled large sums for ventures related to geographical discoveries and colonial expansion into the East. These enterprises later gave rise to vast **colonial trading companies**, which generated substantial profits. Following **World War I**, **joint-stock companies** emerged as the dominant business model in industrial, commercial, and agricultural activities. Eventually, **multinational corporations** with massive capital holdings arose, becoming influential players in the global economy.

In **Sudan**, the first company-related laws were introduced after the arrival of colonial rule in **1899**. The **Civil Justice Ordinance of 1900** was enacted, drawing on principles of **equity and good conscience**, as noted in Article 9, and was heavily influenced by **English law**, particularly its application in other British colonies such as **India** and **Nigeria**. Notably, **Islamic Shariah** was entirely excluded as a source of judicial legislation.

The researcher emphasizes that the development of companies in Europe was driven by both economic and political factors. The Church's prohibition of interest (riba) played a critical role in prompting alternative investment mechanisms, leading to the rise of capital-based companies that funded imperialist expansions. Over time, these companies grew into joint-stock corporations and, eventually, multinational entities that dominate global markets.

Regarding Sudan, the researcher notes that the legal framework governing companies was established under colonial influence, with English law forming the basis for corporate regulation. The exclusion of Shariah principles reflected colonial dominance over the legal system, resulting in corporate laws that diverged from Islamic jurisprudence, despite the latter's comprehensive and socially-oriented vision for economic collaboration.

Therefore, the researcher underscores the need to **review modern corporate legislation in Islamic countries** to ensure alignment with Islamic legal principles, while also accommodating contemporary economic developments. This would facilitate a harmonious balance between tradition and modernity in company governance.

With the growth of commercial activity and the increase in the number of operating companies, **the Companies Ordinance of 1925** was enacted in Sudan. This law laid down the **foundations for company formation**, **registration procedures**, and **general characteristics**, along with **rules on management, capital structure, membership, meetings, oversight, liquidation**, and other regulatory aspects. The legislation was largely derived from the **English Companies Act of 1908** and relevant **English common law precedents**.

Subsequent legislative developments included:

- **The Companies (Winding Up) Rules of 1928**
- **The Public Companies Act of 1969**
- **The Judicial Decisions Principles Act of 1983**, which reintroduced **Islamic Shariah** as a legal foundation. This led to the nullification of certain provisions in the 1925 Companies Ordinance, particularly those relating to **interest-bearing shares and bonds**, as such interest was deemed **usurious (riba)** and therefore prohibited under Shariah. As a result, it became impermissible to issue shares or bonds linked to interest-based financing.

Further legislative reforms included:

- The **Civil Transactions Act of 1984**, whose company-related provisions were judicially interpreted to apply to **partnerships**, viewing them as contractual agreements based on mutual consent among parties.
- Notably, the Civil Transactions Act **did not repeal** the 1925 Companies Ordinance.
- The **Khartoum Stock Exchange Act** was later enacted to regulate the issuance and trading of securities. It established a unified authority to oversee financial instruments and shareholder rights. All companies were mandated to become members of the Exchange, and in case of conflict, its provisions **took precedence** over those of the 1925 Companies Ordinance.
- In **1996**, a **ninth chapter** was added to the Companies Ordinance to regulate **public sector companies**, which are fully owned by the state and subject to special rules. These companies fall under the supervision of the **Ministry of Finance** and are subject to **administrative and technical oversight**, with a designated **minister** appointed by the **Council of Ministers** responsible for their management.

Finally, the **Companies Act of 2015** was enacted to **address economic changes**, **rectify legal gaps**, and **prevent fraudulent practices** that had previously exploited weaknesses in the 1925 law, such as abuse of **voluntary liquidation** procedures.

The researcher observes that the development of corporate laws in Sudan has passed through several distinct stages, with each legislative phase leaving a specific impact on the corporate landscape. It began with the Companies Act of 1925, derived from the English Companies Act of 1908, which laid down the general foundations for corporate operations. This was followed by a series of amendments and additions, such as the Companies Liquidation Rules of 1928 and the Public Companies Act of 1969, all of which were introduced without sufficient consideration for the principles of Islamic jurisprudence.

The researcher notes that a major turning point occurred with the enactment of the **Sources of Judicial Decisions Act of 1983**, which was based on **Islamic Sharia**, leading to the suspension of certain interest-based provisions in the 1925 Act—particularly those relating to dividends and bonds—since it became impermissible to issue financial instruments based on interest. This shift was further reinforced by the **Civil Transactions Act of 1984**, which emphasized the contractual basis of partnerships but did not repeal the 1925 Companies Act. As a result, a duality in legislation emerged.

According to the researcher, the enactment of the **Khartoum Stock Exchange Act** was an attempt to regulate the trading of shares and bonds, requiring all companies to become members of the exchange, which thereby took precedence over the 1925 Act in the event of any legal conflict. In 1996, amendments were introduced to regulate **public sector companies**—companies wholly owned by the government and subject to direct state supervision—thus reinforcing the governmental role in the national economy.

The researcher emphasizes that the promulgation of the **Companies Act of 2015** was essential to keep pace with economic developments and to close legal loopholes, particularly those that had been exploited for voluntary liquidation and other fraudulent practices. However, the researcher argues that this legislation still falls short of achieving a full integration between **Islamic principles** and **modern regulatory frameworks**. There remains a pressing need to harmonize economic legislation with **Islamic jurisprudential foundations** in order to ensure a more just and efficient financial system.

Section Two: The Partnership Contract

The partnership contract is based on the fundamental pillars and conditions common to other financial contracts, which include *formation*, *validity*, and *enforceability*. The partnership contract is not distinguished from other financial agreements in terms of unique features, but rather aligns with them in terms of the requirements related to the *offer and acceptance*, the *contracting parties*, the *subject matter* of the contract, and the *concurrence of the offer and acceptance session*, according to the majority view of Islamic jurists. Additionally, the contract must satisfy the requirements of *legal capacity*, *mutual consent*, and *freedom from vitiating factors* such as coercion or frivolity.

In **positive law**, the same principles apply: the partnership contract must have a lawful *object* and *cause*, just like any other contract. The object must be *possible*, *determinate*, *tradable*, and *lawful*. Similarly, the cause must also be lawful. The object of the contract is the partner's contribution to capital or profits, while the cause is the mutual obligation of each partner to provide their share in the partnership capital.

The intention to establish a partnership contract may be expressed through *spoken words*, *written form*, *conduct*, *gestures*, or *indications*, provided that such expression emanates from a contracting party who is *legally competent*, *sane*, and of *full capacity*, whose legal actions—whether beneficial or detrimental—are recognized under Islamic and statutory law. As Al-Dardir stated:

"The partnership is only valid from those who possess the legal capacity to appoint and be appointed as agents—namely, a free, adult, and rational person."

In most **Arab legal systems**, statutory laws do not provide a broad formal definition of "partnership" in its general sense; instead, they typically address only one type: *contractual partnerships*, a limitation influenced by the **French legal tradition**.

The **Sudanese Civil Transactions Act of 1984** defines a partnership as follows:

"A partnership is a contract whereby two or more persons commit to contribute, each with a share of capital or labor, to a financial enterprise with the purpose of investing it and sharing any resulting profit or loss."

Similarly, **Federal Law of the United Arab Emirates (2015)** defines a partnership as:

1. "A partnership is a contract whereby two or more persons commit to participate in an economic project aimed at generating profit, by contributing capital or labor, and sharing the resulting profit or loss."
2. "For the purposes of paragraph (1), an economic project includes any commercial, financial, industrial, agricultural, real estate, or professional activity, or any other form of economic activity."
3. "By way of exception to paragraph (1), a partnership may be established or owned by a single person in accordance with the provisions of this law."

The UAE legislator adopted the same definition found in **Syrian Law (Article 473)**, **Libyan Law (Article 494)**, and **Iraqi Law (Article 226)**. This contrasts with **Sudanese law**, which uses the term *financial project* rather than *economic project*, aligning more closely with **Egyptian law**, which defines a partnership as:

"A partnership is a contract whereby two or more persons agree to contribute, each with a share of capital or labor, to a financial project with the objective of sharing any resulting profit or loss."

The researcher notes that these various statutory definitions largely converge on the same core understanding of a partnership, with only slight variations in terminology.

Accordingly, the essential elements of a company under the law are as follows:

1. **Contractual Nature of the Company**:

A company must be established through a contract that satisfies the general legal requirements of contract formation. This includes offer and acceptance, legal capacity of the parties, lawful object, and absence of vitiating factors such as coercion or fraud.

2. **Capital Contribution by Each Partner**:

Each partner must contribute a share to the company's capital. This contribution determines the partner's share in profits and losses. The contribution may take various forms, including cash, securities, movable or immovable property, usufruct rights, labor, trade name, patent rights, claims against third parties, or any other asset capable of forming the object of an obligation. There is no requirement for the contributions to be equal or homogeneous. Rather, the aggregate of all partners' contributions constitutes the company's capital, which is distinct and separate from the personal assets of the partners.

3. **Participation in Profits and Losses**:

All partners must share in the profits and bear the losses proportionally. Any agreement excluding a partner from profit or loss sharing renders the contract void. This is expressly stated in Article 515 of the **Egyptian Civil Code**, which provides:

"If it is agreed that one of the partners shall not share in the profits or losses of the company, the contract of partnership shall be void."

A similar principle appears in the **Sudanese Civil Transactions Act (1984)**, which defines a company as:

"A contract whereby two or more persons agree to contribute capital or labor to a financial project with the aim of investing it and sharing any resulting profit or loss."

This description aligns with the concept of partnerships as contracts based on mutual agreement and legal relationships between the parties. Notably, the **Civil Transactions Act (1984)** did not repeal the **Companies Act (1925)**, and judicial practice has continued to apply both laws concurrently.

Furthermore, the company enjoys **legal personality** as stipulated in the **Sudanese Companies Act**, which provides:

"As from the date of incorporation mentioned in the certificate of incorporation, the subscribers to the memorandum of association and all persons who become members from time to time shall constitute a body corporate under the name specified in the memorandum, having legal personality, the capacity to carry out the functions of a joint-stock company, to own property, enjoy perpetual succession, and possess a common seal."

The researcher observes that, from the date of issuance of the certificate of incorporation, the company acquires a **separate legal personality**, enabling it to independently acquire rights and assume obligations distinct from its shareholders.

Company Liability Toward Third Parties:

Article 2 of the **Companies Act of 1925** provides:

"For the purposes of this Act, a company shall mean a company formed and registered in accordance with the provisions hereof, and whose members' liability is limited to the unpaid portion of the value of their shares—if any."

According to this provision, a shareholder's liability is limited to the unpaid value of their subscribed shares. This means shareholders are not personally liable for the company's debts upon liquidation. However, if a shareholder has only partially paid for their shares, they remain obligated to pay the balance—but only to the company, not to its creditors. Creditors may only pursue the company itself, not the individual shareholders.

However, the law allows for **unlimited liability** for members of the board of directors if expressly stipulated in the memorandum of association. The Companies Act states:

"In a limited liability company, the liability of directors or any of them may be unlimited if so provided in the company's memorandum of association."

Nonetheless, shareholders' liability remains limited as previously described, both toward the company and its creditors.

Since the company enjoys **independent legal personality**, it has full legal capacity in its dealings. It may borrow funds from financiers and offer security for its obligations, including **pledging its assets** under either **possessory** or **official mortgage**, pursuant to the **Civil Transactions Act of 1984**.

This law also permits the company to use the mechanism of a **floating charge**, which does not restrict the debtor's ability to dispose of the encumbered property. The company may transfer ownership or otherwise dispose of such assets through any lawful means without obtaining the mortgagee's prior consent. Nevertheless, the proceeds derived from the disposition of the encumbered property remain subject to the floating charge and are themselves considered mortgaged assets. Accordingly, the floating charge ensures that the secured creditor retains **priority status**, making them a **first-ranking creditor** in the event of liquidation or sale of the company's assets.

Chapter Three: Types of Companies in Law and Means of Their Dissolution

Section One: Commercial Companies

The Sudanese Companies Act serves as the legal framework governing the establishment and regulation of commercial companies. It defines the procedures and conditions necessary to achieve the intended objectives while safeguarding commercial and economic interests within the country.

In this context, Article (22) of the Sudanese Companies Act addresses the concept of establishing companies for commercial purposes. The legislator permits the formation of companies to support trade, the arts, charitable activities, or any other objective that serves the public interest. These companies must direct their profits toward achieving these purposes and are strictly prohibited from distributing any portion of their profits to members in companies established for such special purposes.

This legislative direction reflects the Sudanese legislator's vision to promote corporate social responsibility, whereby companies are not limited to profit-making alone but also contribute sustainably to economic and social development. It fosters an integrated approach between economic activity and the public interest.

Furthermore, Article 96 of the Companies Act of 1925 stipulates that a company cannot begin conducting its business immediately upon incorporation but must first obtain a Certificate of Incorporation.

The researcher affirms that public companies are prohibited from commencing their operations without formal authorization from the Registrar of Companies, which is granted only after thorough verification that all legal requirements have been met. This measure embodies a rigorous regulatory approach aimed at enhancing transparency and compliance, thereby protecting the rights of investors and third parties dealing with the company and strengthening confidence in the commercial and economic environment.

Pre-Operational Requirements for Companies

These conditions are laid out in Article (111) of the Sudanese Companies Act of 1925, which provides as follows:

"No public company may commence any of its operations or borrow funds unless the following conditions have been fulfilled:

1. The full cash payment of the value of shares held by the founders, taking into account the minimum subscription level.
2. Each board member must have paid the full value of the shares allocated to them, and not less than the amount payable in cash on each share.
3. A formal declaration must be filed with the Registrar of Companies, submitted by the company secretary or a board member, affirming that all legal conditions have been satisfied.
4. In the absence of a public subscription invitation, an alternative report must be filed with the Registrar of Companies."

Once these requirements are met, the Registrar issues a certificate authorizing the company to commence operations. This certificate constitutes conclusive legal evidence that the procedures have been fulfilled. Any violation of these provisions subjects the company to a fine determined by the court for each day the violation persists.

Through an analysis of Article (111) of the 1925 Act, the researcher concludes that the Sudanese legislator has established a precise framework to regulate the commencement of public companies' activities in the Sudanese market. The conditions set forth in the Act serve as important legal safeguards to ensure the proper conduct of business in accordance with sound legal principles. They help uphold transparency and protect the interests of all stakeholders, including shareholders, consumers, and society at large.

The first of these conditions requires full cash payment of the value of shares, reflecting the importance of financial stability at the founding stage and underscoring the founders' obligation to provide the necessary capital to launch commercial activities. Additionally, each board member is required to fully pay for their allocated shares, reinforcing principles of equity and financial accountability among members.

The third condition involves filing a formal declaration with the Registrar, which is a fundamental step to ensure full legal compliance. This condition illustrates the level of oversight exercised by the legislator to prevent violations that may adversely affect the financial and economic system.

In the case where no public subscription statement is issued, the law allows for the submission of an alternative report. This demonstrates the legislator's flexibility in providing legal alternatives to ensure continuity in the company's incorporation process without disrupting procedural integrity.

The researcher observes that these conditions aim to ensure legal discipline during the establishment phase of companies and enforce ongoing oversight through the Registrar of Companies. Moreover, the penalty for non-compliance—court-imposed fines—is a legal deterrent that promotes adherence to the prescribed conditions.

Thus, it can be concluded that this legal framework aligns with internationally recognized legal standards found in many comparative jurisdictions and represents a significant step toward improving the business climate in Sudan and ensuring stability in the commercial market.

The researcher also notes that the final article of the 1925 Sudanese Companies Act outlines specific exemptions applicable to private companies, granting them greater flexibility in initiating their commercial activities. Unfortunately, the full text of the final article was not available in the accessible sources. Nevertheless, it is well-established that Sudanese law differentiates between public and private companies regarding procedures and legal obligations.

Exceptions for Private Companies:

- **Incorporation Procedures:** Private companies may be exempted from some of the complex procedures required for public companies, such as obtaining a certificate of incorporation or permission from the commercial registrar.
- **Operational Flexibility:** Private companies enjoy greater flexibility in starting their operations and making operational decisions without being bound by certain restrictions imposed on public companies.

The researcher notes that this distinction between public and private companies in Sudanese law aims to strike a balance between regulating commercial activity and ensuring the protection of investors' rights. While strict procedures are imposed on public companies to ensure transparency and accountability, private companies are granted exemptions that help them grow and expand more rapidly.

This balance reflects the legislator's desire to encourage investment and facilitate the business environment in Sudan.

Legislative Developments and Future Directions:

It is worth mentioning that the enactment of the Khartoum Stock Exchange Act in 1994 contributed to strengthening oversight of public companies, as it granted the market council broad powers to monitor the financial and administrative performance of companies, thereby enhancing transparency and increasing confidence in the Sudanese financial market. These measures are considered an important step towards improving the commercial environment in Sudan, as they encourage local and international investments.

The researcher concludes that, based on these observations, the Sudanese legal system still needs continuous updating to ensure that commercial companies can effectively contribute to economic growth—especially in light of the developments in the global financial market and the demands imposed by changes in the digital economy and global financial systems. A more flexible legislative framework would enable companies to interact more effectively with global markets, thereby driving the national economy forward into the future.

Section Two: Private Companies

According to Article (2) of the Sudanese Companies Act of 1925, a private company is defined as a company that meets the following conditions under its articles of association:

1. **Number of Members:** The number of members must not be less than two and not more than fifty, excluding employees of the company.
2. **Prohibition of Public Subscription:** The company is prohibited from inviting the public to subscribe to its shares or bonds. Instead, the shares are allocated directly to the shareholders.
3. **Restrictions on Share Transfer:** The company's articles of association impose restrictions on the transfer of shares from one shareholder to another, due to the private nature of such companies.

The uniqueness of private companies lies in their limited size and small number of members, which allows them greater flexibility in administrative decision-making. This system also helps reduce conflicts of interest and ensures the preservation of balance among shareholders.

However, a private company can be converted into a public company, according to Article (197) of the Companies Act of 1925, which sets out the necessary procedures for such conversion, including:

1. **Issuance of a Conversion Resolution:** The company must issue a resolution to convert into a public company. This requires amending the company's memorandum and articles of association to comply with the legal provisions applicable to public companies, ensuring consistency with the new legal requirements.
2. **Filing the Resolution with the Registrar:** The company must file a copy of the conversion resolution with the commercial registrar, along with a report instead of the statement that would have been filed if the company had originally been a public one.
3. **Filing a Valid Declaration:** The company must submit a properly certified declaration as if it were a public company before starting business.

Once these conditions are met, the commercial registrar records the conversion in the registry, and the company loses its private status and begins to operate as a public company. These procedures aim to ensure a smooth transition from private to public status, which enhances business transparency and contributes to strengthening the national economy.

Amendment to the Companies Act in 1992

In September 1992, the Sudanese Companies Act of 1925 was amended, granting the federal government broad powers to regulate and manage public sector institutions administratively and financially. Article (277) of the amended law defined a public sector company as one that is 100% owned by federal government bodies. This amendment aimed to organize the operations of public sector companies under clear principles, without conflicting with previous laws established under the 1925 Act.

Through this amendment, the relevant ministries were granted the authority to direct and manage these companies via boards of directors appointed by the Council of Ministers. This enhances administrative oversight of public sector companies and ensures their adherence to public policies and national interests.

From the researcher's perspective, the 1992 amendment to the Companies Act is considered an important step toward enhancing oversight of public sector companies in Sudan, particularly by allocating administrative and financial supervision to the federal government. However, the researcher notes that the amendment overlooked certain important aspects in defining a "public sector company." The term is limited to companies that are 100% owned by the federal government, thereby excluding companies that are only partially owned by the government, whether at the state level or jointly owned with the private sector.

It would have been preferable for the amendment to include companies in which the public sector participates at multiple levels, including local governments at the state level, as well as companies jointly owned by the federal government and the private sector. This legislative omission may lead to disparities in the treatment and assessment of public companies, particularly those involving mixed public-private partnerships. Furthermore, such divergence in regulatory and administrative standards between wholly government-owned companies and those involving private sector partnerships may result in inconsistencies in transparency and accountability in the management of these companies.

Based on the above, the researcher concludes that there is an urgent need to reconsider certain aspects of the 1992 amendment to the Companies Act so as to encompass companies that include various components of public sector ownership at different levels. Such a revision would enhance the effectiveness of administrative oversight and ensure a balanced alignment of the diverse economic interests in the Sudanese market. This, in turn, would contribute to the establishment of a more transparent and stable investment environment.

Section Three: Nullity and Dissolution of the Company Contract

First Subsection: Nullity of the Company Contract

The essential elements of a company contract consist of three fundamental pillars: **consent**, **object**, and **cause**. Should any of these elements be absent—whether due to a defect in the consent of one of the partners, a deficiency in legal capacity, or the unlawfulness of the company's purpose—the contract may be deemed **null and void**.

As for the dissolution of a company, it refers to the termination of the legal bond that unites the partners, whether due to the expiry of the company's duration or the occurrence of events that bring about the end of its legal existence. This is affirmed in the relevant provision of the law, which states:

"A company shall be dissolved by operation of law upon the expiration of its fixed term or upon the completion of the objective for which it was established."

Accordingly, the agreement of the partners to operate the company for a fixed term or for the execution of a specific undertaking results in its dissolution once that term ends or the undertaking is fulfilled. A company may also be dissolved upon unanimous agreement of the partners, or due to the death of a partner, interdiction, insolvency, or bankruptcy—unless the partnership contract contains a provision for succession by heirs, the substitution of an interdicted partner, or the settlement of insolvency, whereby the company may continue to exist. Some company contracts may include clauses that preserve the company's continuity.

Additionally, a partner may withdraw from the company, as provided by law:

"The company shall be dissolved by the withdrawal of a partner if its duration is undefined, provided that the partner declares their intention to withdraw to the other partners in advance and that the withdrawal is not made in bad faith or at an inopportune time."

Furthermore, the destruction of the company's assets may render the realization of its objectives impossible, leading to its dissolution by operation of law.

The company may also be dissolved by **judicial decision**, as stipulated in the law:

"The court may order the dissolution of the company upon the request of one of the partners due to the failure of another partner to fulfill their obligations, or for any other cause not attributable to the partners, where the court deems such cause sufficiently grave to justify dissolution. Any agreement to the contrary shall be void."

Additionally, **merger, bankruptcy, and liquidation** are considered causes for the dissolution of a company—issues that will be discussed in detail later.

Through this provision, it becomes evident that the Sudanese Companies Act has established clear frameworks governing the circumstances that lead to the dissolution of a company. These frameworks provide legal protection for all parties involved by ensuring clarity in situations that may result in the company's dissolution, whether due to the expiry of its duration or purpose, or due to difficulties encountered by the partners.

The researcher observes that the legal provisions concerning dissolution afford companies a degree of flexibility and autonomy in defining the conditions for their continuity or termination, while at the same time imposing legal safeguards to protect the rights of the partners in the event of unforeseen changes, such as death or bankruptcy. These provisions contribute to reinforcing a clear and organized legal environment for the corporate sector in Sudan, maintaining stability in the relationships among partners while accommodating changing circumstances affecting any party.

Conversely, the researcher notes that the Sudanese legislator has taken care to provide solutions in exceptional cases—such as the destruction of the company's assets or the withdrawal of a partner—which serves to safeguard the interests of all concerned parties.

Subsection Two: Dissolution of the Company Contract

The **dissolution of a company** refers to the termination of the legal relationship that bound the partners under the contract. This dissolution may occur through various means as prescribed by law, with the causes for dissolution being classified as arising either by **operation of law**, **by the will of the partners**, or **by judicial ruling**. The principal grounds for the dissolution of a company may be summarized as follows:

1. **Expiration of the company's specified term or the achievement of its objective**: If a company was established for a fixed duration or a specific purpose, it shall dissolve upon the expiry of that term or upon the completion of the purpose for which it was formed. Article 253 of the 1984 Sudanese Civil Transactions Act addresses the grounds for company dissolution as follows:
2. The company shall be dissolved upon the occurrence of any of the following:
   - Expiry of the company's term or completion of the objective for which it was formed;
   - Total loss of the company's capital or the loss of a partner's capital share before its delivery;
   - Death, insanity, bankruptcy, or interdiction of a partner;
   - Unanimous agreement of the partners to dissolve the company.

If the partners unanimously agree to dissolve the company, it shall be dissolved accordingly. The partners may agree to dissolve the company at any time, especially if the company was established for an indefinite duration, which means the decision is contingent on the mutual will of all parties involved.

In cases where a partner dies, is interdicted, declared bankrupt, or becomes insolvent, the company shall dissolve **unless** the company contract includes a provision for succession by heirs or stipulates that another person shall replace the incapacitated or insolvent partner. In such cases, the contract remains valid provided these contingencies were addressed contractually in advance.

Additionally, the company may be dissolved if a partner withdraws, **provided** the withdrawal occurs under reasonable conditions. For example, if the company has no specified duration, a partner may withdraw, but must notify the other partners of the intention to withdraw prior to doing so. The withdrawal must not be carried out in bad faith or at an inappropriate time.

Moreover, if the company's capital is destroyed or rendered unusable in a manner that makes the fulfillment of the company's objective impossible, the company shall dissolve by operation of law. A judicial ruling may also result in dissolution. For instance:

"A court may order the dissolution of the company at the request of one of the partners if another partner fails to fulfill their obligations, or for any other significant reason not attributable to the partners. The court shall assess the seriousness of such grounds to justify dissolution, and any agreement to the contrary shall be deemed void."

Merger, bankruptcy, and liquidation are also recognized grounds for company dissolution, and these matters shall be discussed in detail later.

Through these legal provisions, it is evident that the Sudanese Companies Law has established clear and structured mechanisms for handling the dissolution of companies, thereby offering protection to all parties by clarifying the legal consequences of events leading to dissolution—whether due to time, purpose, or unforeseen difficulties affecting one or more partners.

The researcher notes that, as established in legal doctrine, the company contract requires the presence of essential elements for its validity: **consent, object, and cause**. The absence of any of these elements renders the contract void. For example, if a partner's consent is tainted by fraud or coercion, or if a partner lacks legal capacity, or if the company's purpose is unlawful, then the company contract is void—unless rectified either through express contractual provisions or by judicial intervention.

The absence of these elements leads to the **nullity of the contract**, and in such cases, the partners are not bound by any of the obligations arising under the void agreement. If the company contract is declared void, the parties must revert to the pre-contractual status quo—**unless** they agree to proceed with the liquidation of the company according to legal procedures.

As stated in the law:

"The company shall be dissolved by operation of law upon the expiration of its designated term or the completion of the purpose for which it was established."

The agreement of partners to operate the company for a specific term or for the execution of a particular task results in dissolution upon the expiry of the term or completion of the task. Likewise, the company is dissolved upon unanimous agreement of the partners, or in cases of a partner's death, interdiction, insolvency, or bankruptcy—**unless** the company contract provides for the succession of partnership to heirs, or allows for substitution of the incapacitated or insolvent partner, thereby enabling continuity.

As permitted by law:

"The company shall be dissolved upon the withdrawal of a partner if it was established for an indefinite period, provided that the withdrawing partner notifies the others in advance and that the withdrawal is not conducted in bad faith or at an inappropriate time."

In the event of destruction of company assets to the extent that it becomes impossible to achieve its purpose, the company dissolves by operation of law. Additionally, dissolution may be ordered by the court:

"The court may order the dissolution of the company upon the request of one of the partners due to non-performance by another partner or for any other substantial cause deemed sufficient by the court to justify dissolution. Any agreement to the contrary shall be null and void."

Merger, bankruptcy, and liquidation are also causes for dissolution and will be examined in detail later.

Through the analysis of legal provisions concerning **nullity and dissolution of the company contract**, the researcher observes that the law has provided **flexible mechanisms** for resolving disputes among partners that may lead to the company's dissolution. While such mechanisms are necessary for the protection of partners' rights, the researcher believes that company legislation requires **further safeguards** regarding how to address **unforeseen events**, such as the death or bankruptcy of a partner, especially in the absence of clear contractual provisions or prior agreements among the partners.

The researcher further emphasizes that **judicial procedures for company dissolution**, particularly those arising from court judgments, should be carefully considered to **prevent potential abuse** by one party seeking to dissolve the company to their own advantage at the expense of others.

Chapter Four: Concept, Legitimacy, Conditions, and Types of Bankruptcy

Section One: Definition of Bankruptcy

First Requirement: Definition of Bankruptcy Linguistically and Terminologically

First Branch: Bankruptcy in Language

The root verb *aflasa* (أفلس) is derived from the Arabic root *f-l-s* (ف-ل-س). It is a triliteral verb with a hamza added, which conveys the sense of becoming or transformation. The verb *aflasa* means "to become penniless" or "to have no money." For example, the Prophet Muhammad (peace be upon him) said: *"Who do you consider bankrupt?" They said: "One who has neither dirham nor goods."* (Hadith)

The term *aflasa* thus linguistically indicates a state where a person no longer has any money (fils). Similar constructions are used to indicate entering a certain state, such as *aqhara* (to become subdued) or *adhalla* (to become humiliated). From this linguistic usage, it can be concluded that bankruptcy means a change in one's financial condition, specifically becoming so impoverished as to possess only minimal or no monetary value. According to the prophetic hadith, bankruptcy means having no money left.

It is important to distinguish between *taflees* (تفليس), which refers to a legal act or judgment issued by a judge or competent authority, and *iflas* (إفلاس), which generally denotes the state of being insolvent.

Second Branch: Definition of Bankruptcy in Jurisprudential Terminology

Bankruptcy is a **legal mechanism** for enforcing the rights of creditors against a merchant debtor who ceases to pay his commercial debts. This mechanism involves collective liquidation of the debtor's assets, with the proceeds distributed among creditors according to their respective rights and priorities. This procedure applies both to individual commercial enterprises and to commercial companies.

The impact of bankruptcy on individuals tends to be more severe, as it affects their personal and financial status. In the case of commercial companies, the effects are broader due to companies representing a collective effort combining individual inputs, pooled financial resources, and the execution of large projects often unattainable by individual merchants alone. Commercial companies thus serve as key instruments for driving economic and social development at the national level.

Numerous definitions of bankruptcy have been provided by Islamic jurists (fuqaha), yet they largely converge in meaning, as follows:

- **Hanafis:** According to the commentary by Ibn Abidin, bankruptcy means "reaching a state of having no money." Some say it is having money after previously having dirhams (silver coins). Bankruptcy, in this context, is the ruling by the judge declaring the debtor bankrupt. The debt that leads to interdiction (legal incapacitation) in Hanafi jurisprudence—corresponding to bankruptcy in other schools—is a debt exceeding the debtor's assets or likely to do so. The researcher notes that bankruptcy here is a condition attributed to the debtor resulting from debts surpassing his assets, rendering him penniless.
- **Malikis:** Different terms such as *fils*, *iflas*, and *taflees* are used. *Fils* refers to a lack of money; *iflas* means a lack of money exceeding what the creditors can claim; *taflees* is the removal of a man's property for the benefit of his creditors. *Taflees* is defined as the judge declaring a debtor bankrupt by restricting his control over his assets. Some divide *taflees* into general and specific: general is when a creditor's claim exceeds the debtor's ability to pay; specific is the judge's ruling to transfer all debtor assets to creditors due to inability to meet obligations. Al-Qarafi defines it as creditors' request for interdiction over debts exceeding the debtor's assets, similar to the definition in "Jawahir."
- **Ibn Rushd:** Defines bankruptcy as either the exhaustion of the debtor's assets such that debts cannot be paid or the debtor having no known assets at all.
- **Shafi'is:** Use both *taflees* and *fils*. They define *taflees* as the judge's interdiction of the debtor under certain conditions and as the judge declaring the debtor bankrupt by prohibiting him from disposing of his assets. They also describe it as interdiction of one who owes a debt greater than the value of his assets.
- **Hanbalis:** Define bankruptcy as when a person's debt exceeds his assets and his expenditures exceed his income, naming such a person bankrupt even if he owns assets, because his assets are effectively committed to debt payment and thus considered nonexistent. Bankruptcy also occurs when the

judge interdicts the debtor due to debts exceeding assets at the creditors' request. Bankruptcy can mean exhaustion of the debtor's assets by debts, rendering repayment impossible, or having no known assets at all.

In technical terms, bankruptcy is used in two meanings:

1. A person whose assets do not cover his debts.
2. A person with no assets at all or no known assets.

Abu Jayb explains that in Islamic law, bankruptcy refers to either:

a) Debts consuming all the debtor's assets, so no fulfillment of debts is possible; or
b) The debtor having no known assets at all.

It describes a state where the debtor cannot fulfill his payment obligations due to debts exceeding his assets.

The researcher observes that Islamic jurisprudence schools generally do not distinguish clearly between *iflas* (bankruptcy) and *taflees* (the judicial act of declaring bankruptcy). Accordingly, the researcher considers *taflees* as the judicial ruling issued by a judge detailing the debtor's financial condition, whereas *iflas* refers to the debtor's state where debts consume or exceed the debtor's assets, rendering the debtor bankrupt and unable to cover his obligations.

Bankruptcy is a fundamental economic and legal concept related to the debtor's capacity to fulfill outstanding debts. It is an instrument used for liquidating the assets of a merchant debtor or a company that has stopped paying its debts, with the remaining assets divided among creditors according to their shares. While bankruptcy is a tragic event for individuals, its impact on companies can be even more significant, as companies represent a consolidation of human and financial resources and play a crucial role in driving the economy and developing large projects beyond the capacity of individual merchants.

In this context, bankruptcy holds great importance in socio-economic terms. Bankruptcy in large commercial enterprises indicates difficulty in mobilizing available resources for projects, leading to economic slowdown and a decline in investor confidence. On the individual level, bankruptcy may destroy the debtor's personal and financial life; however, its impact on companies may be more destructive, resulting in collapse, job losses, and the erosion of savings for many individuals.

Jurists' definitions of bankruptcy have varied; however, they all converge around the fundamental meaning of bankruptcy, which is the cessation of debt repayment due to the insufficiency of the debtor's assets. Definitions differ among Islamic jurisprudential schools: some regard bankruptcy as a **judicial ruling issued by a judge** to determine the debtor's financial status, whereas others consider it a **description of the debtor's condition** when his debts exceed his assets.

The definitions of bankruptcy vary according to the schools of thought, and it is noteworthy that jurists have not clearly distinguished between *bankruptcy* (**iflas**) and *judicial declaration of bankruptcy* (**taflees**). According to their definitions, *taflees* is the judicial ruling that officially declares the debtor's financial condition, while *iflas* refers to the state in which the debtor's assets are insufficient to cover his debts. Within this framework, it can be asserted that *taflees* is the **legal process** whereby the debtor is interdicted and declared bankrupt, whereas *iflas* is the **financial condition** in which the debtor is unable to fulfill his obligations.

Impact on Commercial Companies:

Bankruptcy in commercial companies constitutes a critical phase that can lead to contraction or even collapse of the market at large. Companies represent an economic force that contributes significantly to national economic growth, especially when these are large enterprises managing substantial projects. When a company goes bankrupt, the broader economy is affected through the destruction of employment opportunities, loss of tax revenues, and damage to investors. Given these severe consequences, economic laws must keep pace with evolving economic realities and implement legal mechanisms to prevent recurrence of such crises.

The researcher views *iflas* (bankruptcy) and *taflees* (judicial declaration of bankruptcy) as interrelated concepts that differ mainly in their practical application. The researcher recommends that legislators improve legal procedures related to bankruptcy in a manner that safeguards the rights of all parties involved—both debtors and creditors—and establishes flexible legal frameworks allowing for fair liquidation of companies without causing major adverse effects on the economy at large. Furthermore, coordination between economic and legal systems is vital to create a stable environment that attracts investment and prevents major financial crises within companies, thereby contributing to economic and social stability.

Additionally, the researcher advocates for the establishment of protective mechanisms for debtors affected by bankruptcy, particularly small and medium-sized enterprises (SMEs), whose owners often face insolvency due to economic crises or unforeseen market fluctuations.

Section Two: Definition of Bankruptcy in Law

Legal Definition:

Bankruptcy is defined as the condition of a merchant's cessation to pay his commercial debts, even if he possesses sufficient funds to settle them. According to the **Bankruptcy Reform Act of 1978** (U.S.), bankruptcy is defined as the inability of a company to fulfill its financial obligations due to the disruption of its financial status. The **Egyptian Commercial Law** defines bankruptcy as: *"Every merchant who is obligated under the provisions of this law to keep commercial books, and who stops paying his commercial debts as a result of disturbances in his financial affairs, is deemed bankrupt."*

Bankruptcy is also defined as the debtor merchant's failure to pay his commercial debts at their due dates, regardless of whether the debtor is solvent or insolvent, whether his assets are plentiful or scarce. The Commercial Law distinguishes between merchants and others; bankruptcy applies exclusively to merchants, whereas insolvency applies to civil debtors.

The Egyptian Commercial Law further states:

"Without prejudice to the application of the provisions of the preceding chapter, every merchant who stops paying his commercial debts or supports financial confidence only through clearly unlawful means is considered bankrupt."

Thus, bankruptcy is established in one of two cases: either the merchant stops paying his due commercial debts, or the merchant artificially supports his financial credibility by unlawful means, such as obtaining bank facilities based on fictitious documents or contracts that purportedly demonstrate involvement in major projects expected to generate profits, enabling him to repay his obligations to the financing bank.

Consequently, the bankruptcy system is designed exclusively for merchants due to the nature of interconnected and complex commercial relationships that require a strict system to preserve their entity and protect them from infiltrators and reckless parties. Since the merchant, while being a creditor, is simultaneously a debtor to other merchants, the failure of one merchant to pay his debts places his creditor merchants at risk of bankruptcy as well. Moreover, commercial life demands trust and creditworthiness among its participants; therefore, the legislator has addressed bankruptcy in detail within the Commercial Law.

The **Saudi Protective Settlement System** provides that:

"Any merchant, whether an individual or a company, whose financial situation has deteriorated such that there is fear of stopping payment of his debts, may request a settlement to prevent bankruptcy."

The **Jordanian Commercial Law** states:

"Every merchant who stops paying his commercial debts, or who supports financial confidence only by clearly unlawful means, is considered bankrupt."

The **Yemeni Commercial Law** provides:

"Any merchant whose financial affairs have deteriorated and has stopped paying his commercial debts may be declared bankrupt."

The **UAE Federal Bankruptcy Law** defines bankruptcy as follows:

"A company is considered bankrupt if: (a) it stops paying its debts on their due dates for more than thirty consecutive business days as a result of disruption in its financial position; or (b) it is in a state of financial insolvency, whereby it becomes evident that the company's assets will never cover its due obligations."

Article 68 of the Bankruptcy Law obligates any bankrupt (as defined above) to file a petition for opening bankruptcy procedures before the competent court. If the bankrupt company is subject to supervision by a regulatory authority, it must notify that authority in writing of its intention to file the bankruptcy petition at least fifteen business days prior to submission. The regulatory authority may submit any documents or defenses regarding the petition to the court.

From these definitions—which largely converge on the concept of bankruptcy with minor differences regarding the notions of debtor and debt—the researcher notes that bankruptcy law was originally limited to merchants only and did not include companies. However, the Saudi bankruptcy system aligns with Islamic Sharia principles and global trends by applying to both commercial and civil persons alike.

Legal Definition of Bankruptcy:

In legal terminology, bankruptcy differs from its linguistic and religious meanings. It is considered an **executive legal mechanism** through which the assets of a debtor who stops paying commercial debts are managed, aiming to enhance credit and uphold trust in commercial transactions. This is achieved through procedures designed to protect creditors' interests and preserve their rights. The system ensures the sequestration of the debtor's remaining assets under judicial supervision to prevent asset concealment or damage to creditors. Its rules seek to achieve justice and equality among creditors, without discrimination.

Upon issuance of a bankruptcy judgment, creditors are prohibited from initiating individual lawsuits or actions against the debtor to ensure equal treatment, making bankruptcy a system applicable to both merchants and non-merchants aimed at collective enforcement on the debtor's assets while safeguarding creditors' rights.

Based on the foregoing, the researcher concludes that bankruptcy is a vital legal concept regulated by various legal systems with the primary objective of maintaining financial and economic stability in commercial relations and safeguarding the rights of all concerned parties. Although bankruptcy definitions vary across jurisdictions, they fundamentally revolve around the debtor's cessation of payment due to financial distress or inability to meet obligations.

The researcher argues that bankruptcy law is not merely a legal procedure applied to merchants facing financial incapacity; rather, it is a fundamental tool within the financial system designed to ensure fairness among creditors by regulating the relationships among parties involved in commercial transactions. In countries where bankruptcy is narrowly applied—such as Egypt, Jordan, and Yemen—it applies only to merchants who cease paying their commercial debts, aiming to protect the market and balance the interests of merchants and creditors.

In contrast, the Saudi bankruptcy system reflects a broader approach, encompassing both individuals and companies, demonstrating greater alignment with Islamic principles and international legal frameworks. In Saudi Arabia, bankruptcy is not limited to cessation of payments by individuals but also incorporates creditor protection mechanisms ensuring transparency and equality among all stakeholders.

As for the UAE law, the definition of bankruptcy relies on a temporal criterion related to the debtor's inability to pay debts for more than 30 consecutive days. The objective is to ensure the protection of creditors' rights through a series of procedures that allow them to seize the debtor's assets. This reflects the UAE legislator's vision regarding the necessity of having effective legal safeguards that maintain the stability of the commercial system and protect it from economic chaos.

In conclusion, the researcher finds that bankruptcy is a legal tool aimed at guaranteeing the rights of creditors; however, it is not limited to that function alone. It also contributes to creating an environment of integrity and fairness in commercial transactions. This system should be applied in a manner that balances the interests of all parties, while ensuring the effective enforcement of laws on merchants and other commercial actors alike.

Section Three: Definition of Bankruptcy in Sudanese Law

The Sudanese legislator did not define bankruptcy as a specific term; rather, it stipulated certain acts that, if committed by the debtor, render the debtor a bankrupt and obligate the declaration of bankruptcy. Article (4) of the Bankruptcy Law of 1929 enumerates acts classified as bankruptcy acts and specifies the conditions under which a person is deemed to have committed bankruptcy. The article states:

"A person commits an act of bankruptcy in any of the following cases:

(a) If he transfers his assets in Sudan or any other country to a trustee or trustees for the benefit of his creditors generally; or if he gifts or transfers all or part of his assets in Sudan or any other country intending thereby to harm or delay his creditors.

(b) If he transfers all or part of his assets or subjects them to a privilege in Sudan or any other country, and such transfer is void under this law or any other applicable law, being deemed a fraudulent preference if he is declared bankrupt.

(c) If, with the intention to harm or delay his creditors, he commits any of the following acts:

- First: Leaves Sudan or remains outside it.
- Second: Leaves his residence or absents himself by any other means.
- Third: Isolates himself to deprive his creditors of means of communication.

(d) If any of his assets are seized and sold pursuant to a judgment issued by any court.

(e) If he requests the issuance of a bankruptcy declaration under the provisions of this law.

(f) If he notifies any of his creditors that he has stopped paying his debts or is about to stop paying them.

(g) If he is imprisoned for a period exceeding twenty-one days by virtue of a judgment or order issued by a civil court for failure to pay a sum of money.

(h) If any creditor obtains a final judgment against him for any amount and, due to the lack of stay of execution of that judgment, notifies him in writing to pay the adjudicated amount according to the judgment or to provide a guarantee for payment or to settle the matter to the satisfaction of the creditor or the court, and he fails to comply within thirty days from the receipt of that notification or fails to convince the court that he has a subsidiary claim against the creditor or a right of set-off or a counterclaim for an amount equal to or exceeding the adjudicated amount, and was unable to raise it in the suit in which the judgment was obtained. Every person who, at that time, has the right to execute a final judgment is considered a creditor obtaining a final judgment as meant in this article."

From the definition, it is clear that the bankruptcy system in Sudanese law does not distinguish between the merchant and the non-merchant. It is noteworthy that the Sudanese legislator did not define bankruptcy as a term per se, but rather limited itself to defining the acts which, if committed by a person, render that person in a state of bankruptcy.

Article (90) of the same law states that bankruptcy is a system of collective execution on the assets of a merchant who fails to meet his debts at their due dates. This system is limited to merchants only, and thus applies exclusively to them. Non-merchants are subject to the civil insolvency regime. Both individuals—men and women—and companies are subject to bankruptcy procedures; however, companies are not subject to these procedures but rather to liquidation procedures according to the Companies Law. This is pursuant to Article (92) of the Sudanese Bankruptcy Law, which states: *(No petition to declare the bankruptcy of any company registered under the Companies Law of 1925 may be submitted).*

From the foregoing, the researcher concludes that the Sudanese legislator has considerably expanded the scope of bankruptcy acts. To reconcile the legal meaning of bankruptcy—represented by the debtor's failure to pay debts at their due dates due to business disruption and deterioration of financial conditions—with the acts enumerated in Article 4 of the Bankruptcy Law of 1929, the researcher sees these acts as restrictions aimed at leading to the debtor's inability to pay his debts at their due dates. Moreover, it is unclear whether the term "person" in the legal article refers to a natural person (i.e., the merchant) or a legal person (i.e., the company). Based on this, the researcher considers that actions by a natural person (merchant) or a legal person (company) which result in harm to creditors due to the debtor's failure to pay—whether caused by factors beyond his control or deliberate conduct intended to harm creditors as outlined in the aforementioned article—are encompassed. A close look at these acts reveals their purpose: to limit the debtor's ability to fulfill debt obligations when due.

The researcher believes that bankruptcy, in its essence under Sudanese law, is the debtor's failure to pay debts at their due dates because of financial disturbances caused by circumstances beyond his control; this can be described as involuntary bankruptcy. However, if the merchant deliberately harms creditors—as the Sudanese legislator states, for example, by concealing or disposing of assets or destroying commercial records—then the merchant or company is deemed a fraudulent bankrupt. This behavior is particularly dangerous and unethical, warranting criminal penalties against the merchant or company in addition to bankruptcy procedures.

The *Judicial Rulings Journal* states:

"Bankruptcy, in its legal meaning, is a special legal system aimed at organizing collective execution on the assets of a bankrupt debtor who stops paying debts at their due dates due to business disruption and deteriorating financial conditions, which undermines trust in his creditworthiness and threatens creditors' interests. In most modern legislations, bankruptcy is a system exclusive to merchants and those akin to them. The Sudanese legislator, however, neglected this distinction and did not accept differentiation between the bankruptcy of a merchant debtor and a non-merchant debtor. This has caused confusion between bankruptcy—which aims to activate credit in commercial transactions, protect creditors' rights, liquidate debtor's assets, and distribute the proceeds among creditors equitably—and civil insolvency, which is based on the imbalance where liabilities exceed assets without resulting in consequences for the insolvent or creditor.

Moreover, adopting a mixed bankruptcy system fails to achieve equality between merchants and non-merchants regarding the consequences and grounds for declaring bankruptcy. There are important differences between civil and commercial transactions that cannot be ignored. At least, bankruptcy of a merchant entails the suspension of the merchant's right to manage and dispose of his assets, as a bankruptcy trustee is appointed to manage them in order to protect creditors' rights. In contrast, non-merchants are not subject to such measures and are free to continue their professions normally.

Bankruptcy is always declared by a court ruling based on a petition from the debtor or creditor. This is a declaratory judgment that does not establish rights like other judgments, but rather establishes a new status—the debtor's bankruptcy. Its issuance triggers collective liquidation of the debtor's assets and the formation of a creditors' committee. Preliminary procedures then follow, assigned to a bankruptcy trustee appointed by the court, who supervises the debtor's assets (movable, immovable, etc.), verifies debts, conducts accounting between debtor and creditors, liquidates and sells assets under court supervision, and distributes the proceeds fairly among creditors without conflict or dispute (pari passu), with no preference except for privileged or secured creditors, whose rights remain unaffected by the bankruptcy declaration and are excluded from the creditors' committee."

From the foregoing, the researcher believes that to distinguish between civil insolvency and commercial bankruptcy and to regulate our legal provisions in this regard, avoiding contradictions and shortcomings present in the current Bankruptcy Law, the key criterion for declaring the debtor bankrupt is his failure to pay due debts at their maturity dates, provided that this failure and inability to pay arise from the deterioration of the debtor's financial situation and disruption of his business, not from negligence or deliberate procrastination.

Regardless of whether the debtor is solvent or insolvent (i.e., whether his liabilities are less than or exceed his assets), the essential factor for declaring bankruptcy is the debtor's inability to pay due debts caused by an acute financial distress that undermines his creditworthiness and exposes his interests and those of his creditors to a real or highly probable risk.

Moreover, the debt in question must be due, definite in amount, and free of any dispute.

Accordingly, the trial court has full authority to determine the state of default in debt payment, its causes, and to verify the fulfillment of other legal conditions required for a bankruptcy ruling, based on all evidence, indications, circumstances, and facts presented.

Applying the above to the case facts, I find that the trial court correctly established the occurrence of bankruptcy with its elements as noted, regarding the bankrupt, based on sound grounds. However, the final judgment contained some shortcomings, particularly in failing to appoint the bankruptcy trustee and neglecting to define his duties and responsibilities as indicated above. It is essential that the judgment explicitly specify the trustee's tasks to ensure the ruling is complete and to empower the trustee to perform his duties as prescribed therein without deviation.

Unlike civil insolvency, bankruptcy entails legal consequences for the debtor and creditors, chiefly the debtor's interdiction from managing his assets, with management entrusted to the trustee, who is granted legal protection. Creditors are thereby prohibited from initiating individual lawsuits against the bankrupt after the bankruptcy ruling and formation of the creditors' committee.

The ruling issued by the primary court declaring the debtor bankrupt is a declaratory judgment, not a final judgment that is irrevocable upon issuance. It is inconceivable that the debtor's assets remain indefinitely frozen and protected legally without end. Once the trustee verifies the bankrupt's debts and satisfies the creditors by liquidating the debtor's assets, or once it is established that the debtor's assets do not cover all debts, the trustee must submit a report to the court that issued the bankruptcy ruling to issue a final judgment closing the bankruptcy and lifting its effects on the debtor and creditors. This restores to the debtor and creditors the freedom to pursue any remaining claims individually as legally permitted.

Given the correctness of the trial court's findings, later upheld by the Court of Appeal in the challenged ruling, the appeal lodged by the appellant, Hafiz Al-Sayed Al-Barbari Company, is without merit, as it is established that the debtor stopped paying his debts due to deteriorating financial conditions and business disruption, which led to his continued imprisonment since 1999 for failure and inability to pay.

Similarly, the debtor's appeal against the ruling concerning the sale of mortgaged properties (real estate and seized goods) in favor of Al-Qadarif Bank is unfounded. The debtor explicitly acknowledges his indebtedness to the bank and does not deny mortgaging the property and goods to the bank to secure the debt.

Legally, such secured rights do not fall within the bankruptcy estate and creditors holding such rights are listed only to the extent that the mortgaged assets do not cover their full debt. The debtor's contrary claims have no factual or evidentiary basis.

Therefore, my conclusion is to dismiss both appeals and uphold the challenged ruling.

It may be that the debtor's default resulted from loss of creditworthiness and inability to continue his trade. The Supreme Court confirmed this in the precedent of *Mohammed Nasser Mohammed v. Al-Qadarif Investment Bank*, stating: *"The criterion for declaring bankruptcy is the debtor's failure to pay due debts at maturity, arising from the deterioration of financial conditions and disruption of business, regardless of whether the debtor is solvent or insolvent. The essence of declaring bankruptcy is the inability to pay debts due to acute financial distress that threatens creditworthiness and creditors' interests with certain or highly probable danger."*

This is the modern concept of default settled by legal doctrine and Latin jurisprudence and adopted by the Egyptian legislator in the 1999 Commercial Law.

Actual default, considering the circumstances under which the debtor stopped paying debts, must indicate acute financial distress and genuine inability to continue trade. Moreover, doctrine and jurisprudence consider the debtor's resort to unlawful or irregular means of debt repayment as an indication of default.

Hence, default is essentially a matter of fact, not law. If the court finds the debtor truly unable to pay due to poor financial condition and that repayment is impossible despite efforts, it must declare bankruptcy. Conversely, if the inability to pay results from temporary financial disruption or a solvable emergency, the court should refrain from declaring bankruptcy.

From the above, the researcher concludes that bankruptcy can be defined as: "The inability of a company or merchant to fulfill its financial obligations to others, and this inability results from the deterioration of its financial condition. Bankruptcy is executed through a legal system in which the debtor's assets are subject to enforcement procedures aimed at equality among creditors so that they receive their rights from the available assets of the bankrupt debtor."

Or it can be defined as:

"A special system for merchants aimed at liquidating the assets of a merchant who has stopped paying his commercial debts when they become due."

The wisdom behind the bankruptcy system lies in the legislator's desire to support trust and credit in commercial transactions through a series of procedures that aim to protect the interests of creditors and preserve their rights proportionally to their debts. This results from the merchant's failure to pay due to a continuous inability to continue his trade or because his financial situation becomes dire and hopeless, rather than due to a temporary, incidental difficulty that can be overcome. In such a temporary case, the merchant cannot be described as bankrupt, and there is no need to declare bankruptcy or issue a bankruptcy ruling in order to liquidate his commercial activities collectively, freeze his control over managing his assets, or apply other related procedures.

In summary, the concept of bankruptcy refers to the legal status reached by a merchant who ceases to pay his debts, or a method of collective enforcement over the assets of a debtor merchant who stops paying his debts when due, which leads to liquidating and selling his assets, in preparation for distributing the proceeds among creditors on a pari passu basis (pro rata).

Both contemporary doctrine and judiciary agree that the cessation of payment is not a temporary financial hardship but must indicate a critical and hopeless financial condition that reflects a genuine inability preventing the merchant from fulfilling his debts when due. Upon issuing a bankruptcy ruling, legal consequences follow, the most important being the debtor's interdiction from managing his assets; all financial transactions performed by the bankrupt since the date he ceased payment become absolutely void, and his assets come under the control of the bankruptcy trustee supervised by the court. If the debtor is not a merchant and stops paying debts, he is considered insolvent (civil insolvency).

From the previous definitions, it becomes clear that bankruptcy requires the following:

- The existence of a person (natural) or (legal), according to Egyptian law defined as: "Anyone engaged in commercial activity, and any company formed under the forms stipulated in the company laws regardless of the company's purpose."

- The state of default must be involuntary, as clarified in Article (4) of the 1929 Bankruptcy Law mentioned above.
- A ruling must be issued declaring bankruptcy due to debts that place the merchant debtor in a state of bankruptcy if he ceases to pay commercial debts. Civil debts do not render a person bankrupt.

Sudanese and Egyptian laws restrict the debts triggering bankruptcy to those where the cause of default is the debtor's financial disruption and the loss of creditworthiness, while Jordanian law does not impose such a restriction.

The bankruptcy system aims to enable creditors to obtain their rights, or as much as possible thereof, on an equal footing concerning all the debtor's assets, and to protect each creditor from other creditors to prevent unfair advantages at others' expense. Bankruptcy also aims to remove the debtor's control over asset management to protect creditors from any harmful acts, appointing instead a bankruptcy trustee or the court. As stated in the Bankruptcy Law: "Upon issuing the bankruptcy order, all the bankrupt's assets revert to the court or trustee as agreed."

Moreover, the bankruptcy system seeks to protect the conflicting interests between the debtor and all his creditors with their different debts. It also aims to protect creditors from one another since bankruptcy inevitably creates competition among creditors, each striving to maximize their own claims regardless of the effect on others. Therefore, bankruptcy rules aim to achieve equality among creditors and organize the distribution of the debtor's assets in a manner that ensures fairness.

To achieve these goals, ensure justice and equality, and guarantee creditors' rights, the legislator established bankruptcy rules that remove the bankrupt's control over his assets and transactions, entrusting the bankruptcy trustee appointed by the judiciary to liquidate the bankrupt's assets, sell them, and distribute the proceeds among creditors according to their respective debts.

The state of bankruptcy for merchants differs from financial insolvency or civil insolvency, as previously mentioned. Bankruptcy is governed by commercial law, which involves collective liquidation of the debtor's assets, whereas insolvency is governed by civil law, which endorses individual rather than collective claims.

Chapter Five: The Legitimacy of Bankruptcy and the Differences Between It and Insolvency

Section One: The Legitimacy of Bankruptcy in Islamic Jurisprudence

Islamic law has paid significant attention to financial matters and specifically regulated the bankruptcy system. Islamic jurisprudence overall has detailed its rulings extensively, indicating that bankruptcy is legitimate and practiced within Islamic jurisprudence. There is ample evidence for this in the prophetic traditions (Sunnah)—both verbal and practical—as well as in the actions of the Companions (may Allah be pleased with them), and also in rational proofs.

Subsection One: Evidence from the Sunnah

It is narrated from Abu Huraira (may Allah be pleased with him) that the Messenger of Allah (peace be upon him) said:

"Do you know what bankruptcy is?" They said, "Bankruptcy among us is one who has neither money nor goods." He said, "The bankrupt of my Ummah will come on the Day of Resurrection with prayer, fasting, and zakat, but he will have insulted this person, slandered that person, consumed the wealth of this one, shed the blood of that one, and struck that one. So some of his good deeds will be given to this person, and some to that person. If his good deeds are exhausted before his debts are settled, then their sins will be taken and placed upon him, and then he will be thrown into the Hellfire."

The reasoning in this hadith is that the Prophet (peace be upon him) asked the Companions about the meaning of bankruptcy. Their answer was what was commonly known to them—that the bankrupt is one who owns neither money nor goods. This concept was firmly established among them. Jurists defined bankruptcy as when a person's debts exceed his assets, meaning his assets effectively belong to creditors and he cannot dispose of them. The Prophet did not negate the Companions' understanding of bankruptcy but rather drew their attention to another kind of bankruptcy—the bankruptcy of the Hereafter. The Prophet (peace be upon him) often used this rhetorical method in his sayings, such as: "The strong is not the one who overcomes the people by his strength, but the strong is the one who controls himself while in anger."

Also, Abu Huraira reported that the Messenger of Allah (peace be upon him) said: "Whoever finds his property with a man or a person who has become bankrupt, he has more right to recover it than anyone else."

The reasoning in this hadith is that it clarifies a ruling in bankruptcy—that the owner of the goods has the right to reclaim them if they are found in possession of the bankrupt.

It was narrated by Saeed ibn Mansour, Abu Dawood, and Abdul Razzaq from the hadith of Abdul Rahman ibn Ka'b ibn Malik, that:

"Mu'adh ibn Jabal was a generous young man who never withheld anything. He continued to be in debt until all his wealth was overwhelmed by debt. He came to the Prophet (peace be upon him) to speak to his creditors. If they had abandoned anyone, they would have abandoned Mu'adh for the sake of the Messenger of Allah. So the Messenger of Allah sold his wealth to them until Mu'adh was left with nothing."

The reasoning in this hadith is that Mu'adh ibn Jabal (may Allah be pleased with him) had reached a state of bankruptcy as the hadith indicates his debts overwhelmed his wealth. Creditors reportedly sought to place him under guardianship as some narrations mention. Mu'adh's coming to the Prophet was not to ask for guardianship on himself but to seek leniency from the creditors. The Prophet then sold Mu'adh's wealth to the creditors and distributed it among them according to their shares. This conduct of the Prophet constitutes many of the bankruptcy procedures, which confirms its permissibility.

In another narration from Abu Sa'id Al-Khudri:

A man during the time of the Messenger of Allah (peace be upon him) suffered a loss in fruits he had purchased. His debt increased, and the Messenger of Allah said, "Charity yourselves on his behalf." People gave charity to help him, but it did not cover his debt. Then the Messenger of Allah said to his creditors, "Take whatever you find, and that is all you have."

The reasoning in this hadith is that a Muslim always strives to help his fellow Muslim, especially in hardships and calamities. These hadiths encourage social solidarity, particularly in times of distress. The bankrupt's remaining assets are taken at their value; he is not imprisoned or punished but is given time and must repay his debts to their owners. This hadith indicates the general rulings related to bankruptcy.

Subsection Two: Evidence from the Actions of the Companions (May Allah Be Pleased with Them)

1. We came to Abu Huraira (may Allah be pleased with him) regarding one of our companions who became bankrupt. He said, "I will adjudicate for you according to the judgment of the Messenger of Allah (peace be upon him): whoever becomes bankrupt or dies, and someone finds his goods in possession of the bankrupt, then he is more entitled to them."

The reasoning in this hadith is that it indicates the legitimacy of a bankruptcy ruling: the right of the owner of the goods to reclaim his property found with the bankrupt. This was a ruling made by Abu Huraira, who judged among the disputants who had chosen him as arbitrator, and none of the Companions objected to his ruling.

2. It was narrated by Abdul Rahman bin Dalaf Al-Muzani that a man from Juhaina used to precede the pilgrim and buy the camels (caravans) at a high price, then hurried his pace to overtake the pilgrim. He became bankrupt, and his case was referred to Umar ibn Al-Khattab. Umar said:

"O people, indeed, Al-Usayfi' (the man) is the Usayfi' of Juhaina. He is satisfied with his debt and trust by saying the pilgrim preceded him, yet he had become indebted and insolvent. Now he is indebted. Whoever has a debt on him should come to us in the morning so we may divide his wealth among them."

Al-Bayhaqi said regarding creditors and debt: "Beware of debt, for its beginning is worry and its end is war."

Reasoning:
This narration explicitly states that Usayfi' of Juhaina fell into bankruptcy, and this happened during the caliphate of the just Umar ibn Al-Khattab. His matter was raised to Umar to judge between him and his creditors. Umar declared his bankruptcy and sought to realize the debts owed to him, asking the creditors to come to him so that his wealth could be divided among them. These are the procedures of bankruptcy, carried out openly before many companions without objection. This indicates the legitimacy of bankruptcy procedures in Islamic jurisprudence.

3. It was narrated by Saeed ibn Al-Musayyib that a freedman (Mawla) of Umm Habiba became bankrupt and a dispute arose about him before Uthman (the Caliph). Uthman ruled that whoever claims his right before the bankruptcy is declared, his right is to be fulfilled, and whoever recognizes his property in kind (the actual goods) is more entitled to it.

Reasoning:

Caliph Uthman ibn Affan ruled on a matter involving a bankrupt person during his caliphate. He clarified the ruling on recovering rights before bankruptcy is formally declared and the ruling concerning goods found with the bankrupt if their owner is known. The ruling was issued in the presence of companions, and no one objected to it, which demonstrates the legitimacy of these rulings as part of bankruptcy law.

Subsection Three: Rational Evidence:

1. Preservation of wealth is one of the five essential necessities (al-daruriyyat al-khams) that Islamic law aims to protect, and the bankruptcy system legislates rules to safeguard wealth.
2. The bankruptcy system works to protect the interests of creditors and preserve their rights. Although this may conflict with the debtor's interests, the public interest takes precedence over private interest.
3. Bankruptcy rulings prevent the debtor from harming some or all creditors by disposing of his assets unjustly or favoring some creditors over others.
4. The majority of jurists permit placing a guardian (conservatorship) over a reckless person to preserve his interest, which is an individual interest. Thus, it is more appropriate to place a guardian over the bankrupt to protect the interests of creditors, which is a collective interest.

Article (235) of the Companies Law of 1925 states:

"Subject to the provisions of Article 239, the rules applied in the Bankruptcy Law of 1929 shall apply to the assets of persons whose bankruptcy has been declared regarding the liquidation of the insolvent company. These rules apply to the secured and unsecured creditors' rights, as well as to debts subject to proof and the valuation of amounts paid annually and future or contingent liabilities. All persons entitled in any such case to prove receipt of shares from the company's assets may participate in the liquidation and present claims against the company as permitted under this article."

Researcher's Opinion on the Legitimacy of Bankruptcy in Islamic Jurisprudence:

From the evidence presented by the researcher, whether from the Prophetic Sunnah or the actions of the Companions, it is clear that bankruptcy is not only legitimate in Islamic law but is an integral part of the Islamic financial and economic system. This system aims to regulate financial transactions and ensure the rights of all involved parties.

The Prophetic hadiths show a broad understanding of bankruptcy, defining it as financial incapacity of the debtor to repay his debts, aligning with modern definitions emphasizing collective creditor rights. The evidence cited includes texts from the Sunnah, such as the hadith of the bankrupt person in the Hereafter, illustrating how debt affects a person's life both in this world and the next. The hadith also emphasizes protecting creditors' rights in this world.

Additionally, several hadiths related to the Companions were discussed, such as Abu Huraira's ruling on reclaiming goods from the bankrupt and the story of Mu'adh ibn Jabal, who was indebted to the point of bankruptcy and sought the Prophet's assistance, reflecting Islamic law's compassion for the bankrupt while safeguarding creditors' rights.

At the rational level, the researcher noted that Islamic law values the preservation of wealth as a fundamental necessity, and bankruptcy laws protect this necessity by preventing harm to others and avoiding debtor evasion of debt repayment. The system emphasizes fairness among creditors by enforcing balance and preventing preferential treatment in bankruptcy cases.

Conclusion:

The researcher concludes that the bankruptcy system in Islamic jurisprudence is legitimate and supported by both legal (Shar'i) and rational evidence. This system is established on the principles of justice and equality among creditors and the protection of their rights from manipulation or evasion. The Islamic system also reflects a profound concern for the preservation of wealth and the fair distribution of rights in a manner that ensures justice for all parties involved. Therefore, the bankruptcy system is considered a fundamental component of the financial structure in Islamic law and must be implemented in accordance with these principles.

Section Two: The Relationship Between Bankruptcy and Insolvency in Islamic Law

Insolvency (Arabic: **i'sar**) is derived from the quadrilateral verb **a'sara – yu'siru – i'sāran** or **'usran**, meaning to become poor or to fall into financial hardship. The word *'usr* (difficulty or hardship) appears in the Qur'an with various meanings.

Allah the Almighty says:

"Rushing towards the caller, the disbelievers will say: This is a difficult day." [Qur'an 54:8]
That is, a hard day—described as difficult due to its horrors and chaos.

"Allah will bring about ease after hardship." [Qur'an 65:7]

Meaning, after a period of straitened circumstances and difficulty in livelihood.

"Allah intends for you ease and does not intend for you hardship." [Qur'an 2:185]

That is, He desires facilitation and not burden.

"And if someone is in hardship, then let there be postponement until ease." [Qur'an 2:280]

Here, *hardship* refers to poverty.

"...and the Ansar who followed him in the time of hardship..." [Qur'an 9:117]

Refers to a time of difficulty and poverty.

"He said: Do not blame me for what I forgot, and do not burden me in my affair with difficulty." [Qur'an 18:73]

Meaning, do not impose difficulty beyond capacity.

"The true sovereignty that Day will be for the Most Merciful, and it will be a hard Day for the disbelievers." [Qur'an 25:26]

Refers to the Day of Judgment and reckoning for their worldly deeds.

"And consult together in kindness; but if you find yourselves in difficulty, then let another woman breastfeed [the child]." [Qur'an 65:6]

Al-Suddi said: "If the mother refuses to nurse her child after divorce, then another wet nurse should be found for him. The mother has more right to nurse the child if she accepts a wage equal to what others would accept, and it is not permissible to take the child from her unjustly."

The Sunnah also highlights the virtue and reward of showing leniency to the insolvent. The Prophet Muhammad (peace be upon him) said:

"Whoever grants respite to an insolvent person or reduces his debt, Allah will shade him on the Day of Judgment under His Throne's shade—on a day when there will be no shade but His."

Islamic jurists from the various schools have defined *al-mu'sir* (the insolvent) as follows:

- **Hanafi definition:** *"The insolvent is the one who is eligible to receive charity and upon whom zakat is not obligatory."*
- **Maliki definition:** *"Insolvency is a state of financial hardship due to lack of money."*
- **Shafi'i definition:** *"The insolvent is one who cannot afford basic expenses either from wealth or from an earning that is sufficient for each day."*
- **Hanbali definition:** *"The insolvent is one who does not possess what he can directly use to repay his debts, nor has any asset which, if sold, would allow him to do so."*

When examining these definitions, we find that most of them are imprecise and not comprehensive in their implications. A person may possess what is considered wealth or what can be sold, yet still be considered insolvent—such as someone who owns household items or clothing that merely covers his body, and yet these do not lift him out of insolvency or poverty. Perhaps the closest definition, in the researcher's view, is that of the Shafi'is. However, understanding the meaning of an insolvent person in their definition depends on understanding the term *bankrupt*. Therefore, a more appropriate definition of the insolvent (*mu'sir*) is: **a debtor who does not own more than what is necessary to meet his essential needs, such as clothing, food, and shelter—only to the extent that sustains him and his dependents—and whose loss of property would result in hardship and distress.** Thus, *'usr* (hardship/insolvency) is synonymous with *fals* (bankruptcy), meaning that all of the debtor's wealth is consumed, or that he has no known assets at all.

The jurists agree that if someone claims insolvency and the creditor believes him, he is not to be imprisoned. Rather, he must be granted respite until ease, as stated in Allah's saying:

"And if the debtor is in hardship, then [let there be] postponement until [a time of] ease" [Qur'an 2:280], and the saying of the Prophet (peace be upon him): *"Take what you find; you have no right to more than that."*

In the **Egyptian Civil Code**, it is stated:

"A debtor may be declared insolvent if his assets are insufficient to cover his due debts."

Legal scholars distinguish between **actual insolvency** and **legal insolvency**. Dr. Abdul Razzaq Al-Sanhouri defined **actual insolvency** as:

"A factual condition arising from the debtor's liabilities—whether due or not—exceeding his assets. It must be declared through a judicial ruling that places the debtor in a state of insolvency."

Legal insolvency, on the other hand, is:

"A legal condition resulting from the debtor's due liabilities exceeding his rights (assets), and must also be declared by a court judgment that places the debtor in a state of insolvency."

Thus, the state of insolvency does not arise unless by a judicial ruling, and the term *legal insolvency* is used to distinguish it from *actual insolvency*, which does not require a declaration.

As for the **Civil Procedures Act of 1983**, it allows the plea of insolvency as a means of releasing a debtor. Article (226) lists the cases in which a debtor must be released and states:

1. If the debtor is imprisoned to fulfill a judgment under Article (142) or (225), he shall not be released except if:

a. The adjudicated amount is paid, or

b. The judgment is fulfilled in any other way accepted by the judgment creditor, or

c. The judgment creditor consents in writing, in the presence of witnesses, or

d. Sufficient evidence of the debtor's insolvency is established.

From clause (d) of paragraph (1), which pertains to the release of the debtor if sufficient evidence of insolvency is presented, the following can be concluded:

- A debtor may be imprisoned.
- Evidence of the debtor's insolvency may be heard.
- The debtor must be released once sufficient evidence of his insolvency is proven.

The researcher notes in this section the influence of **Hanbali jurisprudence** on the Sudanese legislator, which permits the **imprisonment of debtors**.

The Sudanese law does not specify a particular standard for the evidence required to prove insolvency, leaving it entirely to the discretion of the trial court. Insolvency may be established through any means of proof. **Article (4) of the Evidence Act of 1994** defines evidence as:

"Any means by which a fact related to a case or dispute before arbitrators or signatories can be proven or disproven."

It is possible for insolvency to be established by **prolonged imprisonment**, which is known as a *presumption of insolvency*. As stated in the **Judicial Rulings Journal (2003), p. 156**:

"The prolonged detention of a convicted person may be considered a presumption of his insolvency."

It was also stated in the reasoning of a ruling by the **Supreme Court in another case** (Judicial Rulings Journal, 2003, p. 241):

"A person typically does not withhold money when it comes to their freedom. Since no assets were revealed for the debtor (the appellant), and he was unable to pay the adjudicated amount throughout this entire period, this is proof of his insolvency, and his continued imprisonment is of no benefit. Therefore, he should be released. However, if any assets appear after his release and he has not settled his debts or reached an agreement with the creditor regarding repayment, he may be re-arrested."

There is no doubt that reference to **Islamic Sharia rulings** is permitted under **Article (9/2) of the Civil Procedures Act**, which considers **Islamic law the primary source** of legislation and allows courts to refer to it when no statutory provision governs a given matter:

"In matters not governed by any legislative text, courts shall apply Islamic Sharia law, judicial precedents in Sudan, custom, equity, and sound conscience."

From the above, the researcher concludes that:

- The **insolvent debtor** is the one who does **not possess anything beyond his essential needs** that can be used to pay off debts.
- The **bankrupt debtor** is the one whose **assets are insufficient to cover his debts**.
- *Insolvency* and *bankruptcy* are closely related in meaning.
- The Sudanese legislator did **not establish a specific legal framework** for insolvency, nor did it clearly distinguish between **bankruptcy and insolvency**, except in **Article 226**.

The researcher also notes the following differences between insolvency and bankruptcy:

- Insolvency **cannot be declared** for a **non-trader debtor** unless their assets are insufficient to cover due debts.
- Upon declaration of insolvency, **debt maturities become due** in principle, as in bankruptcy. However, unlike the bankruptcy system, the judge may, in the case of insolvency, issue a ruling—at the debtor's request and in the presence of concerned parties.

The researcher believes that there is **significant conceptual overlap between insolvency and bankruptcy**, as both reflect the **debtor's inability to pay debts**. However, the **distinction in terms of legal procedures and practical application** in Sudanese law remains **unclear**. On the other hand, he finds it more appropriate to define the "insolvent" in **Islamic Sharia** as the **debtor who owns only what meets his essential needs**, in line with Islamic jurisprudence, which does not reduce the concept merely to general financial incapacity.

Chapter Six: Types of Bankruptcy

Section One: Simple Bankruptcy and True Bankruptcy

Many foreign legal systems adopt the bankruptcy regime specifically for **traders**, considering it a framework exclusively applicable to this category. However, some legal systems extend its application to include all individuals, whether traders or not, in order to **protect credit generally**. Among the most prominent legislations following this approach are **English, German, and Swiss** laws.

Bankruptcy is considered a **special legal system** with **severe effects and serious consequences**, especially compared to systems that regulate cases of debt default outside the commercial sector. This is due to the **unique nature of commercial activities**, which are characterized by speed in transactions, frequent borrowing, and a reliance on trust in dealings. Therefore, the bankruptcy system aims to **protect credit in the commercial domain** by enforcing strict rules and provisions that compel traders to fulfill their debts on time, thereby ensuring market stability and protecting all parties involved. Bankruptcy procedures are seen as a form of **penalty** that negatively affects a trader's assets, reputation, and commercial future, requiring the trader to exercise caution and diligence in managing their financial affairs.

As for the classification of bankruptcy, legal scholars have divided it into several types based on the reasons that led the trader to fall into bankruptcy. These include **three main categories**, which, despite differing causes, all follow the same legal rules and procedures.

One of these types is **simple bankruptcy**, which occurs when a trader ceases to pay debts due to **circumstances beyond their control**, such as economic crises, price inflation, tax or customs increases, or lack of experience in the commercial field. This type of bankruptcy may still be declared despite the trader's **good faith** and **absence of fraud or negligence**. Examples of such circumstances include: economic recessions, wars, legal restrictions on imports and exports, natural disasters such as earthquakes, fires in the commercial premises, and other uncontrollable events.

Article (104) of the Saudi Bankruptcy Law states that:

"Bankruptcy consists of three types: true bankruptcy, negligent bankruptcy, and fraudulent bankruptcy."

The researcher believes this classification aims to determine the **nature of each bankruptcy case**—whether the trader became bankrupt due to external circumstances, negligence in managing the business, or fraudulent acts intended to evade debt repayment. This classification helps the judiciary assign **appropriate penalties** based on the surrounding circumstances.

In contrast, the **Egyptian law** mentions only two types of bankruptcy. **Article (328) of the Egyptian Penal Code** defines a bankrupt as:

“A trader who has ceased to pay his debts.”

According to the researcher, this article refers to the **general definition of a bankrupt** without distinguishing between different types of bankruptcy, unlike other legal systems. The Egyptian law appears to adopt a **simpler and more generalized definition**, which may lead to **ambiguity** in classifying bankruptcy cases based on causes or consequences.

Article (438) of the Jordanian Penal Code, in its second clause, states:

“Anyone declared as a negligent bankrupt shall be punished with imprisonment not exceeding two years.”

The first clause further states:

“Those found guilty of fraudulent bankruptcy as described in the specific bankruptcy provisions, along with anyone proven to be an accomplice, shall be punished with hard labor.”

Thus, under **Article 438 of the Jordanian Penal Code**, the **punishment for negligent bankruptcy** is imprisonment of up to two years. The same article defines **fraudulent bankruptcy** as an intentional act aimed at **evading debt repayment**, punishable by **imprisonment or hard labor**, and extends the punishment to **any accomplices** involved in the offense.

Researcher's Opinion:

The researcher observes that different legal systems have addressed the issue of bankruptcy in varying ways with respect to classification and the sanctions imposed. While the Saudi Bankruptcy Law offers a detailed classification of the types of bankruptcy, the Egyptian law provides a more concise definition that may not offer sufficient legal protection for distinguishing between the various actions and circumstances leading to bankruptcy.

In contrast, the Jordanian Penal Code emphasizes punitive measures for fraudulent bankruptcy, prescribing penalties including imprisonment and hard labor. This reflects the Jordanian legal system's focus on the penal aspect of bankruptcy. Hence, it is apparent that legal approaches to bankruptcy differ according to the objectives behind such legislation: while some legal systems prioritize the differentiation of bankruptcy types to assign liability appropriately, others place greater emphasis on punishment.

In the researcher's view, differentiating between types of bankruptcy is a critical step toward ensuring justice and accurately assigning responsibility. Proper classification serves as an effective legal tool to safeguard creditors' rights and regulate debtors' behavior.

True Bankruptcy (Bankruptcy Due to Force Majeure):

A **true bankrupt** is one who engages in commerce with a known and customarily sufficient capital for the trade in which they are involved, maintains organized commercial records, does not act recklessly with expenditures, and suffers losses due to circumstances such as fire, flood, or evident economic setbacks. This form of bankruptcy results from external factors beyond the trader's control—such as force majeure, market fluctuations, or economic crises—and not from negligence or failure to protect their trade or assets. These factors collectively absolve the trader of blame, negate bad faith, and rule out intentional harm to creditors or concealment of assets.

Article (439) of the Jordanian Penal Code stipulates that:

"In the event of the bankruptcy of a commercial company, the penalties stated in Article (438), paragraph 1, shall apply to:

a. Silent partners who regularly interfere in the company's operations.

b. Managers of joint-stock or limited liability companies.

c. Directors, board members, authorized agents, supervisory board members, auditors, employees of said companies, and shareholders who themselves commit acts of fraudulent bankruptcy, facilitate or knowingly enable such acts, or who publish false financial statements or distribute fictitious profits."

The researcher notes that **Sudanese legislation does not classify bankruptcy** into true, negligent, or fraudulent categories. Furthermore, **legal persons are held criminally liable**, similar to natural persons, in accordance with Article (3) of the **1999 Sudanese Criminal Act**. As previously mentioned, the **1929 Sudanese Bankruptcy Law**, in Article (4), does not differentiate between traders and non-traders, applying bankruptcy procedures equally to both, based on its general provisions.

Researcher's Professional Legal Opinion:

In this section, the researcher outlines the legal position concerning bankruptcy that occurs due to **external and uncontrollable events**, such as natural disasters, economic crises, or market instability. The text indicates that in these scenarios, bankruptcy is not the result of the trader's negligence or mismanagement, but is instead due to unforeseen circumstances that render them unable to meet their financial obligations. Consequently, the trader is not at fault and cannot be blamed for the resulting losses or hardships.

The researcher emphasizes that this type of bankruptcy distinguishes between cases of failure caused by external forces and those involving debtor misconduct or bad faith. The legislator, in this context, aims to **protect traders facing involuntary financial crises** by excluding presumptions of deceit or asset concealment.

Regarding **Article 439 of the Jordanian Penal Code**, it highlights the penalties for **fraudulent bankruptcy**, targeting individuals who engage in **manipulation, forgery**, or **financial misrepresentation**, whether as company partners, directors, or employees. The Jordanian legislator, through this article, seeks to ensure that no party benefits from fraudulent conduct that could undermine creditors' rights or impede economic justice.

In this regard, the researcher observes that **Sudanese legislation** has taken a different approach from other systems. It does **not distinguish** between true, negligent, or fraudulent bankruptcy. Instead, it holds **legal persons criminally**

accountable for their actions just like natural persons, as per Article (3) of the **1999 Criminal Act**. Moreover, the **1929 Sudanese Bankruptcy Law** does not differentiate between traders and non-traders in applying bankruptcy procedures, reflecting a **broad legal perspective** focused on rights protection and procedural regulation rather than categorization.

Researcher's Conclusion:

The researcher believes that the **lack of distinction** between types of bankruptcy in Sudanese legislation has both **advantages and disadvantages**. On one hand, it simplifies procedures and ensures uniform rule application across all affected parties. On the other hand, it may lead to **ambiguity** in legal classification and hinder the differentiation between bankruptcies caused by external factors and those resulting from **negligence or fraud**.

The researcher advocates for the **adoption of a legal framework that differentiates between various forms of bankruptcy**, thereby enhancing the protection of creditors' rights and offering fair treatment to debtors who fall victim to unforeseen circumstances.

This classification also underscores the **need for flexibility in commercial legislation**. The legal system must accommodate situations involving **force majeure** while allowing debtors the opportunity to recover and resume business activities. However, such leniency must be subject to well-defined procedures to **prevent abuse**, and commercial laws should provide relief to genuine traders or companies, particularly those maintaining **organized financial records** that corroborate the legitimacy of their bankruptcy. These records must demonstrate that no irregular or unethical practices occurred, failing which the debtor becomes subject to legal penalties upon presenting their accounts and documentation.

Section Two: Negligent Bankruptcy and Fraudulent Bankruptcy

Subsection One: Negligent Bankruptcy

A **negligent bankrupt** is a merchant who is wasteful in his expenditures, conceals his financial insolvency from his creditors, and continues to engage in commercial activities until his capital is entirely depleted. Such a person is deemed negligent even if he maintains organized accounting records. Article 4 of the **Bankruptcy Act of 1929** enumerates the acts that constitute bankruptcy without specifically describing such bankruptcy as the result of negligence on the part of the bankrupt, whether a company or a natural person.

Subsection Two: Fraudulent Bankruptcy

A **fraudulent bankrupt** is one who resorts to deception and deceit regarding his capital, records false debts under other persons' names in his books, issues fraudulent instruments, transfers his assets and real estate to others under the guise of ownership transfer, or conceals any part of his property. Such a person operates in trade through fraudulent methods or misleads other traders by any means, whether or not he is wasteful, whether or not he maintains books of account, or whether his books are disorganized or irregular. This type of individual is referred to as "bankrupt" only in terms of the need to distribute his assets among creditors.

If it is proven that a bankrupt has committed any of the acts that legally constitute bankruptcy, **Article 22(1)** provides that:

"Subject to the conditions specified in this law, if the debtor commits an act of bankruptcy, the court may, upon petition from a creditor, the debtor, or the Minister of Justice, issue an order (hereinafter referred to as a bankruptcy declaration order) declaring the debtor bankrupt."

The acts that constitute bankruptcy are detailed in **Article 4** of the **Bankruptcy Act of 1929**, previously discussed.

Any person who, at that time, possesses the legal right to enforce a final judgment is considered a creditor within the meaning of this article. Acts such as transferring the debtor's assets, petitioning for bankruptcy, failing to settle debts, committing fraudulent acts, failing to repay monetary obligations, fleeing the residence or the country (Sudan), changing phone numbers or place of residence, or having a final judgment issued against them—are all considered by Sudanese law to be indicators of **fraudulent or negligent bankruptcy**. This form of bankruptcy is the most severe and is dealt with harshly and strictly due to its serious consequences.

According to **Article 8** of the **Bankruptcy Act of 1929**:

"A creditor shall not have the right to file a bankruptcy petition against a debtor unless:

(a) The debt owed by the debtor is not less than five million Sudanese Dinars, or the combined debts of two or more creditors amount to not less than five million Dinars;

(b) The debt is a specific sum that is due either immediately or at a certain future date; and

(c) The act of bankruptcy upon which the petition is based occurred within the three months preceding the filing of the petition."

Researcher's Analysis and Observations

The researcher concludes that **Sudanese courts face significant difficulties** in understanding the unique nature and objectives of bankruptcy procedures. In many instances, **confusion arises between bankruptcy and civil insolvency**—the latter of which is **not defined** in the **1983 Civil Procedure Act** or any other legislation.

A review of judicial precedents indicates that civil insolvency generally refers to a situation where a person experiences financial hardship so severe that they are incapable of repaying their debts. The root cause of this confusion lies in the **deficiencies and outdated nature of the Bankruptcy Act of 1929**, which has been in force for over nine decades.

To address these shortcomings, **comprehensive legislative reform** is essential. This includes the formulation of **clear and simplified legal provisions** that eliminate ambiguity, modernize procedures, align with contemporary commercial practices, and promote the protection of both creditor and debtor rights. Such reforms are critical for improving credit flow and strengthening the integrity of commercial transactions.

In contrast, the **Egyptian Commercial Law of 1999**, in **Article 249**, defines insolvency as:

"The insufficiency of the debtor's assets to meet due debts."

This definition clearly distinguishes insolvency as a condition affecting the debtor's financial standing, whereby **liabilities exceed realizable assets**.

Islamic jurisprudence, on the other hand, grants the **creditor the right to demand immediate repayment** of due debts and obliges the debtor to fulfill this obligation. If the debtor refuses or delays payment without valid justification, the creditor is entitled to **recover the debt even without the debtor's consent**, as per the Qur'anic verse:

"But if you repent, you may have your principal—neither wronging nor being wronged."

(Surah Al-Baqarah, 2:279)

This means that if a creditor demands repayment of a due debt and the debtor unjustifiably refuses or delays, the creditor has the right to recover it. If the debtor avoids payment—either by **deliberate procrastination or by concealing assets**—the creditor has the right to **seek judicial recourse**, including **detaining the debtor** to compel the fulfillment of the obligation.

Researcher's Final Opinion

The researcher asserts that **bankruptcy law must not conflict with Islamic legal principles**, both in form and substance. **Negligent bankruptcy** is a condition that should receive **special attention** from legal systems. Legislators must adopt **effective monitoring mechanisms** to prevent such bankruptcy from resulting from carelessness or haste.

In contrast, **fraudulent bankruptcy** is among the most dangerous types, necessitating **severe penalties** against the debtor. This form of bankruptcy causes harm not only to creditors but to the **entire commercial system**. Therefore, the law must provide for **strict and unambiguous sanctions** to ensure effective deterrence.

Chapter Seven: Preventive Composition Before Declaration, Conditions and Effects of Bankruptcy Declaration, Company Bankruptcy Declaration, and Management of the Bankrupt's Assets in Terms of the Bankruptcy Parties and Initial Bankruptcy Procedures.

Section One: Preventive Composition Before Declaration of Bankruptcy: Its Concept and Conditions from the Perspective of Civil Capacity

Subsection One: Preventive Composition as a Means to Avert Bankruptcy

Preventive composition from bankruptcy is defined as *"a contract concluded between the debtor and the body of creditors in accordance with procedures prescribed by law, wherein the majority of creditors agree to its terms and the court ratifies it."* This composition constitutes an agreement between a merchant who is unable to fulfill his financial obligations and his creditors. The debtor initiates this agreement by submitting a request to the Civil Court of First Instance in the jurisdiction where their main place of business is located. The creditors express their will by approving the composition, either unanimously or by a legally specified majority.

Preventive composition carries a quasi-judicial character, as it only becomes effective upon ratification by the court, at which point it acquires the status of a judicial decision. According to Syrian law, preventive composition is regarded as a legal mechanism designed to enable a financially distressed merchant to avoid bankruptcy by reaching a financial settlement with their creditors. Thus, it forms a binding contract between the debtor and the body of creditors and only becomes enforceable upon court approval.

In Egyptian Law No. 11 of 2018, Article (30) provides that:

"Any trader may be declared bankrupt. A trader who has ceased to pay their debts—even after filing for bankruptcy—may request preventive composition from bankruptcy, provided they have not committed fraud or a gross error not typical of a reasonable trader. If their financial affairs are in disarray to the point of causing cessation of payments, they must request the composition within fifteen days from the date of such cessation. However, companies undergoing liquidation are not eligible for preventive composition."

The researcher notes that Sudanese law does not provide a specific definition of preventive composition but does acknowledge its applicability both before and after the declaration of bankruptcy. Article (45) of the Sudanese Bankruptcy Act of 1929 affirms the possibility of entering into a preventive composition before or after the issuance of a bankruptcy declaration. A debtor against whom a bankruptcy petition has been filed may propose a composition prior to the issuance of the bankruptcy order. This proposal is submitted to the court, which convenes a meeting of creditors to deliberate on and vote on the proposal, provided that the numerical majority of creditors and holders of three-quarters of the provable claims agree to it.

Article (45)(1) of the Sudanese Bankruptcy Act of 1929 states:

"If a debtor proposes, after the filing of a bankruptcy petition and before the issuance of a bankruptcy order, a composition for the settlement of debts or a scheme for the arrangement of their financial situation, they shall submit such proposal to the court at least one month prior to the meeting set to hear the petition. The proposal shall be considered at the said meeting after being published in the prescribed form in accordance with subsections (3) and (4) of Article (16). If the proposal is submitted less than one month before the scheduled meeting, the court may refuse to consider it or postpone the meeting to another date to allow proper notice to creditors."

The law also requires that creditors representing both the numerical majority and three-quarters of the value of provable claims approve the composition before the declaration of bankruptcy. Article (45)(2) provides:

"At any such meeting, if the proposal is approved by a numerical majority of the creditors and by creditors holding three-quarters of the value of provable claims under the law who appear to file or report their claims, the proposal shall be deemed validly accepted by the creditors. The court or the provisional trustee (if appointed) shall implement the composition or arrangement, subject to Article (41), provided that it does not cause injustice or harm to any of the concerned parties and that there is no reasonable cause to suspect fraud or collusion in the proposal."

As stipulated in Article (45), the composition must not result in harm to any involved party and must be free from fraud or collusion.

Article (46) of the Sudanese Bankruptcy Act allows creditors who represent the numerical majority and hold three-quarters of the total debts to approve any proposal for composition or financial arrangement even after the declaration of bankruptcy. However, such approval remains contingent upon the ratification of the court, which must ensure the protection of creditor rights and verify the fairness of the proposed settlement.

Article (46) states:

"If a debtor is declared bankrupt, the numerical majority of creditors holding three-quarters of the total debts, whose claims have been proven, may at any time thereafter agree to accept any proposal for the composition or arrangement of the debtor's financial condition. In such cases, the same procedures and effects apply as those governing a composition or arrangement proposed before the declaration of bankruptcy."

The researcher concludes that preventive composition is an effective legal mechanism aimed at helping distressed merchants avoid bankruptcy and restructure their financial obligations. It benefits both debtors and creditors, as it may prevent the liquidation of the debtor's assets and instead allow for rescheduling of debts and amicable settlements. However, the success of such a process hinges on the debtor's transparency and good faith, in addition to the judiciary's role in verifying the integrity of the procedures and ensuring that no fraud or manipulation occurs.

Fundamentally, bankruptcy procedures are intended to help creditors recover their claims from the bankrupt debtor. Creditors, even if unable to recover the full amount, hope to obtain the maximum possible recovery. On the other hand, the bankrupt party seeks to resume business operations and generate income. A successful composition agreement may allow for repayment of all or part of the debts. Creditors may prefer this path to avoid the liquidation and division of the debtor's limited assets—especially when those assets are insufficient to satisfy all claims.

Typically, the debtor initiates the proposal for preventive composition, which must then be submitted to the court or the bankruptcy trustee. Approval by the majority of creditors, as defined by law, is required for the agreement to be effective.

From the researcher's perspective, the preventive composition, as previously defined, constitutes a contract between the bankrupt and the collective body of creditors. It may not be concluded between the bankrupt and each creditor individually. The validity of this contract requires the issuance of a judicial ruling ratifying the composition in order to protect the interests of dissenting minority creditors. The composition must be free from deceit and must reflect a high degree of credibility and trust in the debtor. It is characterized as a special type of contract, as it is concluded not with each creditor separately but with the general body of creditors, similar to certain contracts relating to the assets of minors.

Article 46(a) of the Sudanese Bankruptcy Act of 1929 provides:

"If a debtor is declared bankrupt, the numerical majority of creditors holding three-quarters of the value of the proven debts may, if they deem it appropriate, agree at any time after the declaration on any proposal for composition in respect of the debts owed in the bankruptcy or on any scheme for the settlement of the debtor's financial position. In such a case, the same procedures and consequences applicable to pre-bankruptcy compositions or settlements shall apply."

The Bankruptcy Act further requires the court's approval of the composition or settlement, as stipulated in Article 46(2):

"If the court approves the composition or settlement, it may issue an order annulling the bankruptcy and restoring the bankrupt's assets to him or transferring them to another person as may be designated by the court, under such terms as it may determine (if any)."

The composition takes effect upon the court's approval, which aims to protect the rights of creditors who did not consent to the composition. Once approved, the debtor's assets are returned to him or may be entrusted to a custodian appointed to implement the terms of the composition—whether by deferred payment, debt waiver, or payment upon solvency.

- **Deferred Payment:** This entails granting the debtor a grace period to settle debts either in full or in agreed-upon installments, taking into account the debtor's circumstances and capacity—whether he is a farmer awaiting a harvest or a property owner anticipating a market upswing or sale. It is presumed that creditors will assess the timeframe reasonably, without deception or bad faith. Article 45(4) of the Bankruptcy Act provides:

"If any installment due under the composition or settlement is not paid, or if it appears to the court that the composition or settlement cannot proceed without unjustified hardship or delay, or if court approval was obtained through fraud, the court may, if it deems fit, declare the debtor bankrupt and annul the composition or settlement. This shall not affect the validity of any payment or transaction made in good faith under the terms of the composition or settlement. Upon such declaration, all provable debts incurred before the date of the bankruptcy shall be considered provable."

- **Debt Waiver:** Creditors may agree to relinquish a portion of their claims in exchange for partial recovery and investment of the received amounts for mutual benefit. Article 46(6) states:

"Upon approval of the composition or settlement, and after payment of all appropriate costs, privileged claims, procedural expenses, and all fees and percentages due to the court or trustee, the trustee shall immediately deliver possession of the debtor's property to the debtor or to any other person(s) entitled thereto under the terms of the composition or settlement."

- Article 46(7) adds:

"If the composition or settlement is approved but the debtor or the transferee(s) fail to make the required payments, no legal action may be initiated for enforcement. However, any aggrieved party may petition the court for relief."

- If the composition or settlement is annulled, the debtor's property reverts to the trustee originally designated to receive it, without requiring a separate court order unless otherwise determined by the court.
- **Payment Upon Solvency:** This refers to an agreement between the debtor and creditors that repayment will occur once the debtor regains solvency. Under the repealed Egyptian Commercial Code, it was stated:

"A composition may include a condition of payment upon the debtor becoming solvent within a term not exceeding five years from the court's ratification of the composition. The debtor is not considered solvent unless his assets exceed his liabilities by at least ten percent."

This provision allowed the debtor to avoid immediate or fixed-date payment obligations, instead conditioning payment on future solvency. The law defined solvency as the point at which the debtor's assets surpass his liabilities by at least 10%. The five-year term was a strict limit, not subject to extension.

The researcher observes that the Sudanese legislator did not prescribe any of the aforementioned mechanisms for concluding the composition. Instead, it solely required judicial ratification and left the mode of agreement to be freely determined by the debtor and creditors. However, it clarified in Article 46(3):

"If any installment due under the composition or settlement is not paid, or if the court determines that proceeding with the composition or settlement would result in unjustified harm or delay, or if the court's approval was obtained fraudulently, the court may, if it deems appropriate and upon the application of any interested party, declare the debtor bankrupt and annul the composition or settlement. This shall not invalidate any sale, disposition, or payment made in good faith under the composition or settlement. Upon such declaration, all provable debts incurred prior to the bankruptcy shall become provable in the proceedings."

Once the conditions for composition are met and it is ratified by the court, the composition becomes effective and binding, provided that due procedures have been followed. It must then be published in the Official Gazette or as otherwise stipulated by law. The composition must include a list of provable claims and becomes binding on all parties as a judgment, except for alimony claims. It may be annulled if the court later determines that it was tainted by fraud or deceit, in which case the debtor is declared bankrupt and appropriate measures are taken with respect to the prior proceedings. The debtor's assets are then transferred to the interim trustee or the court, and the trustee conducts a review of the debtor's accounts and property.

Section Two: The Nature of Public Declaration and Legal Restraint (Ḥajr) — Linguistically and Terminologically

First Subsection: Definition of Public Declaration (Ishhār) Linguistically, Terminologically, and Legally

1. Linguistic Definition of Ishhār:

The term "ishhār" in Arabic linguistically signifies clarity and making something known. The word "mashhūr" (well-known) refers to something that is widely recognized and mentioned.

In Islamic Sharia, **ishhār** has been defined as: "informing people that a certain person has been subjected to legal restraint (ḥajr), i.e., has been declared bankrupt." It is recommended that such a declaration be made public so that people avoid dealing with that person financially. This is known today as "bankruptcy declaration" or public announcement.

2. Linguistic Definition of Ḥajr:

Ḥajr means prohibition or prevention from action. To say a judge imposed ḥajr (legal restraint) on someone means that the judge prohibited the person from disposing of their wealth. Ibn al-Athīr explained: the judge imposes ḥajr on a minor or someone deemed incompetent to prevent them from mismanaging their property. Ibn Sīda added: *ḥajara ʿalayhi* means to prevent or prohibit, as in the Qur'anic verse:

"Wa yaqūlūna ḥijran maḥjūran"

"And they say: 'A forbidden prohibition'" [Qur'an 25:22],

meaning something absolutely forbidden.

The intellect is also called *ḥijr* because it prevents its possessor from engaging in what is reprehensible. Allah says:

"Hal fī dhālika qasamun lidhī ḥijr?"

"Is there [not] in that an oath [sufficient] for one of reason?" [Qur'an 89:5]

3. Terminological Definition of Ḥajr (Legal Restraint):

From the linguistic meaning, we derive that **ḥajr** refers to the judge's prohibition of the debtor from disposing of their assets upon a creditor's complaint accompanied by valid evidence of the debt. The restrained individual may only use a minimal portion of their wealth for basic sustenance — for themselves and their dependents — until the underlying reason for the ḥajr is resolved.

There are numerous causes that may legally justify imposing ḥajr, depending on the nature of the threat to one's property. These include:

- Ḥajr on the insolvent debtor to protect creditors' rights
- Ḥajr on a person terminally ill to protect heirs
- Ḥajr on minors and the insane to protect their own assets

- Ḥajr on a mortgagor to protect the rights of the mortgagee

Al-Ṣanʿānī's *Subul al-Salām* mentions the statement of a judge to a debtor: *"I have restrained your right to dispose of your property."*

The Qur'an addresses this:

"And do not give the weak-minded your property, which Allah has made a means of sustenance for you..." [Qur'an 4:5]

"Test the orphans until they reach marriageable age; if you perceive sound judgment in them, release their property to them..." [Qur'an 4:6]

These verses indicate the obligation of restraining those who are incompetent or orphaned from managing their wealth to prevent waste and mismanagement. The judge has the right to impose and lift ḥajr upon establishing mental maturity and the ability to manage wealth.

In the Sunnah, the Prophet Muhammad ﷺ imposed ḥajr on Muʿādh's property and sold it to repay his debt, illustrating that it is lawful to restrict a person's property and sell it without their consent to settle debts. A debtor may fall under one of four scenarios:

1. Has more wealth than debt
2. Has more debt than wealth
3. Wealth equals debt
4. Has no wealth

Historical Example:

ʿUthmān ibn ʿAffān imposed ḥajr on ʿAbd Allāh ibn Jaʿfar due to his extravagant spending. Al-Shāfiʿī narrated in his *Musnad* from ʿUrwah ibn al-Zubayr:

"ʿAbd Allāh ibn Jaʿfar made a purchase, so ʿAlī said, 'I will go to ʿUthmān and have a ḥajr imposed on you.' Zubayr said, 'I am your partner in this transaction,' so ʿUthmān said, 'Would I impose ḥajr on someone whose partner is al-Zubayr?'"

Ḥajr is not a degradation of dignity or restriction of freedom. Rather, it is a form of compassion and protection for both individuals and society. It removes hardship and prevents harm, thereby preserving the wealth of the person under restraint. Preservation of wealth is a fundamental objective of Islamic law (*maqāṣid al-sharīʿah*).

Types of Ḥajr according to Legal Scholars:

- **Ḥajr for the benefit of the person restrained:** like minors, the mentally ill, or the financially reckless. The goal is protection of the individual.
- **Ḥajr for the benefit of others:** such as in the case of a bankrupt debtor to protect creditors, or a terminally ill person to protect heirs from excessive bequests.

Focus of this Section: Ḥajr on the Bankrupt Debtor:

This applies when the debtor fails to repay debts, or when debts have overwhelmed their assets. Scholars have differed on this issue:

- **Imam Abū Ḥanīfah**: *Opposed* imposing ḥajr on the bankrupt. He argued that wealth ultimately belongs to Allah and flows from person to person. He viewed ḥajr as a violation of personal liberty and legal capacity. Instead, the debtor is ordered to pay. If they comply, fine; if not, they are detained until they do.
- **The Majority (Ḥanafīs, Mālikīs, Shāfiʿīs, Ḥanbalīs):** *Support* imposing ḥajr on a bankrupt debtor to safeguard creditor rights. They cite the example of the Prophet ﷺ imposing ḥajr on Muʿādh and selling his property to repay creditors.

The Researcher's Position:

The researcher agrees with the majority view: it is permissible to impose ḥajr on a bankrupt debtor and publicly announce it so people are aware and do not engage with the debtor unknowingly. The debtor's financial actions then become invalid.

While Abū Ḥanīfah favored detaining the debtor as a precaution, the majority held that once insolvency is proven, creditors cannot pursue or imprison the debtor, but must instead grant time for repayment, in line with the verse:

"And if someone is in hardship, then [let there be] postponement until [a time of] ease..." [Qur'an 2:280]

Creditors may then request the judge to sell the debtor's assets and distribute the proceeds among them through public auction, prioritizing perishable items like fruits and vegetables.

Conclusion:

Islamic Sharia permits physical coercion and legal restraint to compel a debtor to repay or disclose assets. If the debtor is bankrupt and unable to pay, Sharia permits ḥajr — regardless of whether the debtor is a merchant or not. The reason for the debt does not affect the legitimacy of imposing legal restraint.

Section Three: The Public Declaration of Bankruptcy in Islamic Jurisprudence

Islamic Sharia seeks to achieve the well-being and psychological and material stability of individuals. Through its legislations, it aims to protect merchants, individuals, and the community from falling into bankruptcy. It encourages the merchant or group to act wisely and consciously by exerting every effort to grow their wealth, avoid losses, fulfill their financial obligations, and clear their liabilities before others.

The creditor is granted the right to demand the bankruptcy of the debtor to compel the debtor to repay debts on time. When the debtor knows that the creditor has this right and can exercise it—resulting in the debtor being prevented from disposing of their assets and their bankruptcy being publicly declared—it motivates the debtor to fulfill their debts by the deadline and prevents the creditor from exercising this right unnecessarily. Otherwise, the creditor proceeds with the public declaration of the debtor's bankruptcy to protect their rights, preserve their money, and safeguard the interests of society in general.

When a merchant or a company stops paying their debts, it causes disruption in financial transactions and deprives the state of money flow. Islamic bankruptcy rulings also ensure equality among creditors—there is no favoritism to any creditor over another; all share the debtor's assets proportionally to their debt.

Nevertheless, Islamic Sharia does not neglect the condition of the bankrupt person. The principle is that the creditor is entitled to recover their full debt from the debtor's money, even if nothing remains for the debtor. However, bankruptcy laws grant the bankrupt some care: they are entitled during the bankruptcy proceedings to sustenance for themselves and their dependents; some necessary funds are protected from seizure. The bankrupt is also granted the right to reconcile with creditors to avoid the public declaration of bankruptcy.

Islamic law requires that for bankruptcy to be publicly declared, the debt must exceed the debtor's assets—meaning the debtor becomes unable to pay and stops payment.

The different Islamic jurisprudential schools explain this procedure as follows:

First Branch: The First Approach — The Hanafi School

1. The Hanafi school, according to Abu Hanifa (may God have mercy on him), holds that:

"The debtor should not be subjected to legal restraint (ḥajr), nor should their assets be sold. Instead, the debtor is imprisoned until they sell their assets to repay creditors. If the debtor refuses to sell, then their assets are not sold."

Therefore, according to Abu Hanifa's view, the ruler does not have the authority to impose ḥajr on the bankrupt debtor, nor to sell their assets. Rather, the debtor is detained (imprisoned) until they pay their debts or die in prison.

The conditions for imprisoning the debtor are:

- The debt must be due (immediate). A debtor is not imprisoned for a deferred debt because imprisonment is to prevent injustice caused by delaying payment, and the debtor is not at fault if the creditor voluntarily postponed the right. Likewise, the debtor is permitted to travel before the due date.
- **(b)** Same as above, emphasis that the debt must be due to justify imprisonment.
- **(c)** The debtor must have the ability to pay the debt. Even if insolvent, the debtor is not imprisoned. This is based on the verse: *"And fear a Day when you will be returned to Allah. Then every soul will be compensated for what it earned, and they will not be wronged."* [Qur'an 2:281]
  Imprisonment aims to prevent injustice, which does not apply if the debtor lacks ability. Imprisonment is intended to facilitate debt repayment, not as an end in itself.
- **(d)** The debtor must be delaying payment unjustly. The Prophet ﷺ said: *"The rich debtor who delays payment is unjust."* Thus, the debtor may be imprisoned to prevent this injustice and enforce payment. If no delay or evasion is shown, imprisonment is not warranted.

- **(e)** The debt must be owed by someone other than the debtor's parents. Parents cannot be imprisoned for debt they owe to their child, whether they are ascendants or descendants. This is supported by the Qur'anic verses:

"If there is a particle of mustard seed in a rock or in the heavens or in the earth, Allah will bring it forth." [Qur'an 31:16] and

"Lower to them the wing of humility out of mercy and say: 'My Lord, have mercy upon them as they brought me up when I was small.'" [Qur'an 17:24] It is not considered appropriate to imprison parents over debts to their children unless the parent refuses to support the child when obligated to do so. In such a case, the judge may imprison the parent, but as a disciplinary measure, not because of the debt itself. Conversely, the debtor may be imprisoned for debts owed to parents or other relatives.

h. The creditor must request the judge to imprison the debtor; without such a request, imprisonment does not occur, because the debt is the creditor's right, and imprisonment is a means to achieve that right. A person's right can only be exercised by requesting it, so a request is necessary to justify imprisonment.

Abu Hanifa supported his opinion of not placing legal restraint (ḥajr) on the debtor by arguing that such restraint affirms the debtor's legal capacity, which causes additional harm beyond financial loss. Therefore, the greater harm should not be inflicted to prevent a lesser one.

He based this on the Qur'anic verse:

"And do not consume one another's wealth unjustly, except by trade by mutual consent." (Surah An-Nisa, 4:29)

And on the Prophet's ﷺ saying:

"The wealth of a Muslim should not be taken except with his consent."

Second Approach: The Shafi'i, Maliki, and Hanbali Schools

This approach holds that the bankrupt debtor should be placed under ḥajr (legal restraint). If the creditors demand it and prove the debtor's insolvency, and request the judge to impose ḥajr, the judge complies and restrains the debtor from financial transactions, preventing sales or damage to the debtor's assets to protect the creditors. If the debtor refuses to sell, the judge sells the bankrupt's assets and divides the proceeds among the creditors according to their shares.

The proponents of this view support it by the following evidence:

- From Ka'b ibn Malik from his father: The Prophet ﷺ placed ḥajr on Mu'adh's assets and sold them to repay his debt. This hadith proves that the ruler may place ḥajr on the debtor, manage their assets, and sell them to settle creditors' claims.
- Imposing ḥajr on the bankrupt debtor is to protect creditors from harm due to wasteful spending, acknowledgment of debt, or coercion. This is to prevent the debtor from acknowledging assets then using them personally or hiding them.
- Since a sick person can be placed under ḥajr to protect the heirs, it is even more justified to place ḥajr on a bankrupt debtor to protect the creditors.

Jurists have differed on whether evidence of insolvency should be presented before or after imprisoning the debtor, dividing into two opinions:

- **First opinion:** Evidence is heard before imprisonment. This is the view of Imam Malik, Ahmad, and Shafi'i.
- **Second opinion:** Evidence is heard after imprisonment. This is the view of Imam Abu Hanifa.

Imam Malik's *Muwatta* states:

"... Malik, Shafi'i, and Ahmad hold that proof of insolvency should be heard before imprisonment, whereas Abu Hanifa's view is that it is only heard after imprisonment. The first view is more lenient towards the bankrupt, while the second is stricter. The first is attributed to those cautious about the rights of others; the second to those less so. The matter depends on balancing these considerations."

Abu Hanifa's view is that if the debtor is imprisoned, the imprisonment is lifted once the debtor presents evidence of insolvency. This evidence is not limited to witness testimony but may include any form of proof. Jurists have required that the witnesses be three in number, based on the Prophet's ﷺ hadith regarding the plague, where he asked for three witnesses.

Witnesses must be knowledgeable and well-informed, meaning that testimony cannot be based solely on superficial observation but must be grounded in true insight into the debtor's situation.

From the above, the researcher concludes that the aim of the rules of ḥajr (restraint) in Islamic jurisprudence is to prevent the bankrupt debtor from disposing of their assets after being declared bankrupt. The debtor's transactions are invalid from the date of the bankruptcy ruling onward, so they cannot enter contracts or acknowledge debts after bankruptcy, whether concerning remaining assets or assets acquired afterward.

"Issuing the bankruptcy ruling results in prohibiting the debtor from managing their assets from that date to protect creditors from deliberate harm by the bankrupt, such as wasting funds, transferring them to others, or selling them at undervalued prices. This preserves the general guarantee for creditors over the bankrupt's assets, which would otherwise be diminished by such transactions."

Once a bankruptcy ruling is issued, certain individuals are appointed to manage and dispose of the bankrupt's assets until they are distributed among the creditors. The bankruptcy trustee (Ameen al-Tafleesah) is responsible for publicizing the ruling, managing the bankrupt estate responsibly, and receiving the debtor's assets. Meanwhile, the bankruptcy agent (Wakeel al-Taflees) assumes the role of the bankrupt in managing their financial affairs, safeguarding the interests of both the creditors and the debtor. This requires the agent to be knowledgeable and ethical, as they serve as a legal representative acting on behalf of both parties without their explicit consent.

Article (27) of the Sudanese Bankruptcy Act of 1929 states:

(1) The court may, upon issuing the bankruptcy declaration or at any later time, appoint a trustee over the debtor's assets. Accordingly, the debtor's assets shall transfer to that trustee.

This topic will be discussed in further detail in a separate chapter, God willing.

The researcher concluded that the purpose of a bankruptcy ruling is to achieve a collective liquidation of the debtor's assets by first determining and identifying them, then distributing them among the creditors. This differs from *ḥajr* (legal restraint), which prevents the debtor from engaging in harmful verbal or physical transactions involving their assets, as these are considered a general guarantee for the creditors. Thus, the debtor is not prevented from taking legal action or making necessary claims to preserve their rights, as this ultimately serves to protect the creditors by preserving the general guarantee provided by the debtor's estate.

In Islamic jurisprudence—particularly within the Shafi'i school—there are two opinions on restraining a bankrupt debtor:

1. If the debtor's assets are sufficient to cover due debts, no restraint is imposed. Debts that are not yet due do not justify restraint since the term has not yet come.
2. If the debtor's assets are insufficient to cover due debts, and creditors file a claim before the judge, then the judge imposes restraint.

Hanbali School:

In the Hanbali view, if a person has due debts that exceed their assets, and the creditors request the judge to impose *ḥajr*, the judge must grant it, provided two conditions are met:

1. The debtor's due debts exceed their assets.
2. The creditors request the judge to impose *ḥajr*.

Types of Financial Transactions:

Transactions involving the debtor's property are either **physical acts** or **verbal transactions**, as follows:

A. Physical Acts:

Jurists agree that *ḥajr* on a bankrupt debtor does not affect physical acts, as once they occur, they cannot be reversed. Thus, they remain valid regarding the debtor's assets. Physical acts include acts that entail compensation, such as committing an offense that requires financial restitution or retaliation (*qiṣāṣ*), where the victim opts for financial compensation. In such cases, the victim becomes a creditor. Likewise, if the debtor causes damage after *ḥajr*, they are liable, and the harmed party joins the ranks of creditors.

B. Verbal Transactions:

These are divided into two types:

1. Transactions not involving the restrained assets:

These include obligations on the debtor's person (e.g., purchasing on credit, selling with deferred delivery, or borrowing). Jurists agree such transactions are valid. The debt remains in the debtor’s liability and will be pursued after *ḥajr* is lifted. Creditors from these transactions are not prioritized over existing ones because they knowingly dealt with a bankrupt or took the risk if unaware. The validity stems from the debtor’s full legal capacity and the fact that such dealings do not infringe on the creditors’ rights. This also includes personal legal acts like marriage contracts (for both men and women), provided the *mahr* (dowry) is not monetary.

2. Transactions involving the restrained assets:

These are divided into:

a. Initial financial transactions (e.g., selling, purchasing, manumission, pledging, gifting, bequeathing, endowing, acknowledging debt): Jurists apply the principle: *“Any act that nullifies the creditors’ rights is invalidated by ḥajr.”*

b. Transactions related to acts prior to *ḥajr* (e.g., confirming a previous sale or manumission):
Hanbalis permit the bankrupt to exercise options or annul a contract due to defect if made before *ḥajr*.

Malikis transfer such rights to the creditors. Hanafis allow such sales if at market value.

Some Shafi'is advocate for whichever option (annulment or confirmation) is in the creditors’ best interest.

Preponderant View: The opinion that favors the option most beneficial to creditors is preferred, to preserve their rights and help the debtor clear their debts.

c. New assets acquired after *ḥajr*:

Jurists differ.

- First opinion (Shafi'is): *ḥajr* applies to new assets; the debtor cannot dispose of them.
- Second opinion (Malikis): *ḥajr* does not extend to new assets unless a new *ḥajr* is issued.

Preponderant View: The second opinion is stronger: *ḥajr* does not automatically apply to newly acquired assets.

D. Debtor's Acknowledgment and its Implications:

Jurists analyze the debtor's acknowledgment in two respects:

- **Validity:** Most jurists accept the acknowledgment whether the debt arose before or after *ḥajr*, so long as the debtor remains legally capable.
- **Sharing with Creditors:**

Jurists differed on whether the person acknowledged by the debtor can share in the assets under restraint:

  - **Shafi'is:** Allow them to share.
  - **Hanafis, Malikis, some Shafi'is, and Hanbalis:** Do not allow them to share.

E. Legal Consequences of Unauthorized Transactions:

If a bankrupt violates the restriction and engages in transactions:

- **Malikis (most accurate opinion), Shafi'is, Hanbalis:** Such transactions are *completely void*, even if later approved by creditors or the judge.
- **Hanafis, Malikis (some), and some Shafi'is:** Transactions are *suspended* pending approval by the judge or creditors.

Preponderant View: The second opinion is favored—transactions are suspended, not automatically void—because this protects creditors while recognizing the debtor's legal capacity, unlike minors or insane persons, who lack legal competence entirely.

Travel Restrictions on the Debtor:

The debtor's travel scenarios fall into four cases:

1. **Travel before the debt is due, with a safe return:**
   Jurists agree creditors cannot prevent such travel, as it does not threaten their rights.
2. **Travel before debt is due, but considered risky (e.g., war, sea travel):**

Most jurists: Travel is allowed as the debt isn't due. Some Shafi'is and Hanbalis: Travel can be restricted due to risk, unless the debtor provides collateral, a guarantor, or gets creditor approval.

Third: When the debtor travels before the due date and returns after it has passed, meaning that the debt becomes due while the debtor is away — jurists have expressed two opinions on this matter:

- **First Opinion:**

It is permissible to prevent the debtor from traveling unless he provides a guarantor or pledges collateral sufficient to cover the debt upon its maturity. This view is held by the Mālikī and Ḥanbalī schools. Their justification lies in the potential harm caused by delaying the creditor's right. However, if the debtor provides a guarantor or sufficient collateral that ensures payment when the debt is due, then he may travel, as the harm is thereby eliminated.

- **Second Opinion:**

It is impermissible to prevent the debtor from traveling even if the debt becomes due during the journey. The creditor has no right to demand a guarantor or collateral in such a case. However, it is permissible for the creditor to accompany the debtor and, once the debt matures, prevent him from continuing the journey unless he repays the debt. Nevertheless, the creditor is not entitled to monitor the debtor closely, as this may lead to unjustified harm or humiliation. This opinion is adopted by the Ḥanafī and Shāfiʿī schools, who base their view on the following arguments:

- A creditor has no right to demand from a traveling debtor what he could not demand from a resident debtor, such as immediate payment.
- A debt not yet due cannot be subject to collateralization, just like it cannot be demanded in full.
- If such demands were permitted in loan transactions, they would logically extend to matters like spousal maintenance.
- If the creditor were allowed to make such demands simply because the debtor was traveling and return might be delayed, then similar demands could be made even while the debtor was stationary out of fear of his escape.
- In principle, the creditor has accepted a deferred debt (ajl) with all associated risks. If he wishes to secure his rights, he should stipulate a

guarantee or documentation at the time of contracting. Failing to do so renders him blameworthy for any risk he later incurs.

If the debtor travels after the debt has become due and before repayment: In this scenario, jurists differentiate between two cases:

a) If the debtor is solvent and capable of repaying the debt: In this case, there is consensus among jurists that the creditor may prevent the debtor from traveling until the debt is repaid.

b) If the debtor is insolvent and proven to be incapable of repaying the debt: Here, opinions diverge:

- The Mālikī and Shāfiʿī schools opine that he cannot be prevented from traveling, as the matter is regulated by Islamic law, referring to the Qur'anic verse:
  "And if the debtor is in hardship, then [let there be] postponement until [a time of] ease. But if you give [from your right as] charity, then it is better for you, if you only knew." [Al-Baqarah: 280]
- The Ḥanafīs maintain that the debtor may not be prevented from traveling, but the creditor may accompany him wherever he goes.
- The Ḥanbalīs hold that the creditor may prevent the debtor from traveling unless the latter provides a guarantor for the debt, as the debtor might acquire wealth in the country he travels to, and the creditor might be unable to pursue him. If a guarantor is provided, the creditor can claim the debt through them.

Based on the foregoing, the researcher concludes:

- **Actual actions** undertaken by the bankrupt after being placed under legal incapacity (ḥajr) do not affect the creditors' rights, as such acts are enforceable and cannot be reversed. These include actions that may lead to compensation or fines, such as damage or criminal conduct.
- **Verbal actions** not related to the sequestered estate are limited to those involving the debtor's personal obligations or rights, such as acknowledgments or contracts not involving the sequestered property.

Regarding transactions by the bankrupt that affect the sequestered property:

- The researcher adopts the view that **initial financial transactions**, such as sales or pledges, must take into account the creditors' rights in the sequestered estate, which necessitates the ḥajr.
- As for transactions pertaining to matters predating the ḥajr, such as ratification of a previous sale or manumission, the preferred opinion is that the course most favorable to the creditors should be chosen. This ensures protection of their rights while allowing the bankrupt to reorganize his financial affairs.

In terms of **assets acquired after the imposition of ḥajr**, the researcher supports the view that the sequestration should not extend to such assets. Therefore, the bankrupt may dispose of these new assets provided the judge or creditors consent.

As for the **acknowledgment (iqrār)** of the bankrupt, the researcher notes the consensus among jurists regarding its validity even during ḥajr, provided the debtor's financial liability can absorb the acknowledged right. This determines whether the debtor should contribute to the creditors.

Finally, concerning the **sanction** for violating the ḥajr:

- The researcher holds that any transactions carried out by the bankrupt after ḥajr are invalid if they harm creditors' rights. Such acts must be halted unless approved by the creditors or the judge.

In conclusion, the researcher adopts a view that seeks to **balance the protection of creditors' rights with the bankrupt's interest** in managing his financial affairs post-ḥajr.

Section Four: Conditions for Declaring Bankruptcy in Terms of Civil Capacity

Subsection One: The Merchant in Commercial Legislation

The determination of the term *"merchant"* is a fundamental pillar in commercial laws, as it directly influences the rights and obligations of individuals engaged in commercial activities. Although many jurisdictions adopt similar definitions, variations do exist in the legislative texts among different countries. Below is an overview of the definition of a "merchant" in selected Arab legislations, including Sudanese law:

According to **Article 10 of the Egyptian Commercial Law**, a merchant is defined as:

- Any person who engages in commercial activities professionally, in their own name and for their own account.
- Any company that adopts one of the forms stipulated in the laws governing companies, regardless of the purpose for which it was established.

This definition emphasizes the notion of *professional engagement* in commercial activities, whether by a natural or legal person.

Article 9 of the Syrian Commercial Law provides that a merchant is:

- Individuals whose profession is to engage in commercial activities.
- Companies whose purpose is commercial in nature.

The researcher observes that this definition underlines the idea of engaging in commerce as a *profession* and includes companies operating in commercial fields.

In **the Saudi Commercial Court Law**, a merchant is defined as:

- Anyone who engages in commercial transactions and adopts them as a profession.

This reflects the necessity for commercial activities to be the *primary profession* of the individual in order to acquire the legal status of a merchant.

Article 9 of the Jordanian Commercial Law states that merchants are:

- Individuals whose profession is to conduct commercial activities.
- Companies whose subject matter is commercial.

The researcher notes that this definition aligns closely with that of Syrian law, emphasizing the practice of commerce as a profession.

The **repealed Sudanese Commercial Law** defined a merchant in **Article 3** as:

- Any person who practices an activity temporarily or permanently for profit at a fixed location.

The researcher notes that this definition differs from others, as it includes individuals who engage in commercial activities temporarily, which may lead to inconsistencies in the application of legal provisions.

Under **Article 4 of the 2009 Sudanese Commercial Law**, a merchant is defined as:

- Any natural or legal person (company) who engages in commercial activities on a permanent or professional basis.
- Individuals who conduct commercial activities regularly with the intent to generate profit.

The researcher observes that this definition links the acquisition of merchant status to *regular and professional practice* of commercial activities, and does not recognize *temporary commercial conduct* as sufficient to establish merchant status.

Comparison and Analysis:

While most definitions converge on the necessity of *professionalism and regularity* in conducting commercial activities as a condition for acquiring merchant status, the **Khartoum State Law** deviates by considering an individual who practices commercial activity temporarily to be a "merchant." This approach may conflict with the concept of professional commerce adopted by many other legal systems. In contrast, the **Sudanese Commercial Law of 2009** requires regular and systematic engagement in commercial activities, offering a clearer distinction between occasional participants and permanent commercial practitioners.

Commercial Capacity:

It is noteworthy that most legislations impose certain conditions for commercial capacity. An individual must possess the legal capacity required to engage in commerce, including reaching the age of majority and having sound mental faculties. For example, **Article 4 of the Saudi Commercial Court Law** states that any person who has reached the age of majority and has full mental capacity may engage in commerce.

The researcher concludes that the legal definitions of a merchant in Arab countries align on many core points, though differences remain—particularly regarding whether temporary commercial activity suffices to establish merchant status. These definitions underscore the importance of setting clear standards for commercial professionalism, as the rights and duties arising from commerce may vary depending on such classifications.

Section Five: Declaration of Bankruptcy in Law

The bankruptcy regime is a legal framework designed to regulate the financial status of individuals or commercial entities that are unable to fulfill their commercial debt obligations upon maturity. It serves as one of the principal mechanisms for safeguarding creditors' financial rights by allowing them to recover their claims through the liquidation of the bankrupt debtor's assets. Legislations across various jurisdictions aim to bolster confidence and credit in commercial transactions by ensuring efficient bankruptcy procedures that protect the rights of all concerned parties.

In most legal systems, the declaration of bankruptcy requires that the defendant be a *merchant* who has ceased payment of his commercial debts. Some laws further stipulate that the debtor must not have resorted to unlawful means to maintain financial credibility. However, Sudanese law adopts a different approach: it does not require the debtor to be a merchant. Instead, it permits the declaration of bankruptcy against non-merchants if they commit any of the acts specified in the Bankruptcy Act. This broadens the scope of the bankruptcy system, allowing a wider range of individuals to benefit from its provisions.

Most legal systems stipulate that a bankruptcy judgment may only be issued if the person is a merchant who has ceased paying a commercial debt or has used unlawful means to uphold their financial credit. The researcher notes that Sudanese law does not condition the debtor's classification as a merchant for bankruptcy proceedings to apply. It permits the filing of a bankruptcy petition against a non-merchant, provided they commit one of the acts enumerated in Article (4) of the Bankruptcy Act, which is phrased broadly as: *"A person commits an act of bankruptcy in any of the following circumstances..."*

In the **UAE Bankruptcy Law**, it is stated:

"Subject to the provisions governing preventive composition, bankruptcy may be declared against any merchant who has ceased to pay his commercial debts upon maturity due to financial distress and the deterioration of his credit."

Similarly, the **Egyptian Commercial Law** provides:

"A merchant required under this law to maintain commercial books shall be deemed bankrupt if he ceases payment of his commercial debts due to financial disruption."

It is evident that both Egyptian and Emirati laws restrict bankruptcy to merchants, referencing the definition provided in **Article (10) of Egyptian Commercial Law No. 17 of 1999**, which defines a merchant as:

"Any person who professionally engages in commercial activity in his own name and for his own account, and any company adopting one of the forms prescribed in company laws, regardless of the company's purpose."

In contrast, Sudanese law does not adopt this specific merchant definition. Instead, it incorporates any person—whether a merchant or not—if they engage in acts defined as bankruptcy. In essence, the declaration of bankruptcy under Sudanese law results in the seizure of the merchant's or company's assets, the liquidation of those assets, and the distribution of proceeds to creditors proportionately to their claims.

According to **Article 215 of the Algerian Commercial Code**:

"To declare bankruptcy or judicial composition, the debtor must be a merchant or a legal person subject to private law—even if not classified as a merchant—and must have ceased payment."

From this, the researcher notes that Sudanese legislation recognizes a company as a legal person from the date of its registration in the commercial register and maintains that status until its dissolution. Article (17) of the **Sudanese Civil Transactions Act** states:

"Persons are of two types: natural persons and legal persons."

Article (23) of the same law defines legal persons as:

- The State, public institutions, and other entities granted legal personality by law.
- Religious bodies and sects recognized by the State.
- **Endowments (Awqaf).**
- **Commercial companies.**
- Associations and foundations established in accordance with the law.
- Any group of persons or assets granted legal personality by statutory provision.

The researcher notes that the **Bankruptcy Act of 1929** in Sudan never referred to the bankrupt as a "merchant" but instead as a "debtor" or "bankrupt," focusing solely on the formal conditions for accepting a bankruptcy declaration. It does not address the requirements for acquiring merchant status. Conversely, the **Civil Transactions Act** provides definitions for natural and legal persons, who possess legal capacity to conduct financial and other transactions, without restricting the types of transactions covered. A person is deemed bankrupt if they commit any of the acts listed in the aforementioned Article (4).

Furthermore, **Article 111 of the Sudanese Penal Code (1991, amended in 2000)** stipulates:
"Whoever, with intent to defraud, transfers, conceals, disposes of, or relinquishes property or a right in such property to prevent its seizure or execution based on a judgment or order issued—or anticipated to be issued—by a competent court or public authority, or

(b) Receives, takes, or claims any property or right therein while knowing he has no rightful claim, with the intent of obstructing seizure or execution, shall be punished by imprisonment not exceeding one year, or a fine, or both."

Similarly, **Article 112** of the same law criminalizes filing fraudulent claims to deprive creditors of their lawful entitlements:

"Whoever:
(a) Accepts the issuance of a judgment, order, or execution— or causes it to be issued—based on a fictitious claim in property or a right thereto, with the intent of depriving creditors of legal recourse, or

(b) Obtains a judgment, order, or execution against any person based on a fictitious claim in property or a right thereto, intending thereby to protect a debtor or deprive creditors of their legal rights, shall be punished by imprisonment for a term not exceeding one year, or a fine, or both."

Conclusion:
The researcher concludes that Sudanese bankruptcy law adopts a broader, more inclusive approach than many other legal systems by not limiting the bankruptcy regime to merchants alone. This flexibility allows both individuals and entities—merchant or non-merchant—to be subject to bankruptcy proceedings, provided they commit defined acts of bankruptcy. Additionally, Sudanese law integrates provisions from civil and criminal law to deter fraudulent practices and uphold creditor rights within the bankruptcy process.

Article 22(1) provides:

"Subject to the conditions stipulated in this Act, if the debtor commits an act of bankruptcy, the court may, upon the submission of a bankruptcy petition by a creditor, the debtor, or the Minister of Justice, issue an order (hereinafter referred to as a 'Bankruptcy Declaration Order') declaring the debtor bankrupt."

(2) *If the petition is not dismissed pursuant to the provisions of Article 21, and the debtor fails to propose a composition or a plan acceptable to the creditors and approved by the court in the manner prescribed below, the court shall issue a bankruptcy declaration order.*

(3) *If the bankrupt is imprisoned under subsection (2) of Article 16 or under Article 19, he shall be released. Thereafter, no creditor whose debt is provable under this Act shall have any right to claim against the property or the person of the bankrupt except as provided by this Act. Creditors shall not be permitted to initiate or continue any legal action or proceedings without leave of the court and subject to any conditions it may impose.*

(4) *The bankruptcy declaration order shall take effect and be deemed operative from the date of submission of the petition upon which it was issued.*

(5) *The order shall be published in the prescribed form and in the manner provided for in Article 16 regarding notifications.*

(6) *A bankruptcy declaration order shall not be issued against a partnership in the name of the partnership itself but rather against each individual partner separately.*

Conclusion:

Through a comparative analysis of the bankruptcy laws in Sudan, the UAE, and Egypt, the researcher observes that the Sudanese legislation deviates from the Emirati and Egyptian counterparts regarding the requirement of *merchant status* for declaring bankruptcy. While both Emirati and Egyptian laws explicitly require that the debtor be a *merchant* for bankruptcy proceedings to apply, Sudanese law imposes no such express requirement. Rather, bankruptcy may be declared against any individual—merchant or not—who commits one of the acts listed in Article (4) of the Sudanese Bankruptcy Act. This approach reflects a broader and more flexible application of the bankruptcy regime in Sudan, extending its reach to a wider category of individuals and entities.

In the researcher's view, this flexibility can be beneficial in certain scenarios, particularly in protecting creditors from financially distressed individuals who are not formally recognized as merchants but nonetheless present a risk of default. However, such openness could potentially allow for legal abuse or manipulation by non-merchant individuals not subject to the regulatory frameworks that govern commercial entities. Accordingly, it is imperative that strong and effective safeguards be in place to ensure equitable enforcement of the bankruptcy regime and the protection of all parties' rights. Regulatory oversight mechanisms must also be implemented to maintain the integrity of the process.

On that basis, it may be concluded that the Sudanese legislator has opted to confer broad applicability to bankruptcy proceedings, permitting actions against non-merchant debtors experiencing financial hardship. However, this legislative policy must be complemented by legal guarantees that prevent abuse of the system by non-commercial debtors.

Section Six: Cessation of Payment

A notable aspect of the Sudanese Bankruptcy Act is the ambiguity in its wording, particularly when compared to other Arab laws, which more clearly define the reasons for declaring a merchant bankrupt. Like those laws, the Sudanese legal framework aims to preserve creditors' interests by allowing judicial intervention and the initiation of bankruptcy procedures when a merchant's commercial activities become financially unstable, causing damage to creditors and disrupting their rights to full repayment.

The Sudanese legislature did not define "cessation of payment" in express terms but instead referenced some of its underlying causes. For instance, paragraph (g) of **Article 4 of the Bankruptcy Act of 1929** states:

"That the person has ceased paying their debts or is on the verge of ceasing payment."

Accordingly, "cessation of payment" can be interpreted—pursuant to Article 4—as occurring when a merchant stops paying their debts or is about to stop paying creditors.

Sudanese law adopts a stance similar to that of the English legislator by extending the bankruptcy regime to both merchants and non-merchants. As previously noted, Article (4) of the Sudanese Bankruptcy Act makes no mention of the term “merchant” in its opening clause; instead, it states:

"A person commits an act of bankruptcy in the following cases..."

This is consistent with **Article 243** of the Sudanese Code of Civil Procedure, further confirming the inclusive scope of the bankruptcy framework.

In summary, a merchant is deemed to have ceased payment if their financial situation has deteriorated to the point of hopeless insolvency, rendering them unable to meet their debt obligations on time or if they resort to potentially unlawful means to fulfill their debts. This assessment falls within the discretionary power of the judge, who may determine the existence of financial distress based on presented evidence—such as issuing cheques without sufficient funds, fleeing, closing shops and communication channels, and other indicators of financial default.

In this regard, Sudanese legislation leaves the determination of cessation of payment to practical circumstances and refrains from exhaustively listing all relevant scenarios. Instead, it relies on indicators that may suggest a debtor is no longer fulfilling their obligations, thereby enabling courts to interpret the debtor's financial conduct within the broader framework of insolvency and creditor protection.

Section One: Proof of Cessation of Payment

The burden of proving that the debtor has ceased payment and is unable to meet his debts lies with the party requesting the declaration of bankruptcy. If the petition for bankruptcy is submitted by the debtor himself, he must convince the court that he is indeed incapable of paying his due and payable debts amounting to no less than **50,000 Sudanese Pounds**. Conversely, if the petition is submitted by a creditor or the Public Prosecutor, they must prove that the debtor has failed to pay a due and payable debt not less than **50,000 Sudanese Pounds**.

Insolvency or the inability to pay debts is a question of fact, which may be established through all permissible means of proof. The court may infer it from all facts, circumstances, presumptions, and surrounding conditions. The trial court is obligated to detail, in its ruling, the factual elements constituting the debtor’s insolvency, and its legal characterization of these facts is subject to the oversight of higher courts. This principle was affirmed by the **Supreme Court in the precedent case: The Official Receiver of the Bankruptcy Estate v. Ahmed Babiker Mohamed**, wherein it was held that the trial court’s power under Article

21(1) of the Bankruptcy Act is not an absolute discretionary power regarding the existence or non-existence of sufficient grounds to proceed with a bankruptcy petition. Rather, the court's decision is subject to appellate review, as it does not arise from unfettered discretion but from a judicial duty to investigate and issue a reasoned judgment. Once the court is convinced that the debtor is indeed unable to meet his debt obligations, it must issue an order declaring the bankruptcy; it holds **no discretionary authority** to refuse to do so based on the debtor's good faith or out of sympathy.

This raises the critical question:

What is the legal effect of the cessation of payment coming to an end before the debtor's assets are liquidated?

In response, if the essential substantive condition for declaring bankruptcy is the debtor's failure to pay due debts, Egyptian jurisprudence and case law provide that the **Court of Appeal** may annul the declaration of bankruptcy if it is proven during the appeal proceedings that the state of insolvency has ceased. This position is grounded in considerations of **equity and fairness** to the debtor, as well as a legal principle recognizing the constitutive nature and binding authority of the bankruptcy judgment, as articulated in **Article 568** of the **New Egyptian Commercial Code of 1999**.

In contrast, **Article 57(1)** of the **Sudanese Bankruptcy Act of 1929** provides: *"If the court finds that bankruptcy should not have been declared, or if it is proven to the satisfaction of the court that the bankrupt's debts have been fully paid, or if the court approves a composition or settlement under Articles 45 or 46, it may, upon the request of the debtor or any other interested party, revoke the declaration by a written order. Such revocation shall not affect any prior legitimate transactions, including sales or assignments made by the trustee in bankruptcy."*

This implies that the court has the authority to revoke the bankruptcy order in three specific scenarios outlined in the law.

Considering that the court referred to is the competent court under the Bankruptcy Act, and that under **Article 5** of the same Act, jurisdiction to hear bankruptcy cases is vested in the **Court of Appeal**, the **General Court**, and the **First-Class Magistrate**, it is clear that such jurisdiction is **original** rather than appellate.

In Anglo-Saxon legal systems, the authority to revoke a bankruptcy declaration is confined exclusively to the **court of first instance (trial court)**. However, in Latin legal traditions, this authority extends to **courts of appeal** as part of their appellate function. The Latin approach allows the appellate court to revoke a bankruptcy declaration if it finds during its review that the cessation of payment has ended.

From this perspective, **denying a higher court** the power to revoke a bankruptcy order—even when it is clearly proven that the debtor has fully paid all due debts for which the bankruptcy was declared—amounts to an **unjustified penal classification** of the debtor. This is particularly problematic since the purpose of declaring bankruptcy is to **protect creditors, maintain public credit, and safeguard trust in commercial transactions**. If the debtor has paid off all his debts, these purposes no longer apply, and **there remains no legal justification** for maintaining the bankruptcy judgment.

Conclusion with the Researcher's Opinion:

Through an analysis of the legal provisions related to bankruptcy, the researcher has concluded that the Sudanese legislator has left ambiguity surrounding the definition of *cessation of payment*. The law merely refers to the causes that may lead to such cessation without explicitly defining the specific conditions under which a debtor is considered to have ceased payment. Nevertheless, cessation of payment under Sudanese law may be understood through Article (4) of the **Bankruptcy Act of 1929**, which provides that a person who either ceases to pay his debts or is on the verge of doing so shall be deemed bankrupt.

The Sudanese law adopts an approach similar to that of English law, where the application of bankruptcy proceedings is **not conditional upon the debtor being a merchant**. This approach broadens the scope of the bankruptcy system to include both commercial and non-commercial individuals.

On the other hand, although the Sudanese legislator did not explicitly enumerate the cases of cessation of payment, the law does indicate various **indicators** of such a state, including issuing **bounced cheques**, **absconding**, or **closing down commercial premises**.

Regarding the *proof of cessation of payment*, the legislator places the burden of establishing the debtor's inability to pay on the party requesting the declaration of bankruptcy—be it the debtor, a creditor, or the Public Prosecutor. The court is allowed to infer the state of cessation from relevant facts and surrounding circumstances, and the **Supreme Court** has emphasized the necessity of a thorough factual investigation as a basis for any judicial ruling declaring bankruptcy.

As for the **effect of the cessation of payment ceasing to exist prior to the liquidation of the debtor's assets**, Sudanese law permits the court to **revoke the bankruptcy declaration** in certain instances, such as full repayment of debts by the debtor or an approved composition or settlement. This flexibility is grounded in considerations of **justice** and the **public interest**.

The researcher believes that the **Sudanese legislator should broaden the definition** of the conditions constituting cessation of payment and **strengthen the legal mechanisms** to clarify them. This would help ensure the protection of creditors' rights while maintaining fairness for both parties involved.

Researcher's Opinion:

The ambiguity in the provisions related to cessation of payment under Sudanese law necessitates a more precise legal clarification. The legislator should clearly define the specific conditions under which a person is deemed bankrupt due to non-payment, while also clarifying the responsibilities of all parties involved in establishing bankruptcy. Although granting courts broad powers to revoke bankruptcy judgments in cases of debt repayment is a positive step toward protecting debtors, these procedures should be implemented with **greater rigor** to safeguard creditors' rights and ensure **stability in commercial transactions**.

Section Seven: Conditions for Declaring Bankruptcy in Terms of Commercial Capacity

The Sudanese Bankruptcy Act of 1929, under **Article (57)**, provides that: *"If the court deems that the declaration of the debtor's bankruptcy was unwarranted, or if it is proven to the satisfaction of the court that the debts of the bankrupt have been fully paid, or if the court approves a composition or settlement under the provisions of Article (45) or Article (46), it may, upon the request of the debtor or any other interested party, annul the bankruptcy declaration by a written order."*

Evidently, the primary purpose of this provision is to strengthen credit and foster trust in financial transactions through a series of procedures and rules aimed at protecting the creditors' interests and safeguarding their rights. This enables creditors to seize the remaining assets of the bankrupt debtor and subject them to judicial oversight, ensuring equality among creditors and avoiding favoritism through a fair and equitable distribution. Accordingly, the bankruptcy system serves as a collective mechanism for the liquidation of a debtor's assets when they cease payment.

A **"trader"** (or merchant) in this context is defined as any person who engages in commercial activity in their own name and for their own account, having the required legal capacity. This can refer to either a **natural person** or a **legal entity** engaged in business on a professional basis. As for companies, the applicable standard is the **formal structure** set out in company law, regardless of the purpose for which the company was formed.

It is widely accepted that **professional and habitual engagement in commercial activities** qualifies a natural person as a trader. Even public employees may be considered traders if they independently engage in legitimate, profitable commercial activities recognized under the law. This remains true even if they participate as partners in partnerships, whether visibly or silently. Such commercial status can be proven through any legal means of evidence, including testimony and presumptions, such as the imposition of commercial taxes.

Regarding companies, their classification as commercial entities is based on **formal criteria**, such as their legal form — general partnerships, limited partnerships, or limited liability companies. Since commercial transactions are a type of legal act, the person undertaking them must possess the **necessary legal capacity**, which includes reaching a minimum age as defined by the national law of the country where such acts are performed. Moreover, the individual must not be subject to any condition that diminishes or nullifies their legal capacity, such as **insanity, prodigality, or legal incapacity**. An individual may be fully competent in theory but still restricted from engaging in commercial activity under specific legal provisions.

The researcher has noted a degree of **inconsistency** across various Sudanese laws regarding the **legal age of capacity**. For instance, the **Civil Transactions Act of 1984** uses terms such as "age of majority" and "age of discernment." Article (22) defines the age of majority as **eighteen full lunar years**, granting those who reach it the right to exercise civil rights such as buying and selling. Article 22(4) states: *"Anyone who has not reached the age of seven is considered to lack discernment,"* and Article 22(5) adds: *"Anyone who has reached the age of discernment but not the age of majority, or who has reached the age of majority but is a prodigal or* *of diminished capacity, is considered of diminished legal capacity as defined by law."*

In contrast, the **Criminal Act of 1991** reveals a **lack of clarity and consistency** in dealing with the concept of legal age. The law uses terms like "adult" (Article 3), "legally accountable chooser" (Article 8/1 regarding criminal responsibility and Article 23 on incitement), "age of discernment" (Article 9 on acts of minors), as well as specific age thresholds such as **sixty years** in relation to corporal punishment (Article 35) and **seventy years** (Article 33 on imprisonment and exile).

This legal fragmentation, in the researcher's view, calls for a **comprehensive review and harmonization** of Sudanese laws to avoid inconsistencies and contradictions.

Conclusion and Researcher's Opinion:

In examining the Sudanese Bankruptcy Act of 1929, particularly Article (57), the researcher notes that it identifies the scenarios in which a bankruptcy declaration may be annulled — such as full repayment of debts or court-approved composition or settlement. The Act seeks to **protect creditors' rights** and ensure an **equitable distribution** of the debtor's assets, thus reinforcing **credit** and fostering **trust in commercial dealings**.

Within this framework, a **"trader"** under Sudanese law includes any person who conducts commercial activities in their own name or for their own benefit, whether a natural or legal person. Such an individual must possess the necessary **legal capacity** to engage in these activities, emphasizing the role of **professionalism and habitual conduct**. Companies, by contrast, are assessed based on their **legal structure**, such as general partnerships or limited liability companies, and must also meet the relevant legal capacity requirements.

On another front, the Civil Transactions Act clearly sets the **age of majority at eighteen years**, making it a key criterion for exercising civil rights. However, the researcher has identified **numerous inconsistencies** in how **legal age and capacity** are defined and applied across Sudanese legislation, particularly between civil and criminal law. These discrepancies — such as varying terminology and conflicting age thresholds — pose a risk to **legal clarity and stability**.

The researcher therefore concludes that **better legal coordination and clarity** are required. Sudanese laws should adopt a **uniform and precise standard** for legal age and commercial capacity, especially in relation to bankruptcy proceedings. Harmonizing concepts across civil and criminal law would enhance **legal certainty**, **safeguard rights**, and contribute to the overall **stability of the legal system**.

Chapter Eight:
The Competent Court and the Components of the Bankruptcy Lawsuit

Section One: The Competent Court for Bankruptcy Proceedings

First, it is necessary to clarify the authority before which the bankruptcy petition is filed. It is well established that courts are generally the competent authorities to adjudicate disputes and lawsuits. Since bankruptcy law is a special law, it specifically designates the competent courts to hear bankruptcy cases under Article (5), which provides:

(The competent courts to hear bankruptcy claims are:)

(a) The Court of Appeal,

(b) The Supreme Court,

(c) The First-Degree Magistrate's Court.

These courts have their original jurisdiction defined in the Civil Procedure Code of 1983.

Firstly: The Court of Appeal

This court operates in panels of three judges. Following the amendment of Article (17) in 1987, each state has its own Court of Appeal, with its jurisdiction including:

- Appeals against judgments and orders issued either originally or on appeal by the district courts within its jurisdiction;
- Reviewing administrative decisions issued by central ministers, regional governors, and the capital's commissioner.

The Court of Appeal is presided over by a judge no lower in rank than a High Court judge and includes other Court of Appeal judges. The Court of Appeal's jurisdiction may also be exercised by a single judge delegated by the Court's president.

Secondly: The General Civil Court

According to Article (18) of the Civil Procedure Code (1983), it has jurisdiction as follows:

1. It has original jurisdiction over all civil cases regardless of their value or type except those specifically excluded by law.
2. It has exclusive jurisdiction over:

- Original rulings in cases relating to companies, trademarks, trade names, criminal procedures, bankruptcy cases, and preventive composition (amicable settlements).
- Personal status cases for non-Muslims.
- Appeals against judgments and orders issued by second- and third-degree magistrate courts within its jurisdiction.
- Appeals against judgments and orders of first-degree magistrate courts, which are final.

Thirdly: The First-Degree Magistrate's Court

Pursuant to Article (19) of the Civil Procedure Code (1983), it is competent to hear any lawsuit without value limitation, including appeals against judgments and orders issued by city and rural courts and any other appeals expressly assigned to it by law.

Practical Note Regarding Khartoum:

Although the above courts are designated to hear bankruptcy cases by law, in practice, the capital city of Khartoum has a specialized Commercial Court established under the founding order issued by the Chief Justice on 24 Shawwal 1422 AH (8 January 2002). This order is titled "The Establishment Order of Khartoum Commercial Court" and has been in effect since its signing.

- **Subject-Matter Jurisdiction:** The Khartoum Commercial Court is specialized in civil and criminal cases related to commercial laws.
- **Territorial Jurisdiction:** This court hears all bankruptcy cases arising within the state of Khartoum. In other Sudanese states, bankruptcy cases are heard by any of the courts listed in Article (5).

Local Jurisdiction:

Article (6) of the Bankruptcy Law defines local jurisdiction for filing a bankruptcy petition, stating that the petition should be submitted to the court in the jurisdiction where the debtor ordinarily resides, habitually conducts business, is detained, or imprisoned.

However, despite this provision, its practical application in Khartoum is excluded due to the presence of the specialized Commercial Court.

Article (87) of the Bankruptcy Law (1929) prescribes that, except where otherwise stated, all courts exercising jurisdiction under the Bankruptcy Law must follow the procedural rules set forth in the Civil Procedure Code (1983) when adjudicating bankruptcy matters.

Legal Question:

Is it permissible to depart from the statutory rule and file the bankruptcy lawsuit in the plaintiff's domicile on the basis that rules of local jurisdiction are of a public order nature and therefore can be waived unless the defendant objects before the court?

This argument is rejected since bankruptcy law is a special law; therefore, its provisions on local jurisdiction are mandatory and cannot be overridden except where no such provision exists.

Comparative Reference to Egyptian Commercial Law:

Article (559/1) of the Egyptian Commercial Law currently in force provides that the competent court for declaring the bankruptcy of a merchant debtor is the court in the jurisdiction of the debtor's commercial domicile. If no commercial domicile exists, then jurisdiction lies with the court where the debtor has habitual residence.

Regarding companies, Article (700, paragraph 2) of the same law stipulates that the bankruptcy petition shall be filed with the clerk of the court within whose jurisdiction the company's principal place of business is located, defined by where the company's legal activity is conducted, its main offices, the place where the director exercises his function, and where the board of directors and general assemblies meet. The real principal place, not a mere formal one, governs jurisdiction regardless of the petitioner's identity (creditors or others entitled under Article 700).

The Egyptian Court of Cassation has held that bankruptcy jurisdiction is a matter of public order, limited to courts specialized in bankruptcy. Any disputes outside the bankruptcy scope fall under general civil jurisdiction.

The local jurisdiction in Egypt lies with the primary court in the commercial domicile of the debtor or, in its absence, the habitual residence, as defined by Article (559/1).

Article (4) of the Egyptian Civil Code (1984) defines the commercial domicile as the place where the person carries out trade or craft activities in relation to business management.

Judicial rulings emphasize that bankruptcy procedures are impractical for judges far from the debtor's commercial domicile, where all aspects of the debtor's estate can be effectively managed. This jurisdiction is of public order and cannot be departed from, reflecting the extraordinary nature of bankruptcy litigation and its exceptional consequences.

Summary and Recommendations:

The researcher finds that Sudan's Bankruptcy Law (Article 5) explicitly designates the competent courts to hear bankruptcy cases: the Court of Appeal, the Supreme Court, and the First-Degree Magistrate's Court, with their jurisdiction regulated by the 1983 Civil Procedure Code. While these courts are legally competent, in practice Khartoum has a specialized Commercial Court established in 2002 that hears bankruptcy cases exclusively within its territory.

Local jurisdiction, as defined in Article (6), depends on the debtor's residence, habitual place of business, or detention place, but this provision is practically excluded in Khartoum due to the Commercial Court's exclusive jurisdiction.

In contrast, Egyptian commercial law offers a more flexible approach, allowing jurisdiction based on the debtor's commercial domicile or habitual residence if no commercial domicile exists.

The researcher concludes there is a disparity between Sudanese law's textual rules and practical application, particularly regarding specialized courts and jurisdictional rules in Khartoum. To avoid legal conflicts and enhance clarity, it is advisable to amend Sudanese bankruptcy laws to align with the current practical framework, clarify the relationship between commercial and other courts, and specify jurisdictional rules—especially local jurisdiction—to allow filing in the debtor's habitual residence if no commercial domicile exists, similar to the Egyptian model. Such amendments would promote judicial consistency and legal certainty in bankruptcy proceedings.

Section Two: Contents of the Bankruptcy Petition under the Law

The legislator stipulated in Article (12) of the Bankruptcy Law of 1929 that:

"Every bankruptcy petition submitted by the debtor must include the following details:

(a) A statement that the debtor is insolvent and unable to pay his debts.

(b) The place where the debtor usually resides, or where he conducts his business or personally works for the purpose of gain, or the place where he is detained if seized or imprisoned.

(c) The total amount of all monetary claims made against him and their details, including the names of his creditors and their places of residence as far as the debtor knows or can ascertain by exercising reasonable care and effort.

(d) The total amount of all the debtor's assets and their details, accompanied by the following:

(i) The valuation of all non-monetary assets,

(ii) The place or places where all such assets are located,

(iii) A declaration of the debtor's wish to place all such assets under the court's control, except those legally exempt from seizure and sale pursuant to a judgment for payment of a sum of money, excluding accounting books.

(e) If the debtor is a partnership, the petition must include the full name of each partner. If the petition is signed on behalf of the partnership, it must be accompanied by an affidavit sworn by the signing partner confirming that all partners consent to the submission of the petition."*

Article (13) of the same law stipulates that the petition shall include:

*"In every bankruptcy petition filed by the creditor or creditors, the details relating to the debtor as stated in paragraph (b) of Article (12) shall be included, and also the following:

(a) The bankruptcy act committed by the debtor and the date it was committed,

(b) The amount claimed by the creditor(s) in cash and its details,

(c) The date of any judgment (if any) issued in favor of the creditor(s) against the debtor, including the name of the court that issued it and the amount still due according to that judgment."*

Regarding petitions filed by the Minister of Justice, Article (14) states:

"Every bankruptcy petition filed by the Minister of Justice shall specify the reasons for the request, in a manner that convinces the court."

Concerning jurisdiction, Article (87) of the same law clarifies:

"Except as otherwise provided in this law, every court exercising jurisdiction under this law shall follow the procedural law applicable in civil courts currently in force."

The researcher found that the Bankruptcy Law grants the debtor the right to file a bankruptcy petition because the debtor is best acquainted with his financial situation. To protect the rights of creditors, the debtor is required to include, in addition to the debt amount, specific data proving the debtor's inability to pay debts, which constitutes grounds for the petition as one of the acts of bankruptcy. The petition must specify the debtor's usual residence or place of business or where he personally works for gain, or the place of detention if arrested or imprisoned, to determine the court's territorial jurisdiction. The petition must also detail the total monetary claims against the debtor, their particulars, and creditor identities and residences, to the extent known or reasonably ascertainable.

This means the debtor must specify the aggregate amount of monetary claims against him to confirm that the debt amount reaches at least fifty thousand pounds, granting him the right to submit the petition. It must also identify creditors and their residences for proper court notification. The debtor must declare the total value and details of all assets, whether real estate or movable property, and specify the locations of these assets, along with a declaration placing all assets under the court's control, except those legally exempt from seizure or sale pursuant to a monetary judgment. Accounting books are excluded.

If the debtor is a partnership, the petition must list the full names of all partners. If filed in the name of the partnership, it must be accompanied by a sworn affidavit from the signing partner before a competent court, confirming all partners' consent to filing the petition.

B. Contents of the Creditor's Petition

Article (13) of the Bankruptcy Law of 1929 details the creditor's petition contents as follows:

"Each bankruptcy petition filed by the creditor(s) must include the details specified in paragraph (b) of Article (12) regarding the debtor, and also:

(a) The bankruptcy act committed by the debtor and the date of commission,

(b) The amount claimed in cash and its details,

(c) The date of any judgment issued in favor of the creditor(s) against the debtor, including the issuing court and the remaining amount due."*

The law grants the creditor the right to file a bankruptcy petition against his debtor, which is the natural procedure for declaring bankruptcy, as the creditor is usually the most attentive to the debtor's condition. The creditor may file the petition individually or collectively with other creditors if their combined claims amount to at least fifty pounds. The petition must include the debtor's usual residence or place of business or personal work for gain, or detention place if arrested or imprisoned, to determine the court's territorial jurisdiction. The petition must also specify the bankruptcy act committed by the debtor as per Article (4) of the Bankruptcy Law of 1929, including the date of commission. The petition must be submitted at least three months after the debtor's commission of any bankruptcy act. The amount claimed in cash and its details must be included, along with any judicial ruling against the debtor, specifying the court and the remaining amount due.

C. Contents of the Public Prosecutor's Petition

The Bankruptcy Law of 1929 grants the Public Prosecutor the right to file a bankruptcy petition against any debtor when appropriate, particularly upon the occurrence of a crime involving the debtor and during the investigation, if the debtor has committed an act of bankruptcy justifying the petition to protect creditors' rights.

If requested by the court as the government's legal representative, Article (14) states:

"Every bankruptcy petition submitted by the Public Prosecutor shall include the reasons for the request in a manner that convinces the court."

Although this article does not exhaustively list the data required in the Public Prosecutor's petition, it generally includes the debtor's usual residence or place of business or personal work for gain, or detention place if seized or imprisoned, the amount and details of claims against the debtor with creditor names and addresses, the bankruptcy act committed by the debtor with its date, and the reasons prompting the petition.

In Egyptian Law, the legislator follows a similar pattern to the Sudanese Bankruptcy Law, as follows:

1. **Contents of the Debtor's Petition:**

Article (553) of the Commercial Law requires the merchant debtor to request bankruptcy within fifteen days from the date of cessation of payment, submitting a petition to the court clerk with the following documents: principal ledgers, a copy of the last balance sheet and profit and loss account, a statement of total personal expenses for the two years preceding the petition or the period of commercial activity if less, a detailed statement of real estate and movable property owned and their approximate values at cessation of payment, cash deposits in banks domestically or abroad, creditor and debtor names and addresses, and the estimated value of claims or debts and any guarantees. Protested bills against the merchant within the two years before the petition must be included. The documents must be dated and signed by the merchant. If some documents cannot be provided or data completed, reasons must be explained. If the debtor is a company, the petition is submitted to the court clerk of the company's main office location, or local administration center if abroad. The petition must include names of current and former partners, their residences, nationalities, and dates of departure from the company.

2. **Contents of the Creditor's Petition:**

Article 544(3) of the Commercial Law provides that the creditor requests the debtor's bankruptcy by petition deposited with the competent court clerk, accompanied by a deposit of one thousand pounds in the court treasury as a security for publication expenses. The petition requests precautionary measures, states the circumstances evidencing the debtor's cessation of payment, and specifies the date of the court session for hearing, notifying the debtor. There is no fixed deadline for creditor petitions as long as the cessation of payment continues, except when filing after the debtor's death, which must be within one year after death.

The Sudanese law does not provide explicit provisions regulating disputes arising from bankruptcy or jurisdiction of bankruptcy courts per general rules.

Hearing of Bankruptcy Petitions under the Law:

1. Dismissal of the Petition on Procedural Grounds:

If the bankruptcy petition lacks the required data, the court may request the petitioner to complete it. Failure to do so results in dismissal under Article (38) of the Civil Procedures Law of 1983, especially if no reason for the bankruptcy request is given or if the court lacks jurisdiction. The Bankruptcy Law allows the court to reject, return for amendment, or amend any petition under conditions it deems appropriate if:

- The petition is unsigned or improperly supported,
- The petition fails to specify the required details precisely as per Articles (15/2) and (16) of the law.

Section Three: Procedures Upon Acceptance of the Petition

If the petition is neither rejected nor returned pursuant to paragraph (2) of Article (15) of the Bankruptcy Law, and if accepted after being returned, the court shall then issue an order setting a date to hear the petition in accordance with Article (16). The court shall summon all creditors to notify the court on or before that date of any claims that can be proven under the provisions of the law. Such notification or publication shall be made in the Gazette in implementation of paragraph (3) of Article (16). The court must verify the notices and ensure compliance with the requirements of Article (44) of the Civil Procedures Law of 1983 and must not rely solely on the statements of the petitioner. The court shall resort to publication only after confirming that personal notification to the interested party is impracticable. If the debtor is a known entity such as a company with a known address, the court shall only resort to publication when strictly necessary.

Upon issuing the order for submission of the petition, the court may appoint a provisional trustee to safeguard the debtor's assets, or any part thereof. The court may also order the actual seizure of all or part of the debtor's assets. However, such an order shall have no effect regarding the suspension of lawsuits and ongoing proceedings against the debtor.

In the precedent case of *Yousif Ahmed Babiker and Others v. Al-Sir Hussein Mohammed Zain*, it was held that issuing an order to halt execution proceedings based on a submitted bankruptcy petition is erroneous, since the order declaring bankruptcy has not yet been issued, and the procedures stipulated in Articles 16 and 17 — including hearing the petitioner in the presence of creditors — have not been undertaken. The court further noted that as procedures under Articles 20 and 21 of the law have not yet been followed, it is erroneous to suspend execution procedures based on paragraph (3) of Article 22. Article 22(3) provides that no court order is required once an order declaring bankruptcy is issued.

On the scheduled hearing date, the court shall interrogate the debtor in the presence of any creditors who appear personally or via their representatives. The court shall hear the bankruptcy petition in the presence of creditors, except in cases where their addresses are unknown. This principle was established in precedent case *T.M/212* in the Judicial Rulings Journal 2003, where the court ruled that hearing the petition in the absence of principal creditors is unjustified. The court found no justification for resorting to alternative notification means, especially since the creditor, the National Tobacco Company, is one of the country's largest companies with a known registered office and operational base, making notification feasible. Alternative publication may only be considered if the debtor proves that notification of the creditor's address or residence was genuinely impossible, which was not the case here despite the debtor's claim.

Furthermore, the court noted that the debtor and some creditors admitted that the debtor disposed of real estate, vehicles, and jewelry belonging to certain family members by sale just months before filing the bankruptcy petition. The court failed to give this fact the necessary consideration, although such transactions fall within the scope of Article 49 of the Bankruptcy Law, which addresses the possibility of invalidating certain transfers of ownership by the debtor. The article specifies a two-year period prior to filing the bankruptcy petition during which such transactions are scrutinized. The court should have paid attention to this matter and conducted a thorough investigation into the circumstances of the sales, the beneficiaries of such sales, and whether they included creditors, to prevent the debtor's act from appearing suspicious as preferential treatment of certain creditors with bad faith.

Additionally, the court neglected the evidence regarding the debtor's relocation of his workplace to another city. The court should have verified the nature of the new work, its profitability, and whether the debtor's income therefrom is sufficient to meet his obligations toward creditors.

Legally, the cause of bankruptcy is less important than the effort made by the debtor to prevent it and whether the debtor's current business is adequate to fulfill obligations to creditors. The court failed to give this issue due consideration.

The court must hear objections raised by creditors or their agents against the debtor's petition in accordance with Article (20) of the Bankruptcy Law. The court may, if deemed appropriate, request any evidence necessary to decide on the petition and may grant the debtor or any creditor an extension to submit such evidence.

After reviewing the petition, the court may reject it following the interrogation of the debtor and any further investigations if it concludes there is insufficient basis to proceed, as provided in Article (20). For example, the court may find the debtor's request insincere, the petition motivated by malice, fraudulent intent, or based on incorrect information, or that the debtor caused or contributed to the bankruptcy through reckless speculation.

The court's authority to reject the petition under Article (21/1) of the Bankruptcy Law does not confer absolute discretion regarding the existence or absence of sufficient grounds to proceed. Its decisions are subject to appeal before higher courts, as the decisions must be reasoned.

Fourth: The Effect of Acceptance of the Bankruptcy Petition

If the petition is not rejected pursuant to Article (20/1), and the debtor is unable to propose a settlement or a plan acceptable to the creditors and approved by the court, the court shall issue an order declaring bankruptcy. This order takes effect retroactively from the date the petition—upon which the declaration was based—was submitted, as per Article (22/4). Once issued pursuant to Article (22/1), and by virtue of Article (22/3), no creditor may pursue any debt against the bankrupt person or his estate in any manner inconsistent with this law. Moreover, creditors may not initiate or continue any legal proceedings unless authorized by the court and subject to such conditions as the court may impose.

From the above, the researcher observes the following:

1. Sudanese law grants the debtor the right to file for bankruptcy, given the debtor's superior knowledge of their financial situation. However, it requires the inclusion of precise information regarding assets and liabilities to safeguard creditor rights.
2. The law emphasizes determining territorial jurisdiction based on the debtor's residence or place of business.
3. Sudanese law does not set a specific deadline for a creditor to file a bankruptcy petition, which may result in procedural delays—unlike Egyptian law, which requires filing within one year of the debtor's death.
4. The Sudanese law does not explicitly regulate the jurisdiction of the bankruptcy court over disputes arising from the bankruptcy estate, warranting legislative review to clarify this area.

It is thus evident that while the Sudanese law seeks to protect both debtor and creditor, it requires certain amendments to ensure greater procedural clarity and more precise jurisdictional demarcation.

Chapter Nine: Effects of Declaration of Bankruptcy

Section One: Effects of Bankruptcy Declaration on the Debtor and His Dealings

The issuance of a bankruptcy declaration results in the following:

Subsection One: Dispossession of the Debtor (Loss of Legal Capacity over Estate)

The debtor is stripped of the right to manage or dispose of his assets immediately upon the issuance of the bankruptcy judgment, by operation of law, even if the ruling's text does not explicitly state so. All the debtor's property vests in the bankruptcy trustee, or in the court in the absence of a trustee, except for properties exempt from seizure and sale under judgments for monetary payment. Such exempt property remains part of the debtor's estate but is placed under the control of the trustee or the court for distribution to creditors.

This dispossession includes:

- All goods in the debtor's possession at the time the bankruptcy petition was filed;
- Goods related to the debtor's commercial activities at the time of filing;
- Goods tied to the debtor's business activities with the real owner's consent, where the circumstances would lead others to believe the debtor is the apparent owner.

Moreover, the debtor's dispossession extends to all property acquired **after** the issuance of the bankruptcy judgment, such as:

- Inherited property,
- Testamentary gifts,
- Compensation awards, and other such assets, until full discharge of debts.

Thus, the dispossession encompasses all assets legally or apparently owned by the debtor at the time of bankruptcy and those acquired afterward, up until the debtor is discharged from liability.

Legal Nature of Dispossession

Understanding the legal nature of dispossession resulting from a bankruptcy ruling has been the subject of scholarly debate. The old **French law** viewed it as a **transfer of ownership** from the bankrupt to the trustee (syndic). This approach was similarly adopted by **old English law** prior to the **Bankruptcy Act of 1914**.

However, **modern French law**, which has influenced most Arab bankruptcy laws, maintained the debtor's ownership despite the bankruptcy declaration. Under this model, the trustee merely **acts on behalf of the debtor**, and the assets are transferred to third parties only through sale by the trustee. Ownership remains with the debtor until then. This approach aligns with **Islamic jurisprudence**, which also does not recognize a transfer of ownership upon bankruptcy declaration.

On the other hand, the **English Bankruptcy Act of 1914**, adopted by the **Sudanese Bankruptcy Act of 1929**, provides for the **vesting of all bankrupt assets in the trustee or the court** immediately upon bankruptcy declaration. This is affirmed in **Article (23)**, which states:

"Upon the issuance of the bankruptcy order, all the bankrupt's assets shall vest in the court or the trustee, as subsequently provided."

This principle is also echoed in **Article (72)** of the Land Settlement and Registration Act, which stipulates that upon receipt of a certified copy of a bankruptcy order or an order appointing a manager of a deceased debtor's estate under the 1929 Bankruptcy Act, the registrar must record the bankruptcy court or appointed trustee as the new owner of any land or rights forming part of the bankrupt's estate, thus enabling its distribution among creditors.

Legal Consequences of Asset Vesting

The consequence of transferring ownership of the debtor's assets to the court or trustee is that **any transactions conducted by the bankrupt in relation to those assets after the bankruptcy declaration are deemed void**. This is because the debtor no longer has legal title to those assets.

Before the enactment of the **Civil Transactions Act of 1984**, such acts were considered **absolutely null and void**, as Sudanese law did not recognize the concept of "disposition of another's property." **After** the 1984 Act introduced this concept, the legal treatment of such transactions became more nuanced but still renders unauthorized post-bankruptcy dispositions legally ineffective.

The Debtor's Acts Post-Bankruptcy Declaration Are No Longer Absolutely Void

The acts of a bankrupt concerning his property after the issuance of the bankruptcy declaration are no longer considered absolutely void; rather, they are deemed voidable in favor of the true owner. Thus, the Sudanese legislator has returned to the prevailing concept in Egyptian legislation, which holds that the bankrupt's acts are not effective against the creditors unless ratified by the bankruptcy trustee. This principle was confirmed by the Supreme Court in the precedent *Ibrahim Mohamed Saleh v. Mohamed Saleh and Others*, where it stated: *"An act involving the disposition of another's property without permission is not void, but rather a valid contract pending ratification."* Accordingly, the court or the bankruptcy trustee may approve acts conducted by the bankrupt after the declaration of bankruptcy if such acts serve the interest of the creditors' group, or may annul them if they are detrimental.

Islamic jurisprudence imposes the same effect upon a declaration of bankruptcy—preventing the interdicted debtor from undertaking acts that would harm his creditors. It stipulates that the bankrupt may not discharge his debtors, and if he does, such a discharge is not opposable to creditors with rights in his assets.

The researcher concludes that one of the key consequences of the declaration of bankruptcy concerning the debtor and his acts is the statutory deprivation of the debtor's right to manage or dispose of his assets. All such assets transfer to the trustee or the court, excluding those legally exempt from seizure. This includes assets in the debtor's possession at the time of filing the bankruptcy petition, those related to his commercial activity, and even assets acquired post-judgment, such as inheritance or compensation.

Significant debate surrounds the legal characterization of the debtor's dispossession. As shown, the Sudanese legislator, after the enactment of the Civil Transactions Act of 1984, adopted the theory of disposition of another's property. This made the debtor's post-bankruptcy acts voidable rather than absolutely void and subject to ratification by the trustee if they benefit the creditor body. This aligns with the position of Egyptian legislation and jurisprudence.

The researcher supports the modern trend adopted by Arab legislations, which maintains the debtor's ownership of assets while restricting his ability to act on them to protect creditors. Adopting the theory of disposition of another's property in Sudanese law is a progressive legal development that achieves fairness by allowing the ratification of acts beneficial to creditors instead of nullifying them automatically. The researcher recommends revising Sudanese legislation to establish clear criteria for ratifying such acts, ensuring the protection of all parties' rights in accordance with the principles of justice and the law.

Section II: The Debtor's Inability to Litigate

Following a bankruptcy declaration, the debtor becomes legally incompetent to initiate or be the subject of litigation independently. Instead, all legal actions must be initiated by the bankruptcy trustee. The debtor may not continue in any existing lawsuits; rather, the trustee substitutes the debtor in all judicial proceedings. However, this prohibition does not preclude the debtor from intervening alongside the trustee in lawsuits brought against the bankruptcy estate to safeguard his interests. Conversely, the debtor may not intervene in actions initiated by the trustee against third parties.

As for whether a creditor may intervene in such lawsuits, jurisprudence distinguishes between two cases:

1. **Where the creditor's interest conflicts with that of the creditor body**: Intervention is permitted unanimously by scholars and the judiciary.
2. **Where no such conflict exists**: Opinions diverge on whether intervention should be allowed.

The researcher concludes that a declaration of bankruptcy constitutes a major turning point in the debtor's legal standing, resulting in the loss of capacity to litigate, whether by initiating proceedings or continuing existing ones. The bankruptcy trustee substitutes the debtor in all such matters. Nevertheless, the debtor retains the right to intervene in proceedings against the bankruptcy estate to protect personal interests.

As for creditors' intervention in actions initiated by the trustee, jurisprudence and case law recognize the right to intervene in cases of conflicting interests. In the absence of such conflict, legal opinions are divided—reflecting differing interpretations of the nature of bankruptcy and the role of creditors.

The researcher believes that the general rule vesting litigation powers in the trustee is vital to safeguard collective creditor interests and avoid conflict. However, allowing creditor intervention in the event of a conflict is logical and necessary to protect their individual rights. In cases lacking such conflict, restricting intervention is justified to preserve orderly administration of the bankruptcy estate and avoid disruption of proceedings.

Thus, the researcher recommends the adoption of clear legal standards specifying when a creditor may intervene—namely, where a substantial personal interest is at risk due to the trustee's acts—provided such intervention is subject to judicial approval to balance creditor rights with procedural integrity.

Section III: Exceptions to the Debtor's Dispossession

While the debtor's dispossession from managing his assets renders him unable to litigate concerning them, certain acts classified as judicial safeguards remain permissible. These include precautionary actions designed to preserve his rights, such as filing protests (protesto), renewing mortgage registrations, serving judgments rendered in his favor, and filing appeals or objections to adverse judgments.

Also exempt from dispossession are lawsuits unrelated to the debtor's assets, such as tort claims brought by the debtor for defamation, slander, or damage to reputation, as well as personal actions like spousal obedience claims and criminal proceedings—whether the debtor is the victim or the accused. Nonetheless, the trustee may intervene in such cases when monetary compensation is sought, to preserve creditors' rights. If compensation is awarded in a criminal case in favor of the bankrupt, the proceeds are added to the bankruptcy estate. Where a fine or compensation is awarded against the bankrupt, a distinction must be made:

1. **If the wrongful act occurred before the bankruptcy declaration**: The awarded creditor enters the bankruptcy as a creditor, but the fine is not chargeable to the estate. Compensation is a pre-bankruptcy debt, but the fine arises from a post-declaration judgment.
2. **If the act occurred after the bankruptcy declaration**: The estate is not liable for either the compensation or the fine.

The researcher holds that the debtor's dispossession is one of the most significant consequences of a bankruptcy judgment, as it restricts his ability to act over his assets to protect creditors' rights. However, the law exempts certain judicial acts that the debtor may perform personally, particularly precautionary procedures and personal claims unrelated to his financial assets.

This legal framework demonstrates clear differentiation between compensation and fines in criminal cases, based on whether the underlying act occurred before or after the bankruptcy judgment. Compensation arising from pre-bankruptcy actions is included in the estate, while post-bankruptcy liabilities are excluded—highlighting the principle that the bankruptcy estate represents the liquidation of the debtor's financial position as of a specific date, without burdening it with new obligations.

Therefore, the researcher recommends developing a clearer legal framework that defines circumstances under which the debtor may litigate personally without infringing creditors' rights, thereby ensuring equitable treatment of all parties within the bankruptcy process.

Section Four: The Effect of Bankruptcy on the Debtor's Prior Transactions and Their Regulation under Arab Laws

One of the most challenging and detrimental periods for creditors in bankruptcy proceedings is the *suspect period* (or *twilight period*). During this time, the debtor becomes aware of the deteriorating state of their financial affairs and the imminent risk of bankruptcy. In response, the debtor may resort to various tactics to conceal their insolvency from creditors, including disposing of assets, making fictitious donations to relatives and friends under the guise of gifts but with the intent of asset concealment, or granting preferential treatment to certain creditors over others—by fully settling their debts or providing them with securities over assets, giving them an undue advantage during liquidation.

As such, legislation generally casts suspicion on the debtor's actions during this period. To safeguard the interests of creditors, legislators have established special rules governing the validity and voidability of such transactions. However, differences among legislative approaches are apparent, particularly in defining the suspect period, identifying the types of transactions subject to voidance, and distinguishing between absolute and relative nullity.

In Arab legislation—such as Egyptian and Lebanese laws—the suspect period is clearly and simply defined as the time between the debtor's cessation of payments and the declaration of bankruptcy, with an additional ten days added. These laws also clearly define the transactions subject to voidance and provide a general rule to classify the type of transaction and the applicable form of invalidity.

In contrast, the Sudanese legislator did not adopt a single uniform rule for defining the suspect period. Instead, it varies depending on the nature of the transaction and the surrounding circumstances, structured across three levels:

1. A period of ten years prior to the bankruptcy declaration.
2. A period of two years prior to the bankruptcy declaration.
3. A period beginning three months before the bankruptcy petition is filed and ending with the issuance of the bankruptcy order.

Additionally, contrary to its historical root in English law, Sudanese law does not declare the debtor's transactions during the suspect period as absolutely void. Rather, these transactions are subject to voidability, and the bankruptcy trustee may choose not to pursue annulment if it is deemed not prejudicial to the creditors' interests.

Commentary and Researcher's Opinion:

The suspect period is one of the most sensitive stages in bankruptcy proceedings, as it often involves financially distressed debtors engaging in transactions that may harm creditors—such as asset concealment or favoring some creditors over others. Thus, it is essential for legal systems to implement controls that protect creditors' rights and ensure equitable liquidation.

Researcher's View: The researcher observes that Arab legal systems like those of Egypt and Lebanon provide a clearly defined suspect period, facilitating the application of rules regarding the voidance of dubious transactions carried out by the debtor during this time. In contrast, the Sudanese approach is more complex due to its multiple temporal classifications, which may cause practical difficulties in application, particularly in proving the debtor's intent to harm creditors.

Furthermore, the Sudanese law's position of not rendering transactions during the suspect period absolutely void—but rather voidable at the discretion of the trustee—offers flexibility that might be useful in certain contexts. However, it also opens the door to inconsistent judicial interpretations, potentially undermining the principle of creditor equality.

Therefore, the researcher recommends adopting a unified and clearly defined suspect period, as exemplified by Egyptian and Lebanese laws, to promote fairness and enhance the protection of creditors' rights. It is also suggested that objective criteria be developed to determine when transactions should be considered voidable, based on the impact on the bankruptcy estate rather than leaving such matters solely to the trustee's discretion.

Third: The Suspect Period under the 1929 Bankruptcy Act

Article 49 of the Bankruptcy Act states:

"Any transfer of ownership, unless it was executed before marriage and as a consideration for it, or a transfer made in good faith to a purchaser or lienholder over real estate for valuable consideration, or a transfer made to the transferor's wife or children of property that the transferor received through his wife after marriage, shall be voidable against the bankruptcy trustee if the transferor goes bankrupt within two years of the transfer. It is also voidable against the trustee if the transferor becomes bankrupt at any time during the ten years preceding the transfer and was not able at the time of the transfer to pay all his debts without needing the asset transferred, provided that the transferor's interest in the property was completely transferred upon execution."

From this article, it is evident that:

1. **Valid Transactions:**

- Transfers to a spouse executed prior to marriage as part of the marriage settlement.
- Transfers to a purchaser or lienholder, provided they were made in good faith and for valuable consideration.
- Transfers to a wife or children of property acquired by the debtor through his wife after marriage.

2. **Voidable Transactions Against the Trustee:**

- Any gratuitous transfer made by the debtor within the two years preceding the declaration of bankruptcy, excluding the valid transactions above.
- Any transfer made within the ten years prior to the declaration of bankruptcy if it is proven that the debtor was unable to satisfy his debts at the time of the transaction without relying on the transferred asset.

Article 50 of the Act further provides that any transfer of ownership, creation of a lien, payment of a debt or obligation, or any judicial action against the debtor shall be deemed fraudulent and voidable in favor of the creditors if the following two conditions are met:

1. The transaction was executed within three months before filing the bankruptcy petition.
2. The transaction was intended to defraud or prefer one creditor over others.

This was confirmed by the Court of Appeal in the precedent: *Kyokos Juanios v. Trustee of the Estate of Aristo Lee David*, where it held:

"When a party claims that a property transaction is voidable as a fraudulent conveyance under the 1929 Bankruptcy Act, it is insufficient for the trustee to demonstrate that the debtor was insolvent at the time. The trustee must also prove that the debtor's primary purpose in making the transaction was to prefer the transferee over other creditors."

Moreover, Article 51 of the Act stipulates that:

"Subject to the provisions regarding execution and the avoidance of certain transactions and preferences, none of the following shall be invalid in the event of bankruptcy:

(a) Any payment made by the bankrupt to any creditor;

(b) Any payment or delivery to the bankrupt;

(c) Any contract or transaction entered into with the bankrupt for valuable consideration.

These transactions remain valid provided that:

1. They were concluded before the bankruptcy petition;
2. The other party was unaware at the time of the transaction that the debtor had committed any act of bankruptcy."

Implication: Transactions falling within these categories become voidable against the trustee if they were executed after the bankruptcy petition was filed, and if the counterparty knew at the time that the debtor had committed acts of bankruptcy.

Commentary and Researcher's Opinion:

The 1929 Bankruptcy Act pays particular attention to protecting creditors' rights by placing restrictions on the debtor's conduct during the suspect period. It makes a clear distinction between valid transactions, voidable transactions, and fraudulent ones that require proof of intent to prefer certain creditors.

Researcher's View:

The analysis of Articles 49–51 reveals the legislature's attempt to strike a balance between creditor protection and recognizing certain legitimate debtor transactions. However, several practical challenges can be identified:

1. Complexity in Identifying Voidable Transactions:

The law differentiates between multiple time frames (two years, ten years, three months), depending on the nature of the transaction. This complicates legal proceedings and burdens the courts with cases requiring proof of bad faith or creditor prejudice.

2. Evidentiary Burden on the Trustee:

The aforementioned judicial precedent places the burden of proof on the trustee to demonstrate that the transaction aimed to prefer a specific creditor. This may weaken creditor protection, especially when clear evidence of intent is lacking.

3. Distinguishing Legitimate from Illegitimate Transactions:

While the law validates certain transactions (e.g., marriage-related or those with bona fide purchasers for value), it also allows for voidance if bad faith or fraud is proven—potentially leading to complex disputes between parties.

4. **Challenge of Contesting Transactions Post-Petition:**

Under Article 51, transactions executed after the bankruptcy petition are contestable if the other party was aware of the debtor's bankruptcy acts. Proving such awareness can be difficult and may result in exploitation of last-minute transactions.

Recommendations:

- Simplify the criteria for defining the suspect period by adopting a uniform time frame for all voidable transactions.
- Reallocate the burden of proof so that the debtor must also demonstrate that their transaction was not intended to harm creditors.
- Introduce legal presumptions of fraud, such that gratuitous or preferential transactions are presumed to be in bad faith unless the debtor proves otherwise.
- Promote financial transparency for debtors during the period leading up to bankruptcy, to prevent fraudulent transactions that could harm creditors.

Conclusion:
In light of the above, the researcher concludes that the current legal framework requires reform to strike a better balance between creditor protection and preserving debtor rights, while also streamlining the legal processes surrounding the avoidance of suspicious transactions during the suspect period.

Third: The Nature of Avoidance

It is evident from the provisions of Articles (49), (50), and (51) of the Bankruptcy Law, as well as from comparative legislation, that the term "avoidance" does not carry its traditional legal meaning—i.e., treating the transaction as void *ab initio* and restoring the parties to their pre-contractual positions. Instead, the intention is to render the transaction unenforceable against the bankruptcy trustee. Therefore, a transaction carried out by the debtor during the suspect period remains valid between the parties, but it may be set aside at the request of the bankruptcy trustee. This level of scrutiny is deemed sufficient to protect the interests of creditors. Accordingly, the following consequences arise:

1. A legal action must be initiated to request avoidance of such transactions.
2. Only the bankruptcy trustee has the legal standing to bring an action to annul transactions conducted by the debtor during the suspect period, to the extent necessary to cover the outstanding debts owed by the bankrupt. The purpose of avoidance is to safeguard creditors' rights.

Undoubtedly, subjecting the debtor's transactions during the suspect period to avoidance provides protection to creditors. However, extending the duration of this period may destabilize legal positions, undermine confidence in commercial transactions, and cause harm to bona fide parties who entered into transactions with the debtor, particularly since such transactions may be voided even after ten years—well beyond what those parties may have reasonably anticipated at the time.

Upon analyzing Articles (49–51) of the Bankruptcy Law, the researcher finds that the legislator does not treat transactions carried out by the debtor during the suspect period as absolutely void. Rather, they are deemed voidable against the trustee in bankruptcy. This means the transactions remain valid between the contracting parties unless challenged by the trustee in bankruptcy to protect creditor interests.

Researcher's Opinion:

Although creditor protection is a legitimate interest, the ten-year extension of the suspect period and the risk of avoiding transactions may result in several negative consequences, including:

1. **Legal Uncertainty:**
   A suspect period extending up to ten years may lead to instability in legal positions of those dealing with the debtor, potentially discouraging investors and stakeholders from engaging in commercial dealings for fear of eventual annulment.
2. **Harm to Bona Fide Parties:**
   Those who enter into contracts with the debtor in good faith, without knowledge of the debtor's financial difficulties, may be unfairly subjected to annulment actions, despite acting lawfully and ethically.
3. **Burden of Proof on the Bankruptcy Trustee:**
   As avoidance is not automatic and requires litigation by the trustee, this may complicate proceedings and burden the judiciary. The trustee may also face challenges in proving bad faith or intent to defraud creditors.
4. **Impact on Commercial Activity:**
   This legal framework may discourage financially distressed debtors from entering into lawful transactions, fearing that such actions may later be voided, further exacerbating their financial difficulties.

Recommendations:

- **Reduce the Duration of the Suspect Period:**
  It is preferable to shorten the ten-year period to a more reasonable duration (e.g., five years), to protect bona fide parties and strike a balance between creditor rights and commercial stability.
- **Differentiate Between Bona Fide and Mala Fide Parties:** Legislators could establish legal presumptions to identify good faith, thereby exempting bona fide parties from annulment actions without requiring litigation.
- **Redistribute the Burden of Proof:**
  Instead of requiring the trustee to prove bad faith, a legal presumption of bad faith could apply to gratuitous transactions, while others remain valid unless proven otherwise.
- **Enhance Financial Transparency:**
  Stricter disclosure obligations could be imposed on financially troubled debtors to allow creditors to make informed decisions when engaging with them.

Conclusion:

While bankruptcy laws aim to protect creditors by avoiding suspect transactions, the extended duration of the suspect period may adversely affect legal certainty and trust in commercial dealings. Legislative amendments are necessary to balance creditor protection with the stability and reliability of financial and legal transactions.

Section II: Effects of Bankruptcy on the Debtor's Person

Subsection I: Restriction of the Debtor's Freedom

Restricting the debtor's freedom may be considered a precautionary measure or a consequence of committing an act associated with bankruptcy that constitutes a criminal offense. As a general rule, the declaration of bankruptcy does not in itself restrict the bankrupt debtor's freedom. The commission of acts leading to a declaration of bankruptcy does not, in and of itself, warrant punishment; rather, certain acts related to bankruptcy proceedings may constitute crimes punishable by law.

The legislator's objective is to protect creditors and ensure the swift completion of bankruptcy proceedings. Thus, once the court accepts a petition for the declaration of bankruptcy—and upon the request of any creditor—the court may order the debtor to provide reasonable assurance of appearance at scheduled hearings. The court may also issue a warrant for the debtor's arrest, with detention until the hearing or release on bail. However, once the bankruptcy judgment is issued, the debtor must be released.

If, after being declared bankrupt, the debtor refuses to assist the court or the trustee in collecting, liquidating, or distributing the estate, this constitutes a bankruptcy-specific offense punishable by imprisonment for up to six months, a fine as determined by the court, or both.

It is important to distinguish between **precautionary detention**, which may apply under the Bankruptcy Law, and **executive detention**, which is allowed in certain cases under Article (243) of the 1983 Civil Procedure Act. The latter is intended to compel the debtor to fulfill payment obligations, while the former serves to prevent the debtor from fleeing the jurisdiction or dissipating assets. Therefore, a bankrupt debtor whose assets are under the control of the trustee may not be subjected to executive detention.

Subsection II: Declaration of the Debtor's Bankruptcy

Since the declaration of the debtor's bankruptcy results in the deprivation of their right to manage or dispose of their assets, thereby rendering them unable to provide for themselves or for their dependents, the legislator—taking into account the requirements of justice and humanitarian considerations—has allowed the court, or the trustee with the court's authorization, to periodically grant financial assistance to the bankrupt and their family from the bankrupt's estate. The amount of such assistance is determined by the court or the trustee in bankruptcy based on what is deemed equitable. Furthermore, the court may, upon the request of the debtor, the trustee, or any of the creditors, modify the amount of such assistance at any time. This assistance may also be treated as remuneration for the debtor if they are employed in the liquidation of their own estate.

Commentary and Researcher's Opinion

The consequences arising from the declaration of bankruptcy—including the restriction of the debtor's liberty and the formal declaration itself—are legal procedures aimed at both creditor protection and the fair treatment of the debtor under applicable legal provisions. In the researcher's view, these effects can be summarized as follows:

1. Restriction of the Debtor's Liberty

The legislator in bankruptcy laws stipulates that bankruptcy, in itself, does not necessarily entail restricting the debtor's liberty or punishing them solely for becoming insolvent. This reflects a legal understanding that bankruptcy per se is not a criminal offense. However, the legislator may impose sanctions for acts committed within the context of the bankruptcy process, such as disobeying court orders or failing to cooperate with the trustee in the liquidation of assets.

The researcher notes that **preventive detention**, which may be imposed to prevent the debtor from absconding or dissipating assets, is a necessary measure to preserve the integrity of bankruptcy proceedings. However, such detention must not infringe upon the legal rights of the debtor or unduly affect their personal life.

It is also noted that a clear distinction should be made between preventive detention—which is a protective measure for creditors to ensure the proper administration of bankruptcy—and **executory detention**, which is a coercive tool used to compel the debtor to fulfill payment obligations. Each form of detention has its own legal context, and procedures must be carefully followed to uphold justice.

The researcher further observes that the **declaration of bankruptcy** operates as a legal measure that prevents the debtor from managing or disposing of their assets. This could leave the debtor unable to meet their own and their family's basic needs. Accordingly, the law allows the court or trustee to allocate a **financial allowance** to the bankrupt and their family from the bankruptcy estate as a form of humanitarian relief.

Another humane aspect of bankruptcy law highlighted by the researcher is the provision of financial assistance to the debtor's family to avoid complete deprivation. This reflects a **balance** between the rights of creditors and the protection of the debtor in light of their deteriorating economic situation. The flexibility to adjust the amount of such assistance according to changing circumstances enhances the responsiveness of the law, allowing for a reassessment of the debtor's financial and social conditions.

Recommendations:

- **Ensure a Balance Between Creditor and Debtor Rights:**
  The legal system must constantly maintain a fair balance between creditors' rights to recover their funds and the debtor's right to preserve dignity and secure basic necessities for themselves and their family.
- **Enhance Preventive Measures:**
  The law should strengthen measures aimed at preventing asset dissipation or suspicious transactions by debtors who are aware of their impending bankruptcy.
- **Review Criteria for Preventive Detention:**
  It would be beneficial to establish more specific legal standards for imposing preventive detention to ensure this measure is not misused.
- **Provide Legal Counseling for Bankrupt Debtors:**
  Offering legal advice to bankrupt individuals would help ensure they understand their rights and the legal consequences of bankruptcy, enabling them to make more informed decisions.

Conclusion:

The effects of bankruptcy—particularly those involving restrictions on the debtor's liberty and the formal declaration of bankruptcy—reflect an effort to strike a balance between protecting creditors' rights and safeguarding the debtor's human rights. Legislation must continue to adapt to evolving economic and social conditions and offer debtors a meaningful opportunity for recovery without undermining the rights of creditors.

Section II: Legal Effects of Corporate Bankruptcy on Partners

Subsection I: Company Liability

The management of the company, represented by the general manager and the board of directors, bears responsibility for running the company in a manner that serves the interests of its shareholders and partners, by ensuring profitability and maintaining the company's reputation in the business market. Consequently, these officials are deemed liable for any acts that harm shareholders or partners if such acts lead to the company's bankruptcy as a result of mismanagement, negligence, bad faith, deceit, or fraud. Therefore, they bear the consequences of such conduct under both **civil and criminal liability** frameworks.

It is noteworthy that **Sudanese law does not distinguish** between the bankruptcy of a trader, a company, or an ordinary individual; all are subject to the same general provisions. Based on this legal interpretation, the company acquires **legal personality** upon incorporation, meaning that the effects of bankruptcy should be limited to the company itself as a separate legal entity from its shareholders.

While Sudanese law clarifies the legal consequences of an individual's bankruptcy under **Section 19(2)** of the **Bankruptcy Act of 1929**, which states:

"If the court is satisfied that the debtor acted with the intent to harm creditors, obstruct them, or evade any legal proceedings of the court,
a. by fleeing or leaving the jurisdiction of the court, or is about to do so,
b. or by concealing, destroying, or transferring any document, or removing it from the court's jurisdiction—especially if such document is likely to be useful to creditors—or any asset not exempted by law from attachment and sale to satisfy a monetary judgment (excluding account books), or is about to engage in any of these acts,
then the court may, in addition to appointing a temporary trustee, issue an order with or without bail for the arrest of the debtor and may either detain them until the petition is decided or release them on reasonable and necessary conditions with respect to bail."

As a result, the debtor's assets become subject to court control or the control of the trustee in bankruptcy, and are distributed among creditors in accordance with **general bankruptcy rules**, which entitle every creditor to participate proportionately in the distribution of the debtor's estate.

This raises the question: **Does what applies to an individual bankrupt also apply to a company?**

The answer lies in **Section 23(2)** of the **Companies Act of 2015**, which states:

"Any shareholder who was involved in conducting the company's business with the intent to defraud the company's creditors or creditors of any other person, or for any fraudulent purpose, shall be **personally liable** for all or part of the company's debts and other obligations, as determined by the court, based on a decision rendered upon the request of the liquidator, a creditor, another shareholder, or a person liable for payment, in accordance with Section 246 of the Companies Act of 2015."

Additionally, the company bears **civil liability** in accordance with **Section 24(2)** of the **Civil Transactions Act of 1984**, which grants legal persons all rights except those exclusive to natural persons. The company, therefore, has **legal capacity** within the limits defined by its constitutive document and applicable laws. Based on the above, the company is subject to **civil liability** for any damage it causes or for failing to perform a legally imposed obligation, or under **tort liability** for any act committed by its representatives in the course of performing company business, under the doctrine of **vicarious liability**.

On the other hand, **the consequences applicable to a bankrupt individual—such as loss of political and professional rights, imprisonment, and surveillance—are not applicable to companies** due to their legal personality. However, these consequences **may extend to general partners** who are declared bankrupt alongside the company.

As previously noted, **a company's bankruptcy constitutes a cause for its dissolution, termination, and liquidation**. In partnerships (i.e., companies of persons), bankruptcy generally results in dissolution unless the partnership agreement provides otherwise. In **capital companies (corporations)**, bankruptcy does not automatically lead to dissolution if sufficient assets remain to fulfill the company's purpose. However, if the company's capital is depleted to the point where its continuation becomes unfeasible, it will be dissolved, and the remaining assets distributed among the shareholders upon liquidation.

A shareholder's liability is **contractual** and limited to the **nominal value of their shares** in the company's capital. Therefore, the shareholder is not liable for the company's debts and is not considered a trader. Accordingly, the bankruptcy of the company **does not entail the bankruptcy of the shareholder**, unless the court finds evidence of **fraud or deceit** involving the shareholder, as provided in the aforementioned article.

Researcher's Observations:

The researcher observes that Sudanese law adopts a unified approach to handling bankruptcy, whether concerning traders, companies, or individuals. This raises a question regarding the extent to which such uniform treatment aligns with the **realities of companies as independent legal entities**. Despite this unified treatment, the **main impact lies in holding company officials accountable** for actions that harm the shareholders, thus reinforcing the principle of **collective responsibility in corporate governance**.

The researcher also raises an important question as to whether **similar consequences can apply to companies as they do to individuals** in bankruptcy cases, especially in light of **modern legislative developments** such as Section 23 of the Companies Act of 2015. This provision imposes **personal liability** on shareholders involved in fraudulent activities leading to the company's bankruptcy. Such provisions play a key role in enforcing **civil liability** for harm suffered by creditors and society due to shareholders' misconduct.

Regarding other consequences typically applied to bankrupt individuals—such as loss of political and professional rights, imprisonment, and surveillance—**these cannot be applied to companies** because of their legal nature. However, such consequences may apply to **general partners** who are declared bankrupt alongside the company, serving as an exception that underscores their pivotal role in upholding corporate stability and protecting creditor rights.

Conclusion:

The researcher concludes that a company's bankruptcy **does not automatically lead to the bankruptcy of its shareholders**, unless the court proves the involvement of such shareholders in **unlawful practices**. This highlights the need to **balance creditor protection** with the **legal stability of shareholders' positions** in bankruptcy scenarios.

Subsection II: Liability of the Partner in Solidum (Joint Liability)

In this type of company, the liability of a partner is limited to the amount they contributed to the company's capital and they are not liable beyond that amount unless the company enters liquidation. This position is widely supported by many commercial law scholars. The guarantee serves as a form of protection and assurance for creditors' rights during liquidation. It must be explicitly stated in the articles of association as a pledge by members to contribute up to the value of the company's assets in the event of liquidation.

In a **company limited by guarantee**, the amount of the guarantee may legally be altered. Consequently, such companies may be dissolved, liquidated, or restructured, provided that members are duly informed and held liable for any debts or obligations arising from the distribution of profits. The nature of a partner's obligation is commercial, aimed at investing their capital with the understanding that they are exposed to potential losses and gains depending on the company's performance.

As such, **partners with joint liability** are personally and unlimitedly liable for the company's debts, regardless of their share in the capital. This is consistent with the legal framework governing **general partnerships**, where each partner bears full and joint liability.

In a **limited partnership**, the rules governing general partnerships apply to the general partners. However, **limited partners** are only liable for losses and debts up to the amount of their contributions to the capital or the amount they were obligated to pay. Their liability ends upon fulfilling their contribution, and neither the company nor its creditors may pursue their personal assets to satisfy any debts owed by the company.

The limited liability of such partners means that they do not acquire the legal status of a trader by merely joining the company. As such, the **bankruptcy of the company does not entail the bankruptcy of the limited partner**.

In **unlimited liability companies**, none of the members have limited liability. However, the liability is determined based on the **separation of bankruptcies**, where the company's bankruptcy is distinct from that of the partners—except in general partnerships and limited partnerships, due to the unlimited and joint liability of general partners for the company's debts.

From the foregoing, the researcher concludes that in companies where **partner liability is limited to their contributions**, the liability is strictly confined to the capital invested. This aligns with commercial jurisprudence, which views the guarantee in such companies as a means of protecting creditors' rights during liquidation. In this context, the guarantee amount may be adjusted within certain limits, reflecting the flexibility of the legal framework governing **limited liability companies**.

However, in **general partnerships**, partners bear **personal and unlimited liability** for the company's debts. This renders liability comprehensive and not restricted to the share of capital, thereby creating a system of **joint liability** under which each partner may be required to cover all company debts in the event of bankruptcy. This reflects the unique nature of general partnerships in the legal system, where partners are fully accountable for the consequences of their commercial activities.

As for **limited partnerships**, the situation differs with respect to limited partners. Their liability is **confined to the capital contributed** or any outstanding amounts due. Once these contributions are made, limited partners are shielded from further financial liability and **cannot be held accountable for debts exceeding their investment**. This framework protects limited partners from losses beyond their financial stake and prevents them from acquiring the status of traders or being subject to bankruptcy proceedings due to the company's liquidation.

Regarding **unlimited liability companies**, the researcher finds that liability is limited in the sense that **a company's bankruptcy does not impact individual partners**, except in cases involving general or limited partnerships where general partners have joint and unlimited liability.

Based on this, it may be concluded that **Sudanese legislation clearly delineates** the various legal regimes applicable to general partnerships, limited partnerships, and limited liability companies. This provides a balanced legal framework that ensures **creditor protection** while also **safeguarding partners from liabilities beyond their investments**.

In conclusion, the researcher finds that the distinction between types of companies and the associated responsibilities of partners **reflects a carefully balanced legislative approach** under Sudanese law—one that seeks to protect creditors on the one hand, and safeguard partners' rights on the other. This balance contributes to **commercial stability** and fosters a **flexible and secure legal environment for business operations**.

Section III: Legal Consequences of Company Bankruptcy with Respect to Board Members

Company laws have established stringent liability provisions for members of the Board of Directors due to the extensive powers they are granted. A board member is expected to act as a representative of the company, not for personal gain, and must exercise the level of care that a reasonable person would be expected to apply in such circumstances.

It is a well-established principle that for a company to acquire commercial status, it must engage in commercial activities professionally, possess independence, and be recognized as a separate legal personality. Article 24 of the same law affirms the rights of a legal person, granting it full legal capacity, except for rights inherently linked to natural human attributes, and within the limits prescribed by law. Furthermore, the legal person enjoys the following:

(a) Independent financial liability (patrimony);

(b) Legal capacity within the limits defined by its founding instrument or applicable law;

(c) Right to litigate;

(d) An independent domicile, with its principal place of business deemed its domicile. If it has activities in Sudan, the place of local administration shall be considered its domicile for the purposes of domestic law;

(e) Representation through a person designated in accordance with applicable laws.

Regarding the liability of board members in **joint-stock companies**, legal complexities arise in attributing **collective liability** when the board adopts a resolution that constitutes an offense under the law. However, under the **2015 Companies Act**, the legislature explicitly stipulated that **board members or any other person are not exempt from legal liability** in cases where they exceed their authorized powers. The law provides:

"Articles 28, 29, and 30 do not exempt board members or any other person from legal responsibility in the event of exceeding the powers granted to them."

This raises the question: **Can a dissenting board member be held criminally liable for a decision passed by the rest of the board?** The legal text indicates that the decision, once adopted by the board, represents the collective will of the board, and does not exclude any member from liability. The language of the statute does not differentiate between those who voted in favor or against; therefore, **liability is joint when the board exceeds its delegated authority**, based on the presumption of good faith owed to third parties transacting with the company. Such third parties are not required to investigate whether the board has exceeded its authority when acting on behalf of the company or delegating such authority, in line with **Article 50**, which provides: *"Acts carried out by any board member shall be valid even if a defect in their appointment is later revealed. However, any acts performed after the invalidity of their appointment becomes known shall be deemed invalid."*

Thus, delegation and criminal liability are contingent upon the **validity of the appointment**. Furthermore, under **Section 29(2)** of the **2015 Companies Act**, the board is responsible for exercising its powers in accordance with the company's interest and the public interest.

In this context, **Article 53** of the 2015 Act outlines the **general duties** of board members as follows:

1. A board member owes the following duties to the company:

(a) To act within the scope of the memorandum and articles of association and exercise powers only for their intended purposes;

(b) To act in **good faith** to promote the success of the company for the benefit of all members, with due consideration to fairness among them;

(c) To make decisions **independently**;

(d) To exercise **reasonable care, skill, and diligence**;

(e) To **avoid situations** where they have, or may have, a **direct or indirect interest** that **conflicts or may conflict** with the interests of the company.

(f) To refrain from accepting benefits from third parties that are offered or granted to them in their capacity as board members, or in connection with performing—or refraining from performing—any act in such capacity.

(g) To disclose to the other board members the nature and extent of any direct or indirect interest they may have in any proposed transaction with the company.

(2) A board member whose membership has ended remains bound, for a period of **five years** from the date of termination of membership, by the duties stipulated in **paragraph (1)(e)** with respect to the use of any assets, information, or opportunities that came to their knowledge while serving as a member, and by **paragraph (1)(f)** regarding acts committed or omitted prior to the termination of membership.

Article 54 provides that disclosure of interest by a board member may be made during a board meeting or by written notice. The member must submit a new disclosure if the original becomes inaccurate or incomplete under **paragraph (1)** of the same Article. Such disclosure must be made **prior to the company's approval of the transaction**, and the member in question **shall not participate in the vote**, in order to safeguard the company's financial interests and avoid conflicts of interest.

However, **Article 55** permits exceptions where the board member is not required to disclose an interest, **provided there is no reasonable basis** to believe that such interest may result in a conflict, or if the board members are already **aware** of the interest.

Should a board member **breach the duties** stipulated in **Article 53**, they shall be deemed in **violation** and subject to penalties, as outlined in **Article 257**, as follows:

(1) The Registrar shall impose the penalties prescribed in the Schedule of Offenses and Financial Penalties issued pursuant to this law.

(2) In case of the company's failure to pay the imposed fine, the Registrar may enforce the penalty through the courts.

Prosecution for violations of the Companies Act shall take place before a competent court or any other court designated by the Chief Justice. Arrest warrants for violators may be issued by the police, in accordance with **paragraphs (1) and (2) of Article 258** of the **2015 Companies Act**.

Researcher's Viewpoint

The researcher asserts that **members of the board of directors** bear a **strict legal responsibility**, owing to the broad powers they wield in managing corporate affairs. Board members are obligated to act **in good faith and with reasonable diligence** to ensure the overall interests of the company and its shareholders are met. This includes compliance with the legal and regulatory framework governing their duties, such as acting within their defined powers and according to the company's foundational objectives. Furthermore, the duty to **disclose any direct or indirect interests** that may conflict with those of the company is deemed fundamental.

Researcher's Recommendations:

1. **Clarify legal provisions** concerning the liability of board members in decisions that exceed their authority—particularly in cases where certain members opposed the decision. It must be clearly established that **collective responsibility** applies to unlawful decisions or those conflicting with the company's interests.
2. **Strengthen oversight mechanisms** concerning former board members, especially regarding their duty to **protect confidential information** or **not exploit resources or opportunities** learned of during their tenure. The researcher recommends developing clearer enforcement mechanisms for post-membership obligations.

3. The legal framework governing **penal sanctions** for board violations should be **updated and enforced effectively** through competent judicial bodies. This includes ensuring **collection of monetary fines** imposed for such violations.
4. Mechanisms for **disclosure of interests** should be enhanced to prevent conflicts with corporate interests. Transparency in such disclosures is essential to ensure **fairness** and **protect the company and its stakeholders**.
5. Consideration should be given to providing **protection** for board members against personal liability in the event of **liquidation or bankruptcy**, ensuring that they are not held accountable for matters **beyond the scope of their authority**.

Conclusion:
Board member liability is **collective in nature** and demands strict adherence to **ethical and legal standards**. The legislator should reinforce and clarify the relevant legal provisions to distinguish between individual and collective liability—particularly in the context of **conflict-of-interest disclosures** and the preservation of company interests.

Section Four: Legal Effects of the Declaration of Bankruptcy on Creditors

Subsection One: Formation of the Creditors' Committee

Upon the issuance of a bankruptcy declaration, all creditors of the debtor are brought together into a group known as the **"Creditors' Committee"** or **"Assembly of Creditors."** Legal scholars have differed in defining a precise meaning for this entity. It is generally understood to consist of **ordinary creditors** and **creditors holding general preferential rights**, whose debts arose **prior to the declaration of bankruptcy**.

The decisive factor in determining whether a debt arose before or after the bankruptcy declaration is **the date of contract formation**, if the right arises from a contract, rather than the date of the court's ruling on damages. Therefore, if the contract or wrongful act occurred **prior to the bankruptcy judgment**, the creditor shall be considered part of the creditors' committee—even if the right is later confirmed by a judgment issued after the bankruptcy declaration.

Some scholars define the creditors' committee as:

"An assembly comprised of the creditors of a single debtor, convened to assess the debtor's financial standing in the context of bankruptcy or judicial composition."

The declaration of bankruptcy triggers several legal effects with respect to creditors, primarily:

- The formation of the creditors' committee,
- Suspension of individual claims and enforcement proceedings,
- Cessation of the accrual of interest and deadlines, and
- Establishment of a collective pledge on the debtor's estate.

Accordingly, creditors become a **single unified body**, represented by the **trustee in bankruptcy**, with the primary purpose of preventing disputes and competition in executing judgments against the debtor's assets.

The **Sudanese Bankruptcy Act of 1929** stipulates:

"The trustee may, at any time and by written notice, convene a meeting of the creditors, and shall do so whenever directed by the court." This provision implies a statutory reference to the **creditors' committee** and the obligation of the trustee to convene meetings upon the court's order.

This committee is **compulsorily formed** upon the issuance of the bankruptcy judgment. It is governed by the principle of **equality among creditors** in the distribution of the debtor's liquidated assets. The trustee manages the collective rights of creditors as long as the debt arose from a valid cause **prior to the declaration of bankruptcy**. The determining factor for debt priority is the **date of the act or transaction giving rise to the debt**, not the date of the court ruling, in the event of litigation.

For instance, if a debt arises from damages due to contract rescission or breach, the relevant date is the **rescission or breach date**. Consequently, the creditor is considered part of the creditors' committee **if the act occurred prior to the declaration of bankruptcy**, even if the right is established by a court ruling issued thereafter.

The issue of **multiple creditors** under **Article 30** of the Sudanese law is not explicitly addressed. However, from the context, it is implied that **there must be more than one creditor**. If there is only one creditor, the rationale behind ensuring equality and preventing preferential treatment becomes moot. The

Sudanese legislator uses the term "creditors' committee," inherently suggesting plurality.

Notably, **the Sudanese legislator does not elaborate detailed provisions** regarding the creditors' committee, unlike **English law**, where the committee plays a visible role in administering the bankruptcy estate. In Sudanese law, **the trustee assumes full control**, under court supervision, and the creditors' committee appears to have no active role except in **voting on composition proposals**.

In seeking to **protect creditors** from the insolvent debtor's potentially harmful acts—especially those designed to defraud creditors—the legislator introduces the concept of the **"suspect period"** (or **"period of suspicion"**), although it is **not clearly defined under Sudanese law**. This is the period preceding the declaration of bankruptcy, specifically from the **date of cessation of payment** until the **issuance of the bankruptcy judgment**.

Acts committed by the debtor during this period are **subject to challenge** and may be deemed **unenforceable** in order to protect the creditors, especially if such acts are intended to delay proceedings or conceal the true financial status of the debtor. These acts may be carried out in **good or bad faith**, such as **waiving an inheritance share, gifting assets, or relinquishing part of a debt without consideration**. Such actions are **void by operation of law** in certain jurisdictions.

For instance, under **Article 427 of the Saudi Commercial Law**, any **donation made by a merchant debtor during the suspect period** is **void by law**, falling under the category of **mandatory unenforceability**, on the grounds that the debtor should use this time to settle debts rather than make gratuitous transfers.

Therefore, an **action for unenforceability** may be brought against the debtor to **invalidate such transactions**, allowing the **assets to revert to the bankruptcy estate** for distribution among creditors. The Sudanese legislator has **not explicitly addressed** the rules governing such actions, leaving the matter to **general legal principles**.

Ultimately, the **creditors' committee** and the **bankruptcy trustee** aim to assess creditors' losses, oversee the liquidation of the debtor's assets, and conclude proceedings once that purpose is achieved. The debtor's **inability to pay debts** is the essential reason for the committee's existence, allowing creditors to recover through the enforcement and judicial seizure of the remaining estate—preventing the debtor from dissipating assets to their detriment.

In a **notable court precedent**, where the appellant was the **official trustee in bankruptcy** and the respondent was **Ahmad Babiker Muhammad**, the court stated:

"It must be emphasized that the purpose of bankruptcy, as laid down by law, is to ensure that creditors share the remaining estate on an equal footing, without any fraud in favor of some creditors, and without allowing the debtor to conceal assets or resort to deception that may result in preferential treatment of some creditors over others, thereby frustrating the goal of equitable distribution."

The Sudanese law does not specify the statute of limitations period for claims seeking to supplement the debt, which necessitates referring to the general rules. Since a claim to supplement the debt constitutes a special application of tort liability, it is considered a claim arising from an unlawful act and therefore is subject to a limitation period of **three years from the day the injured party becomes aware of the damage**. The day on which the injured party is deemed to have knowledge is the day the company's bankruptcy is declared, as it is considered the date on which the injured party becomes aware of the insufficiency of the company's assets to satisfy its debts. In all cases, such claims lapse upon the expiry of **fifteen years** from the date of the unlawful act.

Creditors have the right to submit a petition in accordance with the conditions set forth in **Article 8**, namely:

(a) The debt owed to the debtor amounts to **five million Sudanese pounds** or, if two or more creditors join in the bankruptcy petition, their combined debts against the debtor total five million Sudanese pounds;

(b) The debt is a **fixed amount payable immediately or at a specified future date**; and
(c) The act of bankruptcy on which the petition is founded occurred within **three months prior to the submission of the petition**.

Article 13 outlines the contents of creditors' petitions, stating that: *"Every bankruptcy petition submitted by a creditor or creditors shall include the debtor's details as specified in paragraph (b) of Article 12, and shall also specify:*
(a) The bankruptcy act committed by the debtor and the date it occurred;
(b) The amount claimed in cash from the debtor and the details thereof;

(c) The date of any judgment (if any) issued in favor of the petitioner(s) against the debtor, specifying the name of the court that issued it and the remaining amount due under it."*

Article 15, paragraph (2), authorizes the court to **reject any bankruptcy petition, return it for amendment, or amend it under conditions it deems appropriate** if:

(a) It is unsigned or not supported as required above; or

(b) It does not correctly and specifically disclose the multiple required details.

If the petition is accepted, the court sets a date to hear the petition and orders the notification of all creditors in the forms specified in paragraphs (3) and (4), requiring them to notify the court by that date or earlier of any debts they can prove under the provisions of this law. The court may, at the time of accepting the petition or at any time thereafter, upon request of any creditor, order the debtor to provide reasonable security to appear until final orders are issued concerning the petition. The court may also order the debtor's detention if such security is not provided.

The acceptance of the petition is announced and published in the official gazette, with such publication constituting conclusive evidence of notice to any creditor. In addition to publication in the official gazette, the court also notifies creditors either by ordinary notice forms, registered letter, general announcement, or public notice, as decided regarding civil case notifications. The creditor initially bears all expenses incurred for such notification, which are recoverable as costs.

The debtor against whom an order is issued pursuant to Article 16(1) must prepare a **statement of their financial condition and related matters**, supported by an **affidavit sworn on oath**, detailing the debtor's assets, liabilities, names and residences of creditors, their occupations, the securities held by them in order, the dates when the securities were given in order, and any other information prescribed or requested by the court or the interim trustee. This statement shall be submitted to the interim trustee or to the court if no interim trustee is appointed pursuant to Article 17 of the Bankruptcy Law. The debtor is required to do their utmost to convert assets into cash and distribute the proceeds among creditors, and failure to perform these duties deliberately constitutes a breach.

Based on the foregoing, the researcher considers this step necessary to ensure the protection of creditors' rights by consolidating all creditors whose debts arose prior to the bankruptcy ruling into a single committee through which their rights can be handled collectively and equitably. The researcher emphasizes that the decisive factor in determining the debt's inception is the date of the contract or harmful act, not the date of the compensation ruling, thus ensuring the fair distribution of creditors' rights.

The researcher further finds that the role of the creditors' committee and the bankruptcy trustee is to guarantee equality among creditors in the distribution of the bankrupt debtor's assets, ensuring that bankruptcy does not favor some creditors over others. It is noted that the laws may limit the committee's role to voting on composition agreements, while the bankruptcy administration is conducted under the trustee's supervision, which ensures fairness in the process.

Regarding the suspect period, the researcher explains that this period is critically important, as the debtor may engage in unlawful acts adversely affecting creditors' rights, such as donations or attempts to conceal assets. Consequently, the researcher highlights the necessity of protecting creditors from such unlawful acts through legislation that invalidates such transactions.

As for claims to supplement the debt, the researcher holds that such claims should lapse after three years from the injured party's knowledge of the damage, thereby guaranteeing justice and preventing protracted litigation that could disadvantage creditors. The researcher stresses the importance of strict compliance with the petition's detailed requirements to legally secure and protect creditors' rights.

In conclusion, the researcher views the bankruptcy system's purpose as protecting creditors' rights and ensuring justice among all parties through the application of regulated legal procedures that consider creditors' interests and prevent debtor manipulation.

Section Two: Suspension of Individual Lawsuits and Proceedings

A declaration of bankruptcy results in all ordinary creditors and creditors with general privileged rights being treated equally. Therefore, none of them may individually initiate legal action against the bankrupt to recover their debt, nor may they register a mortgage or lien over any of the debtor's real estate after the bankruptcy declaration. Undertaking such measures contradicts the objectives of bankruptcy proceedings, which are designed to preserve creditors' rights, prevent harm among them, and implement collective liquidation procedures that ensure equitable distribution of the debtor's assets.

Accordingly, **Article 22(3)** of the Bankruptcy Law prohibits any creditor from initiating or continuing any legal action or other proceeding unless authorized by the court and subject to the conditions it may impose. However, this prohibition applies only to ordinary creditors and creditors with general privileges. It does **not** apply to secured creditors—such as **mortgagees, holders of special privileges, or creditors with specific liens**—as expressly provided in **Article 22(3)**, which states:

"This article does not affect the rights of any secured creditor to enforce or otherwise dispose of their security in the same manner as if this article had not been enacted."

From the above, the following **types of lawsuits and legal proceedings are exempt** from the prohibition:

1. **Actions and enforcement proceedings by secured creditors** over assets subject to their security interests. These actions do not violate the principle of equality among creditors, as such secured assets fall outside the debtor's general estate. The court or the bankruptcy trustee may, upon court authorization, elect to integrate these assets into the bankruptcy estate. If not, and the secured creditor proceeds with enforcement, **any surplus** value from the asset after satisfying the secured debt **must revert to the bankruptcy estate**.
2. **Actions or proceedings that serve a public interest or benefit the creditors as a collective group.** In such cases, the court has discretionary power to authorize the continuation of proceedings, provided that the **bankruptcy trustee is involved to protect the interests of all creditors**. However, if enforcement proceedings are initiated against the debtor's property, **no party may benefit against the trustee**, except in relation to property that had already been converted into cash via sale or other means prior to the bankruptcy declaration or prior to the notice to the executing court of a bankruptcy petition submitted by the debtor or any creditor, or of notice that the debtor committed an act of bankruptcy. In other words, **enforcement may only proceed on assets that existed before the declaration of bankruptcy**. It is important to note that such enforcement does not prejudice existing mortgages or privileges with priority on the asset. Moreover, **a purchaser of the asset in an enforcement sale acquires valid ownership** even as against the bankruptcy trustee.
3. **Criminal proceedings** may be instituted directly against the bankrupt, as such proceedings are unrelated to the bankruptcy process. Whether the case is

brought by the prosecution or by an injured party, the **bankruptcy does not suspend criminal actions**, since the prohibition applies only to civil claims brought by creditors to assert their debts. Criminal proceedings concern the debtor's **criminal conduct** and remain valid. Nevertheless, if a bankrupt is ordered to pay compensation as a result of criminal conduct, **the injured party may only participate in the bankruptcy estate to claim such compensation if the act giving rise to the compensation occurred before the bankruptcy ruling**.

This was confirmed by the **Supreme Court** in the case of *Bashir Al-Haj Mohammed v. Hussein Ali Al-Khidr*. The bankruptcy court had withdrawn criminal complaints pending before criminal courts (related to bounced checks under **Article 362(b)** of the Penal Code) and consolidated them into the bankruptcy proceedings. However, the **Court of Appeal overturned** this consolidation and **ordered the return of the criminal cases** to their respective courts for adjudication. The bankrupt's attorney appealed to the **Supreme Court**, arguing that the prohibition under Article 22(3) of the Bankruptcy Law extended to criminal proceedings, and that its purpose was to consolidate both civil and criminal liabilities against the bankrupt. The Supreme Court rejected this argument, confirming that the **Bankruptcy Law does not authorize the civil bankruptcy court to withdraw criminal complaints from criminal courts**. Rather, **Articles 58 to 84** of the Bankruptcy Law allow the bankruptcy court to **refer any criminal violations** committed by the bankrupt to the competent criminal court. Furthermore, **Articles 16(2) and 19** pertain solely to bankruptcy-related procedures, whereas the bounced check cases fall under the **Criminal Code**. The Court concluded that **criminal trials are unaffected by the declaration of bankruptcy**, and that **criminal proceedings continue independently** of the bankruptcy process.

Based on the above, the researcher concludes that the relevant laws are intended to **prevent any creditor from initiating individual legal actions** against a bankrupt debtor—such as lawsuits or the registration of secured interests on the debtor's property—after the bankruptcy ruling. Such individual actions undermine the collective bankruptcy process, which is designed to liquidate the debtor's estate and **equitably distribute assets** among all creditors.

The researcher emphasizes that this prohibition does **not** apply to **secured creditors**, such as mortgagees and holders of specific liens, who retain the right to initiate legal action related to the secured assets. The court or bankruptcy trustee may decide to integrate such secured assets into the estate, but **any surplus value beyond the secured debt must revert to the estate**.

Additionally, the researcher highlights other exceptions—namely, lawsuits that aim to serve the **collective interest** of the creditors. In these cases, the court may authorize creditors to proceed, provided the bankruptcy trustee safeguards the rights of all creditors.

Finally, the researcher affirms that **criminal lawsuits against the bankrupt debtor are unaffected** by the bankruptcy judgment. The prohibition only applies to civil claims by creditors, while **criminal proceedings related to the debtor's conduct remain valid and independent**.

In conclusion, the researcher stresses the importance of maintaining **a balance between protecting creditors' rights and prohibiting individual actions** that may harm others. The court plays a key role in determining which actions may proceed in the **collective interest of the creditors**.

Section Three: Acceleration of Debt Maturities

The philosophy behind the acceleration of debt maturities following a debtor's declaration of bankruptcy is based on the notion that these maturities were originally granted based on the creditors' confidence in the debtor and their belief in the debtor's ability to meet obligations. However, upon the declaration of bankruptcy, such confidence collapses. Allowing the original maturities to persist would hinder the liquidation of the bankruptcy estate and prolong the process until the debts become due. This delay inevitably leads to increased bankruptcy administration costs.

For these reasons, the legislator has mandated that, upon the issuance of the bankruptcy judgment, **all debt maturities lapse** and **all debts become immediately due and payable**. This principle is enshrined in **Article 39 of the Bankruptcy Law**, which states:

"A creditor may prove a debt that was not yet due for payment and shall be entitled to a share equal to that of any other creditor."

The acceleration of debt maturities applies to **all debts**, whether **unsecured** or **secured by a mortgage or privilege**, as the wording of the provision is general and comprehensive. Thus, **secured creditors may enforce their claims against the assets of the debtor subject to their security** immediately upon the declaration of bankruptcy. However, this effect applies **only to debts owed by the bankrupt**, and **does not apply to debts owed to the bankrupt by third parties**.

From the foregoing, the researcher concludes that the philosophy behind the acceleration of debt maturities upon bankruptcy is rooted in the collapse of the trust that once justified the granting of extended terms to the debtor. The continuation of those maturities would obstruct the liquidation process and prolong the proceedings, increasing costs to the bankruptcy estate. Consequently, the legislator rightly provided for the **immediate maturity of all debts** upon the bankruptcy declaration.

The acceleration covers **all types of debt**, whether unsecured or secured, as the legal text is broad. Accordingly, **secured creditors are entitled to enforce their security interests** on the encumbered assets upon the declaration of bankruptcy. However, this acceleration applies **only to the bankrupt's liabilities**, and not to **the bankrupt's claims** against others.

The researcher emphasizes the importance of raising awareness among creditors and bankrupt debtors regarding these legal principles to ensure their **effective and fair application**. He further proposes **amendments to provisions regarding bankruptcy expenses**, allowing courts to set **flexible timelines** for handling **exceptional circumstances faced by secured creditors**, with the aim of **streamlining proceedings while preserving fairness** for all parties involved.

Fifth Topic: The Effect of Bankruptcy on Non-Creditors with Other Rights
Section One: Contract Termination

Let us suppose that the bankrupt debtor had concluded a contract **prior to the bankruptcy judgment** and during the **suspect period**. As a rule, **contracts entered into during the suspect period or after the declaration of bankruptcy** may be subject to annulment or ratification based on the **interests of the creditors**.

It must also be assumed that such a contract is **not of a personal nature**, i.e., it does not depend on the personal qualifications of the debtor. For contracts of this kind, the declaration of bankruptcy may **result in automatic termination by operation of law**.

As a general rule, **bankruptcy does not, in itself, lead to the termination or dissolution of a contract**, unless it **prevents the application of the general rules** regarding contract termination or dissolution. Accordingly:

If the contract contains a clause stipulating its termination in the event of bankruptcy, the lessor may invoke that clause, particularly in contracts that are presumed to be executed personally by the debtor. Once the debtor's ability to manage and dispose of his property is removed due to bankruptcy, such clauses become operative. An example of such contracts is a **contract for work (contracting agreement)**.

However, if the contract is not based on personal considerations—which applies to the majority of contracts such as **sale or lease agreements**—the general rule is that the debtor's bankruptcy **does not automatically result in the termination of the contract**. Rather, the counterparty to the contract may request the **bankruptcy trustee** to perform the obligation arising from the contract.

In such cases, **if the trustee finds that performing the contract serves the interests of the creditors' estate, he may proceed with performance**. Otherwise, he may refuse to perform. Pursuant to **Article 34 of the Bankruptcy Law**, if the trustee fails to respond to the counterparty's request within **28 days** from the date of receipt—or within any longer period authorized by the court—**this inaction is considered an affirmation of the contract**.

If the trustee proceeds with the contract, the counterparty is **obliged to fulfill their obligation** under the contract if it has not already been fulfilled prior to the bankruptcy declaration. If the trustee **refuses to perform the contract**, the counterparty may **petition the court hearing the bankruptcy case** to terminate the contract. The court may issue an order terminating the contract **on terms it deems fair**, including ordering either party to **pay compensation for damages** arising from non-performance, among other **equitable conditions**.

If the court awards **damages** to the counterparty, they may **prove such compensation claim** in the bankruptcy and participate as an **ordinary creditor subject to the pari passu distribution**.

These principles may also be **applied to lease contracts** as a model:

- If the **lessor of a property is declared bankrupt**, the mere fact of bankruptcy **does not terminate the lease**. The lessee generally **has no interest in terminating** the lease and may enforce the lease against the

trustee or the **purchaser of the property**, should it be sold. In such a case, **the lessee is liable to pay rent** to the trustee and, subsequently, to the purchaser.

- If the **lessee is declared bankrupt**, this does **not automatically terminate the lease** either. The **trustee is obligated to fulfill the debtor's obligations** under the lease. If the trustee fails to do so—such as by **failing to pay rent or subletting the property unlawfully**—the lease may be **terminated, and the lessee evicted**.

Notably, the researcher observes that under **Article 34(3)** of the Bankruptcy Law—and contrary to the general rules—the legislator permits, **after notifying interested parties** and under conditions the court deems appropriate, the issuance of orders regarding **fixtures and improvements made by the lessee**, as well as any other issues arising from the lease, as the court considers fair.

Researcher's Opinion:

The researcher contends that, as a general principle, **the bankruptcy of the lessee should lead to the termination of the lease**, since bankruptcy causes debts to mature. In other words, allowing the lease to continue would mean the debts owed to the lessor by the lessee remain outstanding, which is **detrimental to the creditors' collective interest**. Therefore, **termination of the lease should be the rule**, and the exception would be **where the trustee determines it is in the debtor's best interest to retain the lease** to complete certain business activities. In such a case, **the lessor has no right to object**, unless the lease contract **explicitly provides for termination upon bankruptcy**.

Researcher's Recommendation:

The researcher notes that the legislator has implemented **flexible mechanisms** allowing courts or trustees to decide on whether to perform or terminate contracts, in line with the **interests of both the creditors and the bankrupt debtor**. This provides the court with the discretion to issue **fair rulings** on contracts that cannot be executed or that may harm the creditors' estate.

The researcher **proposes enhancing bankruptcy legislation** to more clearly define the **mechanism for terminating contracts involving personal obligations of the debtor**, ensuring a **balanced approach between creditor protection and potential opportunities** that such contracts may offer the bankrupt debtor.

Furthermore, the researcher recommends establishing **clearer conditions** empowering the trustee to make **swift and flexible decisions** in such cases—allowing them to determine whether it is in the **collective interest** to maintain or terminate the contract.

Section Two: The Right to Recover Property in the Possession of the Bankrupt Debtor

As a general rule, **property owned by the debtor is subject to bankruptcy proceedings**, liquidation, and distribution. However, any rightful owner may recover their property held in the possession of the debtor **without being affected by the bankruptcy process**. Yet, permitting such recovery **after the declaration of bankruptcy** may harm creditors who relied on the debtor's **apparent ownership** of the assets. Accordingly, **Egyptian law adopts the first view**, which protects the true owner's rights, **provided** that the assets handed over to the bankrupt are **still identifiable and in the same condition in which they were delivered**.

On the other hand, **Sudanese bankruptcy law** prohibits the owner from reclaiming such property and considers it part of the debtor's estate to be distributed among creditors, **if three conditions are met**:

1. That the property is **in the possession, under the control, or at the disposal of the debtor** in the course of their business as of the date the bankruptcy petition was filed.
2. That the **true owner consented** to the property being in the possession, under the control, or at the disposal of the debtor.
3. That the debtor **held or dealt with the property under circumstances giving rise to a belief** that he was the true owner, which the **court shall assess** based on the circumstances of the case.

If these conditions **are not met**, then, according to the general rule, the **owner retains the right to recover the property from the bankruptcy estate** if the asset exists in its original form. If the property no longer exists in specie, the owner may **file a claim equivalent to the asset's value in the bankruptcy estate**, ranking as an **ordinary creditor** subject to pari passu distribution. This legal position is drawn from the provisions of **Articles 23(4) and 24(6) of the Sudanese Bankruptcy Law**.

Article 24(6) provides that:

"Where a request is made to the court by any person claiming an interest in any disclaimed property, or any liability not discharged under this law in respect of such disclaimed property, the court may, after hearing any parties it deems necessary, **issue an order for the delivery and vesting of such property** to the rightful claimant or any other person it deems appropriate, as compensation. Once such vesting order is made, **ownership of the property transfers to that person** without the need for assignment or transfer for that purpose."

However, if the **disclaimed property is of a leasehold nature**, the court **may not issue a vesting order** in favor of any person claiming rights through the bankrupt (whether as sub-lessee or mortgagee of the lease) unless that person:

1. **Assumes the same responsibilities and obligations** as the bankrupt under the lease as of the date of filing the bankruptcy petition, or
2. Assumes **only those responsibilities and obligations which that person had** or to which the lease had been assigned as of that date, **if the court finds this appropriate**.

In either case, the lease shall be deemed to apply **only to the property referred to in the vesting order**, and any lessee or mortgagee who **refuses to accept the order under those conditions** forfeits all interest or security in the property. If **no eligible person accepts** the order, **the court may vest the property in any person, free of all third-party interests**.

Example: Recovery of Property Between Spouses

A notable example is **asset recovery by spouses**, due to the special nature of the relationship and the potential for **collusion** in the event of one spouse's bankruptcy. To protect creditors' interests, the legislature has enacted **specific provisions prohibiting** either spouse from reclaiming property or filing claims as a creditor in the other's bankruptcy.

Article **44 of the Bankruptcy Law** provides:

1. *"Where a **married woman is declared bankrupt**, her husband shall not be entitled to claim, as a creditor, any share of money or other property that he lent or entrusted to her for the purposes of her business, unless and until all other claims by her creditors—supported by consideration of monetary or equivalent value—have been satisfied."*
2. *"Where a **married man is declared bankrupt**, any money or property lent or entrusted to him by his wife for the purposes of any trade or business he*

conducted shall be treated as part of his estate. The wife shall not be entitled, as a creditor, to claim any share of that money or property unless and until all claims by her husband's creditors—supported by consideration of monetary value—have been satisfied."

Judicial Application: ***Amina bint Youssef v. Trustee of the Estate of Mahmoud Abdullah Bassiouni***

This principle was applied early in the enforcement of the **1929 Bankruptcy Law** in the case of *Amina bint Youssef v. Trustee of the Estate of Mahmoud Abdullah Bassiouni*. The facts of the case are as follows:

Mr. Mahmoud Abdullah Bassiouni issued a **private written instrument** to his wife, Amina bint Youssef, stating:

"I am indebted to my wife Amina bint Youssef in the amount of eight and three-quarters ounces of gold, as a loan and debt, and I shall pay her the value thereof upon demand. I have mortgaged the house and land of Mohamed Hassan Miras in her favor as a conventional mortgage against the said amount. If she demands payment and I fail to pay, then the house and land shall become her property."

Upon being declared bankrupt, his wife attempted to **submit the private deed** during bankruptcy proceedings, claiming **£51 as the value of the gold**. However, the trustee **refused to admit the debt into the estate**, ruling that the wife's claim should be **postponed until all other creditor claims had been satisfied**.

Researcher's Opinion:

The **concept of the right to recover property held by the debtor** is a legal principle that seeks to protect the rights of true owners of assets in the possession of a bankrupt debtor. At the same time, however, the law approaches this right with **caution to safeguard the interests of creditors**. The owner is entitled to recover their property **as long as it remains in the possession of the debtor and in its original condition**, which ensures that the assets available to creditors are not depleted by the recovery of property owned by third parties.

Nonetheless, the **Sudanese legal system adopts a more conservative approach**, imposing **specific conditions** on the owner before permitting recovery. These include the requirement that the assets be in the debtor's possession **at the time of filing the bankruptcy petition**, and that such possession must be **clear and linked to the debtor's business or trade activities**. Furthermore, **recovery is**

only permitted in limited circumstances, such as where the debtor possesses the property **with the owner's consent**.

In cases involving **spousal relationships**, the legislature has enacted provisions that are clearly designed to **protect creditor rights and prevent collusion** between spouses. These provisions prohibit a husband or wife from recovering their property from the bankruptcy estate or submitting claims as creditors **until all other creditors' claims have been satisfied**. This approach ensures that **no preferential treatment** is granted to spouses that might **undermine the equal rights of other creditors**.

The researcher proposes **amending and clarifying certain legal provisions** related to the right of recovery, to include more detailed guidance on the conditions under which the debtor's possession of the property may be considered legitimate in **various contexts**, such as within **family relationships** or in cases involving **distressed small businesses**. Furthermore, a **more flexible mechanism** should be established to assess whether the owner can recover their assets in cases where the property forms part of **investments or transactions between family members**, without compromising the creditors' rights.

Upon the declaration of bankruptcy by the court, **the court simultaneously appoints certain individuals** responsible for the management and administration of the bankrupt estate until the assets are distributed to creditors. These include the **bankruptcy trustee, the bankruptcy judge, the court itself, the creditors, and any appointed supervisors**.

Section Six: The Bankruptcy Trustee

In many Arab legal systems, the term **"bankruptcy trustee"** is also referred to as **"creditors' agent"** or **"syndic."** This is the individual appointed to administer the bankruptcy estate once the court issues a bankruptcy order. The primary role of the trustee is to **manage and liquidate the bankrupt debtor's assets** in a way that maximizes returns for the creditors, while simultaneously protecting the rights of the bankrupt debtor, who is no longer able to manage their financial affairs independently. Various Arab laws regulate this position as follows:

1. **Egyptian Bankruptcy Law:**
   Article 120 of the Egyptian Bankruptcy Law stipulates: *"The bankruptcy trustee is the person appointed to manage the assets of the bankrupt debtor, and must exercise due diligence to ensure that the liquidation*

of the estate is carried out fairly and equitably among creditors." It is also emphasized that *"the trustee has the authority to take all necessary legal actions to safeguard the rights of both creditors and the bankrupt."*

2. **Sudanese Bankruptcy Law:**
   According to **Article 23** of the Sudanese Bankruptcy Law: *"The bankruptcy trustee is the individual appointed by the court to manage the bankruptcy and liquidate the bankrupt debtor's assets. He must act in the interest of all creditors, without giving preference to any party over another."*
   Furthermore, **Article 24** states:
   "The trustee acts on behalf of the body of creditors and may not take decisions that affect the interests of any individual creditor without seeking to achieve fairness in the distribution of assets."
3. **Jordanian Bankruptcy Law:**
   Article 29 of the Jordanian Bankruptcy Law provides that: *"The bankruptcy trustee is an individual approved by the court who undertakes the task of managing and distributing the bankruptcy estate to creditors in accordance with the prescribed legal order."*
   Article 31 further provides:
   "The trustee must act with complete neutrality and without bias toward any party involved."

Legal scholars regard the bankruptcy trustee as a **key legal figure** in the bankruptcy system, bearing **significant responsibility** to ensure that the debtor's estate is managed fairly and that the interests of both the debtor and creditors are balanced. As one legal opinion states:

"The bankruptcy trustee must be a person with sufficient legal and administrative experience to manage the assets in a manner consistent with the interests of all parties involved."

It is also noted that:

"The trustee should not be liable for showing preference to any particular creditor, and must comply strictly with the legal order of distribution."

Further commentary states that:

"The trustee's powers should be clearly defined to prevent any abuses that might infringe on the rights of stakeholders. A mechanism should be established to

monitor the trustee's performance to ensure procedural transparency." And that:

"The trustee must remain entirely impartial in administering the bankruptcy and focus on balancing the interests of both the bankrupt and the creditors."

The **researcher believes** it is essential to **precisely define the trustee's powers** within the legal texts to ensure fairness for all parties. The trustee should be a person of **good reputation and experience**, and there must be **periodic oversight mechanisms** to prevent favoritism or bias. Clearly assigning responsibilities and expanding the trustee's powers in a manner that guarantees neutrality and transparency would improve the **management of the bankruptcy estate** and protect the rights of all stakeholders—especially given the complexities that often arise in bankruptcies involving multiple parties.

The trustee is considered to be a **representative of both the bankrupt debtor and the body of creditors**. He represents the debtor because the debtor, having been stripped of the ability to manage his assets, can no longer undertake any legal acts that could be enforceable against the creditors. At the same time, the trustee represents the creditors as a group, which is recognized as having legal personality and thus must have an agent to act on its behalf. However, **the trustee does not represent each individual creditor separately**.

Section Seven: Appointment, Jurisdiction, and Conditions for Appointing the Bankruptcy Trustee

Upon the declaration of bankruptcy, the bankrupt is divested of control over his assets. A person is appointed by the court, either temporarily or permanently, to manage these assets until a decision regarding the bankruptcy is finalized. If the assets are liquidated and the proceeds distributed to settle debts, it is the trustee who handles the sale and distribution process. In other words, the bankruptcy trustee remains involved from the initiation of the bankruptcy until its conclusion.

The Sudanese Bankruptcy Act of 1929, under Article (27), provides that: "The court may, upon the issuance of the bankruptcy adjudication order or at any subsequent time, appoint a trustee over the bankrupt's property, and consequently, such property shall vest in that trustee.

When the court appoints a trustee pursuant to the provisions of this Article, it may remove any person who was previously entrusted or placed in possession of any of such property in accordance with the provisions of Article (19)."

Similarly, the UAE Commercial Transactions Law states:

"The court shall, in its bankruptcy adjudication judgment or in a subsequent judgment, appoint a paid agent to administer the bankruptcy estate, known as the bankruptcy trustee. The bankruptcy judge may, at any time, either on his own motion or upon request by the bankrupt or the supervisor, order the addition of one or more trustees, provided the total number does not exceed three."

The Egyptian Commercial Code, under Article (571), provides that: "The court shall appoint, in its bankruptcy judgment, an agent to manage the bankruptcy estate known as the bankruptcy trustee. The bankruptcy judge may, at any time, either on his own motion or upon request by the bankrupt or the supervisor, order the appointment of one or more additional trustees, provided the total number does not exceed three."

The profession of bankruptcy trustees is regulated by a decision issued by the competent minister. Furthermore, Article (561) stipulates: "The court shall, in its bankruptcy adjudication judgment, determine a provisional date for the cessation of payments, appoint a bankruptcy trustee, and select one of its judges to serve as the bankruptcy judge. It shall also order the sealing of the bankrupt's business premises."

Article (564) also states:

"The court registry of the court that issued the bankruptcy judgment shall notify the bankruptcy trustee immediately upon issuance of the judgment by registered mail with acknowledgment of receipt, to commence the administration of the bankruptcy estate. The trustee shall then register the judgment and any amendment of the cessation of payments date in the commercial register. The trustee shall also publish a summary of the judgment in a daily newspaper designated by the court in the bankruptcy adjudication. This publication must occur within ten days from the date of notification and shall include the name, domicile, and commercial register number of the bankrupt, the court issuing the judgment, the date of issuance, the provisional date of cessation of payments, the names and addresses of the bankruptcy judge and trustee, and an invitation to creditors to submit their claims. In the event of an amendment to the date of cessation of payments, the publication shall include the new date as determined by the court.

Within thirty days from the date of notification of the bankruptcy judgment, the trustee shall register a summary of the judgment in the name of the body of creditors at every land registry office within whose jurisdiction the bankrupt owns real property. This registration shall not confer any additional rights upon the body of creditors."

Based on the above, the researcher proposes the following:

1. Arab legislation should more precisely define the criteria for selecting bankruptcy trustees to avoid appointing individuals lacking the necessary qualifications. Specialized skills in legal and financial management should be a basic requirement. Additionally, individuals with direct ties to any party involved in the bankruptcy should be disqualified.
2. A continuous oversight mechanism should be established to monitor the trustee's performance and ensure compliance. The court or relevant supervisory bodies should review periodic reports submitted by the trustee to ensure adherence to legal and ethical standards in bankruptcy administration.
3. The rights of the bankrupt must be safeguarded. While the trustee primarily represents the creditors, it is also essential to ensure the bankrupt's rights are not unjustly exploited. The court should be granted wider powers to oversee and ensure a fair distribution of the bankruptcy estate.
4. The role of the media in publishing bankruptcy decisions and summaries should be enhanced for greater transparency and to safeguard the interests of both creditors and the bankrupt. Publishing such summaries in newspapers and commercial registers, as stipulated in Egyptian law, enables all stakeholders to track the proceedings.
5. Caution must be exercised in appointing the bankruptcy trustee, as this role is central to the fair administration of the bankrupt's estate. Implementing a transparent appointment mechanism and ensuring continuous oversight will significantly enhance the effectiveness of the bankruptcy system. It is equally important to consider the interests of the bankrupt alongside those of the creditors, ensuring that asset liquidation and distribution are conducted fairly and objectively.

Conditions for Appointment of the Bankruptcy Trustee:

The conditions for appointing a bankruptcy trustee are critical to ensuring the integrity and efficiency of the bankruptcy process. These conditions vary by jurisdiction but generally focus on avoiding the appointment of individuals who may have conflicts of interest with the bankrupt or the creditors. Statutory requirements in bankruptcy legislation aim to prevent the appointment of individuals whose personal interests may interfere with their fiduciary duties.

1. **Egyptian Commercial Law:**
   According to Article (572) of the Egyptian Commercial Law (2021), a person may not be appointed as a bankruptcy trustee if they:
   - Are the spouse or relative of the bankrupt up to the fourth degree;
   - Were a partner, employee, accountant, or agent of the bankrupt within the two years preceding the bankruptcy adjudication;
   - Have been convicted of a felony or a misdemeanor involving dishonesty or breach of trust.

The researcher finds that this provision highlights the importance of severing any personal ties between the trustee and the bankrupt to ensure impartial administration and protect the rights of the parties involved.

2. **UAE Bankruptcy Law:**
   Article (19) of the UAE Bankruptcy Law, issued by Federal Decree-Law No. (9) of 2016, sets similar conditions, prohibiting the appointment of the following as trustees:

- A creditor;
- The spouse, in-law, or relative of the debtor up to the fourth degree;
- Any person convicted by a final judgment of a felony or misdemeanor involving theft, embezzlement, fraud in commercial dealings, breach of trust, forgery, perjury, or economic crimes;
- Any person who was a partner, employee, or auditor of the debtor within the two years preceding the initiation of settlement proceedings.

3. **Sudanese Bankruptcy Law:**
   The researcher observes that the Sudanese Bankruptcy Act of 1929 does not address the qualifications or conditions required for appointing a bankruptcy trustee. This legislative gap may result in uncertainty regarding the eligibility of individuals to assume this role, particularly if they have had prior relationships with the bankrupt or situations that could lead to conflicts of interest.

Scholarly Opinions on the Conditions of the Bankruptcy Trustee:

The researcher finds that most legal scholars agree on the importance of strict conditions for appointing a trustee to preserve the integrity of the process and prevent conflicts of interest.

"The requirements stipulated in Arab legislation serve as a safeguard against appointing individuals with personal interests that may compromise the integrity of the bankruptcy, thereby protecting the rights of both creditors and the bankrupt."
Additionally, "the condition barring the appointment of relatives or former business associates of the bankrupt is among the most critical guarantees of impartial administration. Any violation of these conditions could undermine the credibility of the legal process."

Based on the shortcomings of the Sudanese Bankruptcy Act regarding the appointment conditions of trustees, the researcher recommends updating the legislation to include such provisions, aligning it with other Arab legal systems. This would enhance the credibility of bankruptcy proceedings and minimize the risk of mismanagement.

Furthermore, the researcher suggests the establishment of an official supervisory registry containing the names of qualified individuals eligible to serve as bankruptcy trustees. This registry would contribute to transparency and prevent the appointment of unqualified individuals. It should also include information on any prior legal judgments against prospective appointees. The researcher also recommends implementing periodic training programs for trustees to keep them informed of legislative updates and best practices in the field. Additionally, a mechanism should be put in place to monitor their activities and ensure the proper implementation of decisions.

If a violation of trustee appointment criteria is discovered, such as appointing an unqualified individual or identifying a conflict of interest, there should be strict legal measures to hold violators accountable. This may include the possibility of appealing bankruptcy decisions and postponing any related asset distributions until the matter is reviewed.

Conclusion:

The researcher concludes that appointing the bankruptcy trustee is a crucial step in bankruptcy proceedings and must be handled with utmost caution to ensure procedural integrity. Legal safeguards preventing the appointment of individuals with close ties to the bankrupt or the creditors—such as spouses or relatives—are essential to achieving fairness among all parties involved. Therefore, updating legislation and expanding appointment criteria to meet modern legal and economic demands would contribute significantly to improving administrative performance and establishing justice in financial insolvency cases.

Section Eight: Types of Bankruptcy Trustees or Agents

Throughout the stages of bankruptcy proceedings, the role and classification of the bankruptcy trustee (or agent) vary according to the function they perform and the procedural phase. These classifications include the following:

1. Temporary Trustee

A **temporary trustee** is the agent appointed by the court in the bankruptcy adjudication judgment. This appointment is made by the court without consulting the creditors, and the trustee's role is considered provisional. This is because, at the early stage of the bankruptcy, it is not feasible to consult the creditors as they may not yet be identified or known.

Functions of the Temporary Trustee:

The duties of the temporary trustee are limited to **preservative measures**, such as:

- Placing seals on the bankrupt's assets,
- Verifying the bankrupt's financial records,
- Preparing a balance sheet for the bankrupt, if one has not already been submitted.

The researcher views the appointment of a temporary trustee as a preliminary and necessary step to **safeguard the bankrupt's assets from dissipation or waste**. The researcher concurs with the legal opinion that:

"The role of the temporary trustee must be subject to strict oversight to ensure that the conservatory measures do not prejudice the rights of either the bankrupt or the creditors."

2. Permanent (Definitive) Trustee

The **permanent trustee** is appointed following a meeting of the creditors, which is convened upon request by the bankruptcy administrator within fifteen days from the issuance of the bankruptcy adjudication. During this meeting, the creditors may present their views regarding the temporary trustee. These views are then submitted to the court, which may either confirm the appointment of the temporary trustee or replace them. Once appointed, the permanent trustee assumes **full administrative responsibility for the bankruptcy estate**.

Functions of the Permanent Trustee:

- Administering the bankrupt's assets;
- Initiating lawsuits to claim the bankrupt's rights;
- Receiving claims filed against the bankruptcy estate;
- Challenging certain transactions made by the bankrupt, if necessary;
- Selling perishable goods;
- Seeking judicial authorization to continue the bankrupt's commercial activity;
- Preparing the bankruptcy estate for dissolution.

The researcher believes that the **permanent trustee must be qualified and experienced in managing financial and commercial affairs**, especially given the complexity of such tasks. Some jurists emphasize that the decision to retain or replace the temporary trustee must be made with careful consideration to ensure the proper progression of the proceedings.

3. Trustee of the Creditors' Union

If the creditors decide to **form a union** and proceed with the liquidation of the bankrupt's assets, they must appoint a **Union Trustee** ("Ameen Al-Ittihad"). The court's approval is required for this appointment. The Union Trustee is responsible for **overseeing asset sales and distributing the proceeds to the creditors in accordance with the statutory order of priority**.

Functions of the Union Trustee:

- Selling the bankrupt's assets;
- Distributing the sale proceeds to the creditors;
- Concluding the final liquidation of the bankruptcy estate.

The researcher considers the appointment of the Union Trustee a **critical phase in the bankruptcy**, requiring specialized expertise in **asset management and equitable distribution**. It is widely believed that **judicial oversight** of the Union Trustee's actions is essential to prevent manipulation or misconduct that could harm creditors' interests.

Key Duties Performed by the Bankruptcy Trustee

The bankruptcy trustee is entrusted with a range of core responsibilities that are essential for the lawful and orderly administration of the bankruptcy estate. These include:

- **Managing the bankrupt's assets:**
  The trustee is responsible for preserving the bankrupt's assets and preventing any unauthorized use. This includes classifying assets and protecting them from harm or loss.
- **Distributing proceeds among creditors:**
  After liquidation of assets, the trustee distributes the proceeds among the creditors according to the legally prescribed order of priority.
- **Initiating legal proceedings on behalf of the bankrupt:**
  The trustee may file lawsuits to recover the bankrupt's entitlements from other parties.
- **Challenging certain acts of the bankrupt:**
  If the trustee discovers that the bankrupt engaged in transactions that could harm creditor interests, such acts must be challenged in court.
- **Continuing commercial activity:**
  In certain cases, the permanent trustee may be authorized to continue the bankrupt's commercial operations if it serves the interest of the bankruptcy estate. Judicial permission is required for such continuation.

Observations on Egyptian and Emirati Legislation

The researcher notes several **commonalities** between Egyptian and Emirati laws concerning bankruptcy trustees:

1. Both laws establish **clear procedures** for the appointment of bankruptcy trustees;
2. Both laws **prioritize the protection of creditor and debtor rights**;
3. Both systems require **legal oversight mechanisms** to ensure the integrity and fairness of bankruptcy proceedings.

The statutory provisions under both Egyptian and Emirati law help **regulate bankruptcy administration, define the legal responsibilities of trustees**, and safeguard creditor rights. These provisions also **prevent unlawful acts by the bankrupt**. Legal scholars emphasize that **clear and specific criteria for trustee appointments** are crucial to ensuring procedural fairness. For instance, **excluding the bankrupt's spouse or relatives up to the fourth degree** from being appointed as trustee is deemed essential to avoid personal interference in the proceedings. Moreover, it is widely accepted among scholars that **any prior criminal record** should disqualify a person from being appointed trustee, as it undermines the credibility and integrity of the process.

The Researcher's View on Sudanese Bankruptcy Law

The researcher observes that the **Sudanese Bankruptcy Act lacks sufficient detail** regarding the qualifications and requirements for appointing a bankruptcy trustee. Although the law addresses some general aspects of legality, **it requires modernization** to align with contemporary legal developments. The researcher recommends that **the Sudanese legal framework incorporate more detailed criteria** and establish **an effective supervisory mechanism** to monitor trustees and prevent misconduct.

It is evident from the researcher's analysis that the **1929 Sudanese Bankruptcy Act lacks critical provisions** on trustee eligibility criteria. Ideally, Sudanese lawmakers should have adopted a model similar to modern legislation, emphasizing **competence and integrity**. Furthermore, the researcher highlights the **absence of continuous oversight** provisions, which could lead to violations or mismanagement. There must be **enhanced judicial supervision** to ensure the fair and transparent administration of the bankruptcy estate.

Chapter Ten: Termination of Corporate Bankruptcy and Liquidation through the Sale of Assets and Distribution Among Partners, and Methods of Ending Bankruptcy Proceedings

Section one: Termination of the Company's Bankruptcy and Its Liquidation

Subsection One: Dissolution of the Company and Its Causes

There is no doubt that companies play a significant and vital role in the economic, political, and social life of societies and nations. They contribute greatly to job creation, the increase of national income, and the development and advancement of society. Accordingly, a network of legal relationships arises among all parties connected to the company—its management, shareholders, and business partners. When a company ceases to exist for any reason, numerous legal issues arise in relation to its dissolution.

Despite the proliferation of companies in the modern era—particularly in Sudan—many lawsuits and disputes remain active in courtrooms. The dissolution of a company for any reason does not eliminate its obligations toward third parties. Rights do not lapse with the mere cessation of the company, as this could lead to injustice and a denial of rights for those dealing with the company—whether they are other companies, administrators, or individual stakeholders.

The general causes of a company's dissolution apply to all types of companies. Some causes arise by operation of law, such as the loss of capital or the expiration of the company's term, or the death of a partner in partnerships. Other causes are based on the will of the partners, such as the decision to dissolve the company voluntarily. Still others result from court rulings, such as declaring the company bankrupt, declaring the bankruptcy of a partner in a partnership, or the court-ordered liquidation of the company.

The application of bankruptcy provisions in Sudan is governed by the Bankruptcy Act of 1929. As previously noted, this law does not distinguish between bankrupt individuals based on whether they are traders or non-traders. This aligns with the perspective of Islamic jurisprudence, which applies the rules of bankruptcy to all insolvent individuals regardless of whether their activities are commercial, because Sharia does not differentiate between commercial and non-commercial debts—rather, it considers them all as debts that must be paid.

In Sudanese law, bankruptcy procedures are outlined in the Bankruptcy Act of 1929 and the Civil Procedure Act of 1986. Article 253 of the Civil Transactions Act of 1984 addresses the causes for the dissolution of a company, stating:

1. A company is dissolved upon the occurrence of any of the following:
   a. Expiration of its term or the completion of the purpose for which it was established.
   b. Loss of all the capital or the loss of one partner's capital before it was delivered.
   c. Death, insanity, bankruptcy, or interdiction of a partner.
   d. Unanimous agreement among the partners to dissolve the company.
2. The term of the company may be extended before the expiration of its original term, in which case the company continues. If the extension occurs after the expiration of the term, it is deemed a new company.
3. If the company's term expires or its intended purpose is fulfilled, and the partners continue their business activities, this shall be considered an implicit extension of the company under the original terms.
4. A creditor of any partner may object to the extension of the company. Such objection will suspend the effect of the extension as to that creditor.

Subdivision One: Expiration of the Term Specified in the Company's Contract or Articles of Association

A company contract is considered a fixed-term contract. The founding partners may specify a certain duration for the company in its incorporation documents. The company dissolves upon the expiration of this period, even if its objective has not been fulfilled.

According to Article 526(1)(2) of the Civil Code, partnerships terminate automatically upon the expiration of the specified term, unless the partners agree to extend the company prior to the term's expiration. If the term expires and the partners continue their business activities, a new company is formed under the same conditions as the original.

Most legal systems do not specify a maximum duration for any type of company, with the notable exception of French law, which sets a maximum lifespan of 99 years. In general, the duration of the company is left to be determined by its management, provided that it does not exceed a reasonable period for human activity or the time needed to complete the company's purpose.

Accordingly, the expiration of the company's term is one of the valid reasons for its dissolution. The term may expire before the company achieves its intended goal, or the partners may wish to continue the business after the original term has ended. The law permits the extension of the company's duration either explicitly—by mutual agreement before the expiration date—or implicitly through continued activity after the term has expired.

If the extension is agreed upon before the term expires, the company continues, and the contract must be amended accordingly. Legal procedures must be followed to validate the amendment. However, if the extension is agreed upon after the term ends, the company is treated as a new entity under the same previous conditions, and it must undergo registration and publication procedures as required by law.

In cases where the partners do not expressly agree to an extension, but continue operating within the company's objectives, the company is deemed to have been implicitly extended under the same conditions as before. It is undeniable that such an extension—whether explicit or implicit—may harm creditors of the company. After the term is extended, creditors may no longer execute against a partner's share, as it remains part of the company's assets. In contrast, execution would be possible once the company is dissolved and each partner's share of the assets is determined.

To balance the interests of partners and creditors, the law allows a creditor to object to the extension of the company. Upon objection, the extension has no effect on that creditor, who may execute against the partner's share and thus force the partner out of the company unless the partner offers a substitute share. As for the other partners and the company as a whole, the company remains intact, and the creditor's objection does not affect its continuity—unless the partners agree otherwise.

Section two: Termination of the Company's Bankruptcy and Its Liquidation

Subsection One: Dissolution of the Company and Its Causes

There is no doubt that companies play a significant and vital role in the economic, political, and social life of societies and nations. They contribute greatly to job creation, the increase of national income, and the development and advancement of society. Accordingly, a network of legal relationships arises among all parties connected to the company—its management, shareholders, and business partners. When a company ceases to exist for any reason, numerous legal issues arise in relation to its dissolution.

Despite the proliferation of companies in the modern era—particularly in Sudan—many lawsuits and disputes remain active in courtrooms. The dissolution of a company for any reason does not eliminate its obligations toward third parties. Rights do not lapse with the mere cessation of the company, as this could lead to injustice and a denial of rights for those dealing with the company—whether they are other companies, administrators, or individual stakeholders.

The general causes of a company's dissolution apply to all types of companies. Some causes arise by operation of law, such as the loss of capital or the expiration of the company's term, or the death of a partner in partnerships. Other causes are based on the will of the partners, such as the decision to dissolve the company voluntarily. Still others result from court rulings, such as declaring the company bankrupt, declaring the bankruptcy of a partner in a partnership, or the court-ordered liquidation of the company.

The application of bankruptcy provisions in Sudan is governed by the Bankruptcy Act of 1929. As previously noted, this law does not distinguish between bankrupt individuals based on whether they are traders or non-traders. This aligns with the perspective of Islamic jurisprudence, which applies the rules of bankruptcy to all insolvent individuals regardless of whether their activities are commercial, because Sharia does not differentiate between commercial and non-commercial debts—rather, it considers them all as debts that must be paid.

In Sudanese law, bankruptcy procedures are outlined in the Bankruptcy Act of 1929 and the Civil Procedure Act of 1986. Article 253 of the Civil Transactions Act of 1984 addresses the causes for the dissolution of a company, stating:

1. A company is dissolved upon the occurrence of any of the following:
   a. Expiration of its term or the completion of the purpose for which it was established.
   b. Loss of all the capital or the loss of one partner's capital before it was delivered.
   c. Death, insanity, bankruptcy, or interdiction of a partner.
   d. Unanimous agreement among the partners to dissolve the company.
2. The term of the company may be extended before the expiration of its original term, in which case the company continues. If the extension occurs after the expiration of the term, it is deemed a new company.
3. If the company's term expires or its intended purpose is fulfilled, and the partners continue their business activities, this shall be considered an implicit extension of the company under the original terms.

4. A creditor of any partner may object to the extension of the company. Such objection will suspend the effect of the extension as to that creditor.

Subdivision One: Expiration of the Term Specified in the Company's Contract or Articles of Association

A company contract is considered a fixed-term contract. The founding partners may specify a certain duration for the company in its incorporation documents. The company dissolves upon the expiration of this period, even if its objective has not been fulfilled.

According to Article 526(1)(2) of the Civil Code, partnerships terminate automatically upon the expiration of the specified term, unless the partners agree to extend the company prior to the term's expiration. If the term expires and the partners continue their business activities, a new company is formed under the same conditions as the original.

Most legal systems do not specify a maximum duration for any type of company, with the notable exception of French law, which sets a maximum lifespan of 99 years. In general, the duration of the company is left to be determined by its management, provided that it does not exceed a reasonable period for human activity or the time needed to complete the company's purpose.

Accordingly, the expiration of the company's term is one of the valid reasons for its dissolution. The term may expire before the company achieves its intended goal, or the partners may wish to continue the business after the original term has ended. The law permits the extension of the company's duration either explicitly—by mutual agreement before the expiration date—or implicitly through continued activity after the term has expired.

If the extension is agreed upon before the term expires, the company continues, and the contract must be amended accordingly. Legal procedures must be followed to validate the amendment. However, if the extension is agreed upon after the term ends, the company is treated as a new entity under the same previous conditions, and it must undergo registration and publication procedures as required by law.

In cases where the partners do not expressly agree to an extension, but continue operating within the company's objectives, the company is deemed to have been implicitly extended under the same conditions as before. It is undeniable that such an extension—whether explicit or implicit—may harm creditors of the company.

After the term is extended, creditors may no longer execute against a partner's share, as it remains part of the company's assets. In contrast, execution would be possible once the company is dissolved and each partner's share of the assets is determined.

To balance the interests of partners and creditors, the law allows a creditor to object to the extension of the company. Upon objection, the extension has no effect on that creditor, who may execute against the partner's share and thus force the partner out of the company unless the partner offers a substitute share. As for the other partners and the company as a whole, the company remains intact, and the creditor's objection does not affect its continuity—unless the partners agree otherwise.

Subdivision Two: Completion of the Work or Purpose for Which the Company Was Established

Article 253 of the Sudanese Civil Transactions Act of 1984, Article 265(1) of the Egyptian law, and Article 90(d) of the Jordanian Companies Law stipulate that if a company is established for a specific project—such as constructing an airport or digging a canal—it is automatically dissolved upon the completion of that project. It must be stated in the company's articles of incorporation that the company is established for a specific task and is to be dissolved upon its completion.

In some cases, a company may be founded to complete a specific task, yet its contract includes a set duration. In such cases, the company will not be dissolved upon the expiry of the stated duration unless the intended purpose has been fully achieved. Likewise, a company may be dissolved before the expiration of its term if its objective has been fulfilled earlier, since the partners intended the company to exist only as long as necessary to accomplish its purpose.

If the purpose for which the company was established has been achieved, but the partners wish to continue operations or undertake similar activities, creditors of any partner have the right to object to such continuation. In this case, the same legal rules apply as in cases of term expiry with third-party objections. The creditor's objection results in suspending the effect of the extension with regard to that creditor.

Subdivision Three: Destruction of Company Assets

A company is also dissolved if its capital is entirely or substantially destroyed to the extent that the remaining assets are insufficient to continue operations. This destruction may be physical or moral (legal/institutional). Capital is one of the essential pillars of a company's existence; without it, the company cannot function. The legislator thus stipulated that a company shall be dissolved "if all or a significant portion of its assets are destroyed such that continuing operations becomes pointless."

Material destruction may involve, for instance, a fire that consumes all of the company's assets. Moral destruction might involve the company losing a concession or patent it relied upon, or engaging in an activity later deemed illegal—such as the government banning the product it produces.

However, such destruction does not necessarily lead to the dissolution of the company if its objectives can still be achieved—for instance, if the partners agree to compensate for the loss by increasing their capital contributions, or if the company receives compensation from an insurance company for the lost assets.

Destruction of a single partner's share does not automatically dissolve the company unless that share is essential for continued operations—such as when the share's value is so large that continuation becomes unfeasible. Conversely, the company is dissolved if a partner's share is destroyed before being contributed and the share consisted of specifically designated assets, as fulfilling the obligation to provide the share becomes impossible, rendering the company contract invalid due to the absence of a fundamental element: the capital contributions.

It is up to the court to determine the significance of the lost portion of capital and whether the remaining amount is sufficient for continued operations. This applies to general partnerships and limited partnerships. As for joint-stock companies and limited liability companies, the legislator did not specify a percentage of loss that mandates dissolution, nor the procedures to be followed in such situations.

Subdivision Four: Consolidation of All Shares in the Hands of One Partner

The law sets a minimum number of partners for every type of company. Private or partnership companies must have at least two partners, while public or joint-stock companies require at least seven. If all shares come under the control of one partner, or the number of partners drops below the legal minimum, the company is dissolved by operation of law due to the absence of a key element—plurality of partners.

Article 8(2) of Egyptian Companies Law No. 159 of 1981 states:

“If the number of partners drops below the legal quorum, the company shall be deemed dissolved by operation of law unless the partners restore the quorum within a maximum period of six months. In such a case, the remaining partners shall be personally liable for all obligations of the company during that period.”

Similarly, Article 140 of the Sudanese Companies Act of 1925 stipulates:

“If at any time the number of members in a private company falls below two, or in any other company below seven, and the company continues its operations for more than six months with such deficiency, then any member aware of this situation who continues to conduct business after the six-month period shall be personally liable for all debts incurred by the company during that time, and may be sued individually without the inclusion of any other members in the lawsuit.”

Subdivision Five: Company Merger

In Arabic lexicons, the term "merger" (*اندماج*) is derived from the verb *اندمج*, which originates from the triliteral root دمج. Ibn Faris, in his dictionary *Maqayis al-Lughah*, explains that دمج implies folding and concealment. Al-Fayruzabadi, in *Al-Qamus Al-Muhit*, defines دمج دموجًا as "entering into something." Similarly, *Al-Mu'jam Al-Wasit* states: *Damaja al-layl damujan* means "the night became dark," or "something entered and became integrated into something else." Hence, the linguistic meaning of *اندماج*—"the merging of one thing into another"—closely aligns with its legal and technical definition.

In legal terminology, a merger is defined as a contract under which one or more enterprises are incorporated into another, resulting in the dissolution of the merged entity’s legal personality and the transfer of its assets and liabilities to the absorbing entity. Alternatively, it can involve the combination of two or more entities, resulting in the dissolution of all their legal personalities and the transfer of their assets and liabilities to a newly established entity. It is also defined as the consolidation of two or more legally existing enterprises into one entity, based on the agreement of the shareholders of the merging companies, such that the resulting entity forms a unified economic unit.

According to **Article 4 of Law No. 244 of 1960** concerning mergers in joint-stock companies, when one company merges into another, the absorbing company is considered the universal successor of the merged company, assuming all its rights and obligations as stipulated in the merger agreement.

The **Sudanese Competition and Anti-Monopoly Regulation Law** defines a merger as:

"The act of two or more persons joining under the name of an existing or new person, or the act of one or more enterprises acquiring direct or indirect control over another enterprise or part thereof—whether by purchasing its shares, assets, or acquiring the ability to effectively influence decision-making. This includes horizontal, vertical, or conglomerate mergers as specified by regulations."

Although the **1925 Sudanese Companies Act** did not address mergers, **Article 2 of the 2009 Competition and Anti-Monopoly Regulation Law** reiterates the above definition and specifies various forms of control and merger.

The **new Companies Act of 2015** provides detailed provisions on mergers from **Articles 121 to 130**. According to **Article 121**, a merger project is defined as a process whereby one or more companies transfer all their undertakings, assets, and liabilities to another existing or newly established company. The "merged company" is the transferring entity, while the "absorbing company" is the one receiving these transfers.

Article 122 outlines the merger requirements as follows:

1. The boards of the merging companies must prepare and approve the proposed terms of the merger project, which must include:

(a) The name, headquarters, and whether each company involved is a limited liability company (LLC) for both the transferring and receiving companies.

(b) The number of shares in the receiving company to be allocated to members of the transferring company, the share exchange ratio, and any monetary compensation.

(c) Conditions related to share allocation in the receiving company.

(d) The date from which the members of the receiving company are entitled to participate in profits and any conditions affecting that entitlement.

(e) The date from which the financial transactions of the transferring company will be treated as those of the receiving company for accounting purposes.

(f) Any rights or restrictions related to the shares in the receiving company to be granted under the merger and the proposed measures to address them.

(g) Any benefits paid, given, or intended to be given to experts or board members of the merging company and the justification for such benefits.

Articles 123 and 124 specify that the merger project must be approved by a special resolution of each merging company. The board members must submit a copy of the proposed merger terms to the **Registrar of Companies**, who must then publish a notice of receipt in the **Official Gazette**. Additionally, merging companies are required to publish this notice in a widely circulated economic daily newspaper for three consecutive days before the general meeting convened to approve the merger.

According to **Article 125**, each merging company's board must prepare and approve an explanatory report outlining any substantial interests of board members—whether as shareholders, creditors, or otherwise—as well as the legal and economic basis of the proposed terms, especially the share exchange ratio and any valuation difficulties.

Notably, **Article 14 of the 2004 Banking Regulation Act** states:

"No bank operating in Sudan may merge with or be absorbed by another bank(s) without the approval of the Bank of Sudan."

Article 11 of the 2009 Competition and Anti-Monopoly Regulation Law further provides:

"Despite the provisions of the Companies Act of 1925, no enterprise may proceed with any merger without notifying the Competition and Anti-Monopoly Council and obtaining its written approval. The Council must issue a decision—either approving, rejecting, or suspending the merger or setting conditions for its approval—within two months of receiving the notification. This period may be extended by an additional 30 days if further information is required. Failure to issue a decision within the specified period constitutes implied approval."

Under **Article 12** of the same law, the Council may revoke its explicit or implicit approval of the merger at any time if it is proven that the notification contained materially false information or was tainted by fraud or deception.

Section three: Dissolution of the Company by Judicial Ruling

A company may be dissolved by a judicial ruling based on a request by one of the partners or a third party. The dissolution may result from a court decision: *"The court may order the dissolution of the company upon the request of one of the partners due to the failure of another partner to fulfill their obligations, or for any other reason not attributable to the partners. The judge shall assess the seriousness of the cause to determine whether it justifies dissolution. Any agreement to the contrary shall be considered void."*

Certain cases are specified in various corporate laws that may lead to the liquidation of companies. For example: if the company commits serious violations of the law or its articles of incorporation, if it is unable to meet its obligations, if it ceases its operations for one year without a valid reason, or if its accumulated losses exceed 75% of its total capital—unless the general assembly decides to increase the company's capital. The law grants the court discretionary power in such matters.

When a company is unable to fulfill its financial obligations to third parties, its assets may be seized and liquidated. The proceeds are then distributed to creditors proportionally to their claims. According to the Companies Act of 1925, any company may voluntarily enter into liquidation procedures for reasons such as:

1. *(If the company resolves by an extraordinary resolution that it cannot continue its operations due to its obligations and that liquidation is advisable).*

Furthermore, the company, its contributors, or its creditors may petition the court for its liquidation.

2. *(If the court is convinced by evidence that the company is unable to pay its debts, taking into consideration its current and future debts and contingent liabilities when determining its financial capacity).*

The **Companies Act of 2015** outlines specific circumstances under which liquidation is permissible:

A. If an event occurs that is stipulated in the company's memorandum as a reason for its dissolution, and the company passes a resolution in a general meeting for voluntary liquidation.

B. If the company resolves in a general meeting, by special resolution, to undergo voluntary liquidation.

A company may also be dissolved through deregistration if it ceases operations for a certain period, uses a name or trademark already registered to another company, or adopts a similar trademark that may cause confusion, deception, or fraud. The Sudanese law provides: *(If the company does not commence business within one year from its incorporation, or ceases operations for a full year)*.

The law further outlines the procedure for deregistration:

1. The registrar must have a reasonable cause to believe that the company is not conducting business.
2. The registrar will contact the company to verify the status of its operations. If no response is received within a month, a second notice is sent after 24 days, reminding the company of the previous notice. If there is still no response within a month of the second notice, the registrar will publish a notice in the official gazette announcing their intention to strike the company off the register.

According to **Article 203** of the Companies Act of 2015, any company seeking voluntary liquidation must comply with the following:

A. A majority of the board members (if there are more than two) must, within one month before the liquidation resolution, sign a notarized declaration stating that they have reviewed the company's assets and liabilities and believe the company can pay all its debts within one year from the start of the liquidation process. This declaration must be accompanied by a statement of the company's full assets and liabilities, certified by a legal auditor. The liquidation resolution, the declaration, and the statement must be filed with the Registrar of Companies within fifteen days from the date of the resolution, along with the name of the appointed liquidator.

Appointment of a Liquidator by the Registrar:

Article 242 gives the registrar the authority to appoint a liquidator in a voluntary liquidation under the following conditions:

1. If the registrar has reason to believe that the company is in liquidation but has no appointed liquidator.
2. If the company's affairs have been wound up, but the reports required from the liquidator have not been prepared and three months have passed.

In such cases, the registrar must send a notice by registered mail or other means to the company and the liquidator (if any), inquiring about the situation. If no response is received within a month, a second notice is sent. In addition, a notice must be published in an economic section of a widely circulated daily newspaper for three consecutive days, stating the registrar's intention to appoint a liquidator if no reply is received within three months.

After this period, the registrar may appoint a liquidator or strike the company off the register under **Article 255**. A liquidator appointed by the registrar is deemed to have been appointed by the company. Any stakeholder (e.g., a creditor or contributor) may request the court to remove the liquidator in accordance with the law.

Under the **Companies Act of 1925**, a company may enter voluntary liquidation for the following reasons:

- *(If the company resolves by an extraordinary resolution that it cannot continue its operations due to its obligations and that liquidation is advisable).*
- *(If the court is convinced by compelling evidence that the company is unable to pay its debts, considering both its actual debts and contingent or future debts).*

Sudanese law also stipulates: *(If the company does not commence business within one year from incorporation or ceases operations for a full year).*

The **2015 Companies Act** defines permissible liquidation circumstances as follows:

- If an event specified in the memorandum occurs and the company passes a resolution for voluntary liquidation.
- If the company decides in a general meeting, by special resolution, to undergo voluntary liquidation.

Section four: Company Bankruptcy

Company bankruptcy is a ground for its dissolution, liquidation, and the distribution of liquidation proceeds among creditors as pari passu (pro rata), regardless of the company's type or legal structure—whether it is a capital company or a partnership. Bankruptcy in partnerships constitutes a reason for dissolution unless the partners agree otherwise in the partnership agreement. As for capital companies, bankruptcy does not necessarily lead to dissolution if the remaining assets are sufficient to fulfill the purpose for which the company was established. However, if no such assets remain, dissolution becomes inevitable.

The **Companies Act of 1925** prohibits declaring bankruptcy for companies, as stipulated in Article 92: *"No petition shall be presented for the declaration of bankruptcy of any company registered under the Companies Act of 1925."* In contrast, both **Egyptian and Jordanian laws** operate on the principle that bankruptcy is based on the commercial status of the person, whether natural or legal. Commercial companies are considered traders, and if they cease payment of their debts, they may be declared bankrupt in accordance with **Article 316** of the Jordanian Commercial Code, which states: *"Subject to the previous chapter's provisions, any trader who ceases to pay their commercial debts shall be considered bankrupt, as shall any trader whose financial credibility can only be sustained by unlawful means that clearly lack legitimacy."*

Article 477 of the same code further provides: *"Companies licensed or registered under the applicable Companies Act are subject to the liquidation and dissolution procedures contained therein. This does not exempt commercial companies from bankruptcy proceedings."* Therefore, if a company ceases to pay its commercial debts, it may be declared bankrupt, provided the following conditions—derived from Article 316—are met:

1. The company has legal personality.
2. It is a commercial enterprise.
3. It has ceased payment of its debts.

Bankruptcy must then be pursued as a cause for dissolution, extending its legal consequences to the general partners in partnerships, in addition to the company itself. Jurisprudence and court decisions affirm this position. One school of thought holds that the basis for extending bankruptcy effects to partners lies in their joint liability, while another view maintains that it is the partners' status as traders that underpins such consequences.

Section five: Unanimous Consent of Partners to Dissolve

According to **Article 253(a)** of the Egyptian Companies Act and **Article 601** of the Jordanian Civil Code, a company may be dissolved by unanimous agreement of the partners unless the partnership agreement specifies a different majority requirement. This is referred to in Egyptian legal doctrine as "facilitated dissolution." Since the partners agreed to establish the company, they likewise may agree to dissolve it—even before the expiration of the period stipulated in the partnership agreement.

However, if the agreement includes a clause prohibiting dissolution before the company's term ends, partners must resort to the judiciary. The legal bond between partners is subject to two key constraints:

1. A resolution to dissolve a partnership must be unanimous unless the partnership agreement provides otherwise. For capital companies and limited liability companies, where unanimity is difficult to obtain, the law requires a resolution passed by the qualified majority needed to amend the articles of incorporation.
2. The agreement to dissolve must occur while the company is solvent. If the company has ceased debt payments or is on the brink of bankruptcy, such an agreement is disregarded, as it is presumed to aim at evading bankruptcy proceedings. In this case, the company must first settle its debts, and creditors are entitled to object to the dissolution. Such cases fall under the jurisdiction of the competent court.

Thus, any decision to dissolve a company that has stopped paying debts or is financially incapable must follow procedures consistent with the requirements for amending the articles of incorporation, as the dissolution resolution is effectively a modification of the company contract.

Section six: Nationalization

Nationalization refers to the transfer of private enterprise ownership to the state, with compensation awarded to the owners of the nationalized entities. It constitutes one of the causes for the company's termination, leading to the extinction of its legal personality and the emergence of a new state-owned legal entity. The motives for nationalization may be political, social, or economic. Often, the law enacted to nationalize a company specifies the fate of the nationalized company's legal personality. If the nationalized entity retains its legal personality, nationalization does not constitute a ground for dissolution.

Researcher's Opinion

Undoubtedly, the dissolution of a company—regardless of the cause—entails significant legal, economic, and social consequences, as it leads to the redistribution of rights and obligations among the parties involved, whether they are partners, creditors, or government authorities. Among all causes, **bankruptcy** has the most profound impact, as it often results in the loss of economic rights for many parties. This necessitates the application of precise legal procedures to safeguard rights and ensure equitable treatment of creditors and debtors alike.

The researcher believes that the **1929 Sudanese legal position**, which does not differentiate between the bankrupt trader and non-trader, aligns with **Islamic Sharia principles**, which do not distinguish between commercial and non-commercial debts. However, there is an urgent need to **modernize relevant legislation** to reflect developments in the modern economic system, particularly in light of the evolving nature and diversity of corporate activities.

Additionally, **Article 253** of the **1984 Civil Transactions Act** requires greater clarity regarding **creditor protection**, especially in cases of **implied continuation** of a company after the expiration of its term or the fulfillment of its original purpose. The lack of legal clarity on this matter may lead to recurring legal disputes over the partners' liabilities toward creditors when the company continues to operate implicitly without proper registration.

In conclusion, the researcher proposes **amending Sudanese company legislation** to include clearer provisions regarding **company liquidation procedures**, granting courts broader powers to protect creditor rights, and preventing partners from exploiting legal loopholes to evade financial obligations after the company's dissolution

Section seven: Specific Grounds for the Dissolution of a Company

The term "partnership companies" appears in **Latin legal systems**, unlike the **Anglo-Saxon legal system** from which the now-repealed **Sudanese Companies Act of 1925** was derived. However, some companies share similar characteristics with partnerships—namely, **companies with unlimited liability**. These were referenced in the **2002 Companies Act**, specifically in **Article 3**, which provides:

"The liability of its members or board members shall be unlimited. The transfer of its name is restricted. The number of its members shall be no less than two and no more than fifty. The company is prohibited from inviting the public to subscribe for its shares."

In the **2015 Companies Act**, the first chapter sets out the **types of companies**, with **Article 6** stating:

“A company may be either limited or unlimited in liability as follows:

(a) The liability of the members of a limited liability company shall be:

> (i) If the company is limited by shares, each member’s liability is limited to the unpaid amount on the shares held by them.
>
> (ii) If the company is limited by guarantee, each member’s liability is limited to the amount they undertake to contribute to the company’s assets in the event of its liquidation.

(b) There shall be no limit to the liability of members in an unlimited liability company.

(c) Both limited liability companies by shares and unlimited liability companies shall be registered with capital divided into equal shares.”

Article 8 of the same law further provides:

“(1) A company may be either a private or a public company, regardless of its type under Article 6(a).

(2) A private company is one that is prohibited from inviting the public to subscribe for its shares. Its bylaws may also limit its membership to fifty and may restrict the transfer of its shares.

(3) Any other company shall be considered a public company and may not restrict the transfer of its shares.”

As for **partnership companies**, the specific causes for their dissolution can be summarized as follows:

- The **death of one of the partners**,
- The **bankruptcy** of a partner,
- The **placing of a partner under guardianship or interdiction**,
- Or a **partner’s withdrawal** from the company.

These causes reflect the **personal nature** of partnerships, which rely heavily on mutual trust and the individual characteristics of the partners.

First: Death of a Partner

Article 253 of the Sudanese Civil Transactions Act of 1984 provides that:

"A company is dissolved by any of the following: ... the death, insanity, bankruptcy, or interdiction of one of the partners."

Similarly, Article 528 of the Egyptian Civil Code states:

"A company is dissolved upon the death of one of the partners, or upon their interdiction, insolvency, or bankruptcy."

In partnerships (Sharikāt al-Ashkhās), the death of a partner results in the **dissolution of the company** with respect to the remaining partners. This is based on the principle of *personal trust* among partners, who contract with one another in reliance on each other's individual characteristics.

An agreement to continue the company with the deceased partner's heirs is only valid if concluded *in advance* among the partners **prior** to the death. Any subsequent agreement—whether express or implied—between the surviving partners and the heirs **does not prevent dissolution**, as this is the general rule.

However, **Jordanian law** departs from this position. In partnerships, the **death of a partner does not constitute a ground for dissolution**, **unless** the partnership agreement explicitly provides otherwise. This is confirmed by Article 11(a) of the **Jordanian Companies Law**.

In the event of a partner's death, **Article 30(2)(a)** of the same law allows any heir to join the partnership in proportion to their inherited share, **as general partners**, **provided they meet the qualifications** for general partnership.

If the company continues with the heirs, the founding contract must be **amended** to reflect the exit of the deceased partner and the entrance of new partners (the heirs), while the company **retains its legal personality**. If the heirs **do not wish** to join as general partners, they are entitled to **receive their share** of the company's assets. In such a case, the company must be dissolved unless the remaining partners wish to continue and the number of remaining partners does not fall below the legal minimum.

Thus, continuation of the company after the death of a partner is not a matter of public policy, and the partners are free to agree otherwise.

What About Minor Heirs?

According to **Article 9** of the Jordanian Companies Law, **minors (under 18 years of age)** may not become general partners in a partnership. To address this, **Article 30** provides that:

"If the heir joins the partnership as a **limited partner**, the general partnership shall automatically convert into a **limited partnership**."

Legal Consequences of Heirs Joining the Company:

1. A heir joining as a **general partner** becomes liable for the company's obligations from the date of their admission.
2. They remain liable for pre-existing obligations to the extent of the share inherited from the deceased.
3. A heir joining as a **limited partner** is only liable **to the extent of their share**. However, they remain responsible (along with other heirs) for the deceased partner's liabilities to third parties in proportion to their inheritance.

Procedural Requirements for Heirs' Admission under Jordanian Law:

- Submission of a **Change Request** signed by all partners, including heirs, before the Companies Registrar, notary public, or licensed attorney.
- Determination of each heir's share per the **certificate of inheritance** or **waiver agreement (takhārūj)**.
- Any fractional shares must be consolidated into whole numbers through a **written agreement** among heirs.
- The heirs' admission **does not require** consent from the remaining partners.
- If there is a **minor** among the heirs, an amendment must be filed converting the company into a **limited partnership**, along with the relevant agreement and documentation.

Sudanese Perspective

Article 254 of the **Sudanese Civil Transactions Act (1984)** provides:

1. *"It is permissible to agree that if one partner dies, the company shall continue with their heirs, including minors. In such a case, the heirs shall replace their predecessor with the consent of the guardian or trustee of the incapacitated, and with the approval of the remaining partners."*

2. *"It is permissible to agree on the continuation of the company between the remaining partners upon the death, interdiction, insolvency, bankruptcy, or withdrawal of one partner. In these cases, the affected partner or their heirs are entitled only to their share in the company's assets, valued on the date of the triggering event. This share must be paid in cash, and they shall have no claim to future rights unless such rights arise from operations conducted prior to the event."*

It is noteworthy that **the Sudanese Civil Transactions Act** does not distinguish the applicable procedures by company type.

Egyptian Judicial Position

The Egyptian Court of Cassation has held:

"A partnership company is dissolved upon the death of one of the partners, pursuant to Article 528 of the Civil Code. It does not continue with the heirs, as such companies are founded on mutual personal trust. An agreement to continue with the deceased partner's heirs must be made in advance by the partners. Any agreement made after the partner's death—whether express or implied—between the heirs and surviving partners does not preclude the company's dissolution."

Companies Law of Sudan (2015)

Article 96 addresses the transfer of shares from the legal representative of a deceased member as follows:

"A transfer made by the legal representative of the heirs of a deceased member in respect of that member's share or interest in the company shall be valid, as if the representative were a member at the time of executing the transfer, even if not personally a member of the company."

This comparative review reflects the varying legislative approaches toward the effect of a partner's death on the continuity of partnerships and highlights the importance of anticipating such events in partnership agreements.

Second: Bankruptcy of One of the Partners

The bankruptcy of a partner in a partnership is considered a fundamental reason for the dissolution of the partnership, unless the partners agree otherwise in the partnership agreement. In partnerships, a partner is personally liable for the company's debts with their private assets. These specific grounds for dissolution are not considered part of public order, thus the partners may explicitly exclude any of them by agreement in the contract. In a general partnership, a partner bears unlimited and joint liability for the debts of the company, not only up to the value of their share, but also with their personal property. Additionally, each general partner acquires the status of a merchant merely by joining the partnership and is personally liable for its debts, which are considered as if they were their own.

The Egyptian Court of Cassation ruled that:

"If the defendant is a general partner, then the declaration of the partnership's bankruptcy necessarily entails the bankruptcy of the partner as well, since general partners are liable for the partnership's debts with their personal assets. If the company ceases to pay its debts, it means that its partners have also ceased to pay."

It is well established that general partnerships are built upon the personal considerations of the partners, who attract the trust of third parties due to their good reputation and financial capacity to meet company obligations. The declaration of a partner's bankruptcy may undermine this trust and weaken the company's financial standing. Since all partners' assets are liable for company debts, the bankruptcy of one may jeopardize the whole partnership unless the remaining partners are capable of continuing without the bankrupt partner. However, a partner's bankruptcy does not automatically result in the bankruptcy of the company or other partners, because the company's legal personality and estate are separate from those of its partners. The partner is liable for the partnership's debts, while the partnership is not liable for the partner's personal debts. Conversely, when the partnership itself is declared bankrupt, general partners are also declared bankrupt due to their liability for the partnership's obligations.

The Egyptian Court of Cassation further ruled:

"A general partnership has a distinct legal personality from its partners, meaning it exists independently and its assets are separate from those of the partners and serve as security solely for its creditors. A partner's share exits their personal ownership upon contribution and becomes company property. Creditors of individual partners may not enforce against the company's assets. They may only claim the partner's portion of company profits or capital share upon dissolution. The declaration of a partner's personal bankruptcy does not entail the company's

bankruptcy, as the company is not liable for personal debts of its partners. The effect of declaring a partner bankrupt is limited to the dissolution of the partnership, unless otherwise agreed in the contract."

Article 807 of the UAE Commercial Code (Law No. 18 of 1993) states:

1. *"If the company is declared bankrupt, all general partners must also be declared bankrupt. This includes any general partner who left the company after its cessation of payments, provided no more than one year has passed since the official registration of their withdrawal from the company."*
2. *"The court shall issue a single ruling declaring the bankruptcy of the company and all its general partners, even if it lacks jurisdiction over the partners' personal bankruptcies."*
3. *"A single judge shall be appointed for the company's bankruptcy and the bankruptcies of all general partners. However, each bankruptcy is administratively and procedurally independent regarding management, debt verification, and termination."*

In **limited partnerships**, which also rest on the personal qualities of the partners, the bankruptcy of any partner leads to the dissolution of the company. Scholars agree that: *"Since limited partnerships are classified as partnerships based on personal considerations, they are dissolved upon the death, incapacitation, bankruptcy, insolvency, or withdrawal of any partner—whether general or limited."*

The Qatari Companies Law of 1999, in Article 36, stipulates: *"Subject to Articles 37, 38, and 39 of this law, the rules applicable to general partnerships apply to limited partnerships with respect to their formation, management, dissolution, and liquidation."*

Similarly, Article 48 of the Jordanian Companies Law of 1976 provides: *"The provisions of general partnerships shall apply to limited partnerships in all cases not expressly addressed in this chapter."*

The Egyptian Court of Cassation also ruled:

"When a limited partner in a limited partnership engages in management activities to an extent that affects third-party confidence, they may be deemed personally liable for the company's debts alongside general partners, and may be declared bankrupt upon the company's bankruptcy."

In **silent partnerships (Shirkah al-Muhasah)**, the bankruptcy of one partner does not affect the others due to the financial independence of each. If bankruptcy proceedings target one or some silent partners, the remaining partners retain the right to participate in the bankruptcy proceedings to claim their shares.

As for **capital companies (corporations)**, the bankruptcy of a shareholder is considered a private matter and does not affect the company. In **joint-stock companies**, the identity of shareholders is irrelevant, as the emphasis is on the value of the shares they contribute. Shareholders usually do not know each other and are not bound by mutual agreements. Hence, the company is unaffected by personal events such as a shareholder's death, bankruptcy, or legal incapacity. The same applies to **partnerships limited by shares**, unless the company's articles of association or a general partners' agreement provide otherwise and are approved by the general assembly. The rationale for the possible dissolution in this case is the element of personal trust among general partners. However, the bankruptcy of a shareholder does not, in the researcher's view, result in the dissolution of a partnership limited by shares, as the shareholder bears no personal liability for the company's debts, and personal consideration is not a relevant factor—similar to shareholders in joint-stock companies.

Limited liability companies (LLCs) are also unaffected by reasons stemming from personal considerations. The company does not dissolve upon the death of a partner, as their shares are transferred to heirs. Nor is it dissolved by a partner's bankruptcy, insolvency, or legal incapacity.

Legal Incapacity (Guardianship):

We previously discussed legal incapacity resulting from bankruptcy under the topic of bankruptcy declarations. However, legal incapacity as a ground for company dissolution also includes the partner's insanity, mental deficiency, or profligacy. These are causes for dissolution under Egyptian Civil Code Article 528(3) and Article 32 of the Jordanian Companies Law, due to the loss of personal trust central to partnerships. A guardian or legal representative cannot become a partner in such companies, as they do not possess the personal qualities upon which the company was founded. Nonetheless, the partnership agreement may provide for continuation among the remaining partners. In such cases, the incapacitated or bankrupt partner is entitled to their share of the company's assets, valued at the date the event leading to their exit occurred, and to be paid in cash.

Third: Withdrawal of a Partner

The Egyptian legislator stipulates that: *"A company shall be dissolved upon the withdrawal of one of the partners if its duration is not specified, provided that the partner notifies the other partners of their intention to withdraw before doing so, and that the withdrawal is not made fraudulently or at an inappropriate time."*

From the above text, it is evident that the dissolution of the company due to the withdrawal of a partner — and hence the termination of the personal consideration — is subject to a set of conditions and limitations, as follows:

(a) The legislator requires that the company be of unspecified duration. The partner's right to withdraw from a company of indefinite duration is considered a matter of public order. Therefore, a clause in the partnership agreement that deprives the partner of this right would be invalid.

(b) The right of a partner to withdraw is not absolute; the legislator requires several conditions that essentially reflect the principle of *non-abuse of rights*. These conditions serve as constraints on the unilateral exercise of the withdrawal right to ensure it is not used arbitrarily:

1. **The company must be of unspecified duration.** This includes situations where no time limit is defined, no purpose is specified that would terminate the company upon its completion, or if the company's duration is tied to the lifetime of the partners or set for an exceptionally long term that effectively spans a human lifetime.
2. **Withdrawal must occur at an appropriate time.** A partner may not withdraw when doing so would expose the company to significant financial losses — for instance, during a crisis. Determining the appropriateness of the timing is a matter of fact assessed by the trial judge. Generally, a withdrawal request is presumed to be timely unless proven otherwise.
3. **The right of withdrawal must not allow the partner to evade obligations.**
   Withdrawal cannot be a way to escape liabilities by merely relinquishing the partner's share. Hence, a partner should not be granted an unrestricted right to withdraw unilaterally, as this could lead to the company's collapse.
4. **The partner must act in good faith.** The request for withdrawal must not be made with the intention to harm the company or other partners. Fraudulent intent could render the legal action voidable.

5. **The partner must notify the others of the intention to withdraw before doing so.** The legislator does not mandate a specific form or deadline for this notification, which means general legal principles apply. Since no written form is required, the notification can be proven by any legal means.

It is worth noting that **if the company is of a fixed duration**, any partner may petition the court to allow their withdrawal prior to the company's dissolution date, provided they have valid grounds. Acceptable reasons may include a breakdown in cooperation with other partners or severe financial hardship requiring liquidation of their share.

Company dissolution is only enforceable against third parties once it is officially registered.

The dissolution must be registered in the same manner as the original company contract. If it is not registered, it has no legal effect on third parties.

Article (256/2) provides that:

"Any partner may petition the court to be removed from the company if the company is for a fixed term and they present reasonable grounds. In such a case, the company is dissolved unless the other partners agree to continue."

For companies of indefinite duration, unilateral withdrawal is permitted, provided the partner notifies the others of the intention to withdraw.

This is confirmed in Article (28) of the Jordanian Companies Law No. 22 of 1997 (as amended), which states:

"A partner in a general partnership may unilaterally withdraw if the company is of an indefinite duration..."

Similarly, Article (440) of the Algerian Civil Code states:

"A company is dissolved upon the withdrawal of a partner, if the company's duration is not specified, provided the partner notifies all others in advance, and the withdrawal is not made in bad faith or at an inappropriate time."

Sudanese law also addresses withdrawal from companies of fixed duration if reasonable and acceptable grounds exist. In such cases, the company is dissolved unless the remaining partners agree to continue. This aligns with Article (531) of the Egyptian Civil Code No. 131 of 1948, which states:

"A partner in a company with a fixed term may petition the court to be removed if they have reasonable grounds. In such case, the company is dissolved unless the remaining partners agree to continue."

However, Sudanese legislation does **not** address withdrawal from companies of indefinite duration, whether in the Civil Transactions Act of 1984 or the Companies Act of 2015. Under the current Companies Act, some amendments could be made to cover this gap.

Researcher's Opinion:

The specific reasons for the dissolution of partnerships reflect their legal nature, which is based on personal consideration and mutual trust among partners. This is clearly shown in how a partner's death, bankruptcy, interdiction, or withdrawal can lead to the company's dissolution — unless the partners have agreed otherwise in advance.

The researcher believes this approach aligns with established principles of Latin legal tradition, which places significant weight on the personal relationships among partners. However, modern economic developments necessitate a re-examination of certain rules, particularly those governing the dissolution of partnerships due to a partner's death or bankruptcy. Under modern legal frameworks, these events can be addressed without immediate dissolution, for instance, by allowing the remaining partners to continue operations or offering heirs the option to join under specific conditions.

The Sudanese Companies Act of 2015 rightly distinguishes between limited and unlimited liability companies — a necessary step to protect the rights of third parties dealing with the company. Still, the researcher finds that more legal safeguards are needed to ensure the stability of partnerships and protect the rights of creditors and other partners when a member exits.

Recommendations:

The researcher recommends introducing legal provisions that allow partners to agree in advance on the continuation of the company in the event of a partner's death or bankruptcy. Creditors should be granted the right to challenge such agreements if their financial rights are compromised. Additionally, alternative mechanisms should be adopted, such as converting partnerships into limited liability companies once they reach a certain level of commercial activity — a move that would ensure business continuity and protect the rights of all stakeholders.

Section eight: Special Causes for the Termination of a Company's Legal Personality

First Requirement: Liquidation and Its Types

Subsection One: Definition of Liquidation

Liquidation is defined as *"a set of actions aimed at winding up the current affairs of the company and settling all its rights and debts in order to determine the net assets for distribution among the partners."*

To carry out a company's liquidation, one or more liquidators must be appointed to manage the process and perform all the necessary actions, as the legal consequences of the company's dissolution must be addressed.

Liquidation is also defined as a collection of procedures and actions intended to terminate all activities of the dissolved company. It involves selling its assets and converting them into cash with the purpose of ending the company's existence — a process referred to by legal scholars as *"realization."* This means putting an end to all legal effects left behind by the company, settling all its rights and obligations, determining the net remaining assets, and then distributing the proceeds to the partners in proportion to their shares.

In other words, liquidation is the legal mechanism through which a company contract is terminated and dissolved. Liquidation may occur in one of two forms: either **voluntary**, based on mutual agreement among the partners, or **compulsory**, by judicial order.

As a general rule, liquidation should follow the procedures agreed upon by the partners in the company contract. If the contract lacks provisions on liquidation procedures, then the rules set forth in the **Commercial Law** and **Civil Law** must be followed.

Liquidation is mandatory for all types of companies that are in a state of dissolution, *except for joint ventures* (شركة المحاصة), which do not undergo liquidation in the strict legal sense, but rather a financial settlement between partners.

Company contracts typically stipulate how liquidation and distribution should occur. If no such provisions exist, the legal rules governing liquidation must be applied.

The **Egyptian legislator**, in Article 351(2), defines liquidation as: *"Liquidation refers to the set of actions aimed at winding up the company's ongoing operations, collecting its dues, converting its assets into cash, and paying its debts, in order to form a positive net value that allows for distribution among the partners."*

Once the company is dissolved — whether due to general or special causes or by court ruling — important legal effects follow, most notably the initiation of liquidation procedures. These actions aim to collect the company's rights, pay its debts, and inventory its assets to determine the net amount to be distributed among the partners.

The **Sudanese Companies Act of 2015** does not define liquidation explicitly. However, it refers to it as the totality of procedures and actions undertaken to collect the company's receivables, settle its debts, and inventory its assets for the purpose of determining its net worth to be distributed among the partners.

According to this law, the liquidation of the company must follow the provisions outlined therein, unless the company's memorandum or articles of association specify a different method, or the partners agree otherwise at the time of dissolution.

The **Dubai Court of Cassation**, in Judgment No. 405/2002 dated 2/2/2003, stated that:
"It is established that liquidation refers to the set of procedures prescribed by law for inventorying the company's assets, collecting its dues, settling its debts, selling its assets, and allocating to each partner an amount proportional to their share in the capital. Profit and loss are distributed among partners according to the agreed ratio or as prescribed by law."

Liquidation may be:

- **Voluntary liquidation**, which is conducted amicably among partners and is not subject to direct court supervision.
- **Compulsory liquidation**, in which the court exercises broad powers and strict oversight over the implementation of the procedures.

The specifics of each type will be discussed in detail in the following subsections.

Subsection Two: Types of Liquidation

Cases of company liquidation are considered one of the reasons for its dissolution or entry into the liquidation phase. These reasons may be general, such as the dissolution of capital companies, which are evaluated based on their financial status and thus are not subject to the same dissolution methods as partnerships. Partnerships may dissolve due to the death of a partner or the imposition of seizure on one of them. According to the Iraqi Companies Law, a company may be dissolved for any of the following reasons:

1. Failure of the company to commence its operations for a continuous period not exceeding one year.
2. Completion of the project for which the company was originally established.
3. Merger or transformation of the company in accordance with the provisions of the law.
4. When the company loses 75% of its nominal capital and fails to take the necessary legal measures, or upon a decision by the company's general assembly to liquidate it.

Article (164) of the Companies Law of 2015 states the methods of liquidation as follows:

"The liquidation of companies may be carried out through:

(a) the courts,

(b) voluntarily, or

(c) under court supervision."

The provisions of the Companies Law of 2015 concerning liquidation apply regardless of the method used unless otherwise provided.

According to the above, there are three forms of liquidation:

A. Voluntary Liquidation by Agreement of the Partners

This type of liquidation is initiated by a resolution of the company's extraordinary general assembly and by agreement among the partners. A liquidator is appointed, and their powers, rights, obligations, and fees are defined.

Voluntary liquidation occurs when the company is solvent and the partners appoint a liquidator to carry out the liquidation procedures. Article (202) of the Sudanese Companies Act of 2015 permits voluntary liquidation in the following cases:

- If the event specified in the company's articles of association for its dissolution occurs, and the company decides in a general meeting to proceed with voluntary liquidation.
- If the company, in a general meeting and through a special resolution, decides to undergo voluntary liquidation.

The motive behind such liquidation may be to settle the company's legal and financial status and identify the available assets for distribution among the partners. The partners should refer to the general assembly in accordance with the Companies Law and the company's internal regulations concerning liquidation procedures.

Under Iraqi law, Article (92) establishes that a decision by the general assembly to liquidate a company must be taken by a special majority. These are general dissolution cases that apply to all types of companies, regardless of the variations in dissolution causes based on company type. Some causes apply specifically to partnerships and are not covered by law.

In joint-stock companies, due to the large number of shareholders, consensus on liquidation is not usually possible. In Egypt, dissolution before the expiry of the company's term requires a resolution by the extraordinary general assembly.

The Jordanian Companies Law (Article 259) outlines the cases in which voluntary liquidation may occur with partner approval. If any of these causes arise, the partners may still agree to continue the company through a resolution of the extraordinary general assembly. The article states:

"A public joint-stock company may be voluntarily liquidated in any of the following cases:

a) Upon expiration of the company's term unless the general assembly decides to extend it.

b) Upon completing the purpose for which the company was established unless extended.

c) By a resolution from the general assembly to dissolve and liquidate the company.

d) In other cases provided in the company's bylaws."

Under Jordanian law, a company may also dissolve if it becomes impossible to carry out its activities or upon the expiry of its term as per the incorporation contract. In such cases, the company automatically terminates and must be liquidated to settle the rights of shareholders and third parties unless the general assembly decides to extend its term. Dissolution may also occur based on a resolution of the general assembly to liquidate the company, with or without reason, as long as the reason is not contrary to law.

Conditions for Voluntary Liquidation (According to Article 203 of the Sudanese Companies Act 2015):

Before initiating voluntary liquidation, a company must comply with the following:

- The majority of board members (if there are more than two) must, one month before the liquidation decision, sign a notarized declaration stating that they have reviewed the company's assets and liabilities and believe that the company will be able to pay off all its obligations within one year of commencing liquidation.
- The declaration is only valid if:

1. It is accompanied by a statement of the company's full assets and liabilities certified by a legal auditor.
2. The liquidation decision and notarized declaration (and its attachments) are submitted to the Registrar within fifteen days of the liquidation resolution, including the name of the appointed liquidator.
    - Any board member who signs this declaration without reasonable grounds to believe the company can meet its obligations within one year is considered to have committed the crime of making a false declaration and may be punished by imprisonment of up to seven years or a fine.
    - The declaration is deemed false if one year passes from the filing date and not all obligations have been met.

The voluntary liquidation of the company is considered to have commenced from the date of the liquidation resolution.

Appointment of the Liquidator by the Company:

The **liquidator** is the person tasked with performing the necessary operations for the liquidation. If the company resolves to liquidate voluntarily, as per the aforementioned article, an **optional liquidator** is appointed. This liquidator is responsible for converting the company's assets into cash, paying off debts and expenses, and returning the remaining funds to the shareholders. The optional liquidator holds the same authority as the court-appointed liquidator.

Once the liquidation decision is issued, the company must cease its operations, except those necessary for the benefit of the liquidation. However, the company retains its legal personality until the liquidation is complete.

It is important that the appointed liquidator is not the current financial auditor or someone who audited the company's accounts in the five years preceding their appointment. In practice, liquidation carried out by partners usually only occurs in partnerships due to the small number of partners. In capital companies and those with many shareholders, it is impractical for the shareholders themselves to act as liquidators. Instead, the general assembly that issued the liquidation resolution appoints one or more liquidators. If no liquidator is appointed, the provision in the Civil Transactions Law may apply, which gives any interested party the right to request the court to appoint a liquidator. The chosen liquidator is the one approved by the majority of the partners.

Section nine: The Registrar's Authority in Appointing a Voluntary Liquidator

Article (252) of the Companies Act of 2015 provides that:

1. The registrar must, if he has reasonable grounds to believe that a company in voluntary liquidation does not have a liquidator, or that its affairs have been liquidated but the required reports have not been prepared within three months of that, send a notice by registered mail or other means to the company and the liquidator (if any) inquiring about the matter.
2. If the registrar does not receive a response within one month of sending the letter, he must send another letter to the company and the liquidator (if any), and publish a notice in the official gazette and in the economic section of a widely circulated daily newspaper for three consecutive days, stating his

intention to appoint a liquidator if no response is received within three months.

3. Upon the expiration of the period mentioned in the notice, the registrar may appoint a liquidator to undertake the liquidation procedures in accordance with his powers under the provisions of this law, or delete the company in accordance with Article (255).
4. A liquidator appointed under paragraph (3) shall be deemed to have been appointed by the company, and any interested party may petition the court for his removal pursuant to the provisions of this law.

Powers of the Voluntary Liquidator:

Since the liquidator is considered a representative of the company, he is granted powers enabling him to perform his duties accurately and honestly. The company is bound by all acts carried out by the liquidator in its name if they are necessary for the liquidation process. The liquidator is liable to the company for any damage caused by his actions, and thus he is responsible for any harm caused to shareholders or partners due to his errors.

The Sudanese Companies Act of 2015 grants the voluntary liquidator the powers outlined in Article (208) as follows:

1. Upon the liquidator's appointment, all powers of the board members cease, except to the extent permitted by the company in a general meeting or by the liquidator himself.
2. The liquidator may, without court permission, exercise all powers conferred upon a court-appointed liquidator under this law.
3. The liquidator may also exercise the powers granted to the court under this law regarding the preparation of the list of contributories, making claims, paying company debts, and settling the rights of contributories among themselves.
4. If multiple liquidators are appointed, one or more of them may exercise any of the powers granted under this law, as determined by the company at the time of appointment. If no such determination is made, any two or more may act jointly.
5. If, for any reason, no liquidator exists, the court may appoint one upon the request of any contributory or creditor.

Section ten: Liability of the Voluntary Liquidator

According to company law, the company is bound by the liquidator's acts within the scope of liquidation and his lawful powers, and he bears no liability for such acts. However, if the liquidator acts beyond his authority or outside his scope of duties, he is personally liable to third parties for such actions, and general civil liability rules apply.

The liquidator is liable to the company for negligence or failure in fulfilling his duties, and any partner may claim against the liquidator for such failures. Third parties harmed by the liquidation may also seek compensation. Where multiple liquidators are appointed, they are jointly liable under tort law. If the liquidator's actions amount to criminal offenses such as fraud, forgery, or breach of trust, then criminal liability applies.

Article (233/1) of the 2015 Companies Act states:

"The liquidator may, with court permission in court-supervised or court-based liquidation, or by special resolution in voluntary liquidation, undertake any or all of the following acts:

- Pay any class of creditors in full.
- Enter into compromise or settlements with creditors or claimants, or those who may have present or future claims against the company.
- Settle all claims, obligations, debts (actual or potential), whether present or future, between the company and any contributory or party potentially liable to the company, and resolve any disputes related to the company's assets or its liquidation on agreed terms, and accept securities or full settlements for any claims, debts, or obligations."

The liquidator performs his duties under court supervision, and any creditor or contributory may appeal to the court regarding the exercise of any power or proposed action.

Term of the Liquidator's Work:

Determining the duration of the liquidator's role is primarily subject to the will of the partners. However, a prolonged duration may harm third-party interests.

Article (216/1) of the Sudanese Companies Act of 2015 provides:

"If the liquidation lasts more than a year, the liquidator must call a general meeting of the company at the end of the first year from the start of liquidation and at the end of each subsequent year or whenever feasible thereafter, to present a report in the prescribed format including all required details regarding the liquidation process."

The Sudanese legislator did not specify a precise duration for the liquidation process. In contrast, the Algerian legislator, under Article (785), stipulates:

"The liquidator's mandate shall not exceed three years, but may be renewed by the partners or by the court president, depending on whether the liquidator was appointed by the partners or by judicial decision. If it is not legally possible to convene a partners' meeting, the mandate may be renewed by court decision at the request of the liquidator. The liquidator must, when requesting renewal, state the reasons that prevented the conclusion of the liquidation and the measures to be taken along with the timeline required to complete the process."

Section eleven: Effects of Pure Voluntary Liquidation

According to Article (207), when a company is liquidated through **pure voluntary liquidation**, the company's assets are used to meet its obligations in accordance with Article (239). Any surplus is distributed among the members in proportion to their shares in the company. The liquidation process ends once the partners approve the account submitted by the liquidator. At that point, the legal personality of the company ceases permanently, and the liquidator is discharged from liability.

Once the liquidator collects the company's receivables from third parties, settles its debts, converts its assets into divisible capital among the partners, and prepares a statement of account accordingly, and once this statement is approved by the partners, the liquidation is deemed complete.

The liquidator must include in the statement of account a list of the company's assets, rights, and debts, as well as a full explanation of the actions taken and the final outcome of the liquidation. Upon completing their duties, the liquidator is obligated to deliver all the company's books, correspondence, papers, and documents to the office of the Registrar of Companies.

From the above, it becomes evident to the researcher that if there is dissatisfaction with the course of the voluntary liquidation — whether due to internal reasons such as misconduct by the liquidator or undue influence from majority shareholders, or due to external factors such as refusal by certain entities to deal with the liquidator or multiple court actions and attachments on the company's assets — and even if confidence in the voluntary liquidation process is not completely lost, then the parties may resort to the court under Article (221) of the Companies Act of 2015. This article stipulates the court's authority to order that the liquidation continue under its supervision:

"If a company resolves by special resolution to voluntarily liquidate, the court may, upon request by the company, a creditor, a shareholder, a contributory, or the liquidator, order that the voluntary liquidation continue under the supervision of the court. All parties shall have the right to approach the court, and in general, the liquidation shall proceed according to the conditions the court deems fair."

This supervised voluntary liquidation retains the nature of voluntary liquidation and the liquidator continues to exercise the full powers of a voluntary liquidator. Its advantage lies in suspending attachments and lawsuits and facilitating access to the court.

Section twelve: Removal of the Liquidator

Article (208/7) states:

"The court may, upon a justified request submitted to it, remove the liquidator and appoint another liquidator."

Accordingly, the liquidator may be removed in the same manner in which they were appointed. Additionally, the court may, upon the request of any partner and for reasonable cause, decide to remove the liquidator even if the liquidator was not appointed by the court. Any decision or judgment for the removal of a liquidator must include the appointment of a replacement.

In all cases, the decision to appoint or remove a liquidator, as well as the method of liquidation, must be registered with the Registrar of Companies. Such decisions have no effect against third parties until the date of registration.

Furthermore, Article (209) obligates a company that has chosen voluntary liquidation to announce the appointment of the liquidator within **twenty-one days** of the appointment in the prescribed manner with the Registrar.

As per Article (206/1), any resolution to liquidate the company voluntarily must be announced within **ten days** of issuance by publishing it in the **official gazette** and in the **economic section** of a **daily newspaper for three consecutive days**, while also notifying the registrar.

Second Requirement: Compulsory Liquidation

Section One: Permissibility of Liquidation

This type of liquidation is also referred to as **judicial liquidation**, which is one of the causes leading to the dissolution of a company when it becomes impossible for the company to continue its activities—particularly due to the loss of its capital. If a company loses 75% of its nominal capital, it effectively loses its legal personality, thus justifying its liquidation.

A petition for judicial liquidation may be submitted by one of the persons entitled to do so, based on one or more of the grounds stated in **Article (165) of the Companies Act of 2015**, which provides for liquidation through the court as follows:

"A company may be liquidated by the court in the following cases:

(a) If the company resolves by special resolution to be liquidated by the court; or

(b) If the inaugural meeting is not held, or the incorporation report is not filed; or

(c) If the company does not commence business within one year of its incorporation, or if it suspends its business for a whole year; or

(d) If the number of company members falls below two; or

(e) If the company is unable to pay its debts; or

(f) If the court finds that it is just and equitable to liquidate the company."

In these cases, the court may issue a judgment for liquidation if it considers it appropriate based on its discretionary authority. It is not sufficient merely to submit a petition by someone with legal standing or to establish that one of the statutory grounds applies—especially in cases where the partners are unable to agree on appointing a liquidator, or where there are valid reasons preventing the assignment of the liquidation task to the individuals specified in the partnership agreement.

Judicial liquidation may be initiated by any of the partners, or when the court orders the dissolution of the company and appoints a liquidator under the law to handle the winding-up process. However, this alone does not compel the court to issue a liquidation order—the decision is entirely discretionary.

Upon issuing the liquidation order, the court appoints a **liquidator under its supervision** who is responsible for verifying debts, liquidating the company's assets, allocating funds to cover expenses and debts, and distributing any remainder to the shareholders.

As the name suggests, **judicial liquidation** entails **close and direct supervision by the court**. The stakeholders involved—creditors, shareholders, board members, and the company as a legal entity—are all affected by the proceedings. Judicial liquidation differs substantially from **pure voluntary liquidation**, where the court has no authority over the liquidator's actions. In voluntary liquidation, the liquidator operates independently and is accountable only to the partners who appointed them.

Generally, the court does not interfere in voluntary liquidation unless the stakeholders are dissatisfied with the liquidator's conduct or if a minor or technical issue arises that requires judicial intervention. In such cases, stakeholders may apply to the court, while the liquidation remains voluntary. This **limited judicial intervention** is allowed under **Article (215)** of the Companies Act, which states:

(1) "If the company is in the course of voluntary liquidation, the liquidator, any creditor, shareholder, or contributory may apply to the court to resolve any dispute arising during the liquidation, or to exercise with regard to claims or other matters any or all of the powers it may exercise as if the liquidation were by the court.

(2) If the court is satisfied that resolving the dispute or exercising the requested authority is fair and beneficial, it may approve the application in whole or in part on such terms as it deems appropriate. The court may also issue any other order it considers just in relation to the application."

If there is dissatisfaction with the liquidation procedures and complete loss of trust in the voluntary liquidation, a petition for compulsory liquidation may be submitted, even if the company is already undergoing voluntary liquidation. This is in accordance with **Article (218) of the Companies Act**, which states:

"Voluntary liquidation does not deprive any creditor, shareholder, or contributory of the right to request liquidation by the court, if the court is satisfied—based on the request of a creditor, shareholder, or contributory—that their rights would be prejudiced by the voluntary liquidation."

Moreover, **Article (266) of the Jordanian Commercial Code** provides:

"The court may order the compulsory liquidation of a company based on a lawsuit filed by the Public Civil Prosecutor, the Companies Registrar, or their designee, in any of the following cases:

1. *If the company commits a serious violation of the law or its articles of association;*
2. *If the company is unable to meet its obligations;*
3. *If it ceases operations for a year without a justified or legitimate reason;*
4. *If the company's total losses exceed 75% of its subscribed capital, unless its General Assembly resolves to increase its capital."*

However, **the court's decision to liquidate a company is not final and may be appealed.** This principle was affirmed by the **Jordanian Court of Cassation**, which held:

"The decision of the Court of First Instance ordering the liquidation of a public shareholding company may be appealed."

Section thirteen: Who Has the Right to File for Court-Ordered Liquidation

Under the **Sudanese Companies Act**, the right to submit a petition for court-ordered liquidation is granted to one or more of four categories. Three of these are outlined in **Article 167(1)**:

"A petition for the liquidation of a company may be submitted to the court by the company, any creditor, any contributory, any shareholder, or any party authorized by law, whether individually or collectively..."

These categories are:

1. **Creditors**
2. **Contributors and shareholders** (treated as one group)
3. **The company itself** as a legal entity
4. **The Registrar**

According to **Article (145) of the Companies Act**:

"If the Registrar determines, based on the findings of an inspector's report, that the liquidation of the company is warranted, they may file a petition with the court for its liquidation in the interest of justice and fairness."

The **Sudanese legislator** has addressed the provisions of **court-supervised liquidation** in **Articles (221–225)** of the **2015 Companies Act**, which include the following clause:

"If the company resolves by special resolution to continue with the voluntary liquidation under the supervision of the court, the court may issue an order for such supervision. All parties shall retain the right to resort to the court, and the liquidation shall generally be conducted under conditions deemed just by the court."

This shows that **the court's power to place voluntary liquidation under its supervision is discretionary**. However, **nothing prevents the company** from applying to the competent court requesting supervision. In such a case, the company is only required to comply with the obligations set forth in the relevant article.

Thus, **the right to request court-supervised liquidation is not exclusive to the company**. It is also a legitimate right of the **creditor or shareholder/contributor**, whenever the court is satisfied that their rights may be adversely affected if the company continues under voluntary liquidation.

Section fourteen: Appointment of a Liquidator by the Court

Article (177) of the 2015 Companies Act states:

(1) *The court may appoint one or more persons as official liquidators to carry out the procedures of liquidation and fulfill the duties imposed by the court. Upon their appointment, all powers of the company's board members shall cease.*

(2) *The court may appoint a provisional official liquidator at any time after the liquidation petition has been submitted and before the liquidation order is issued.*

(3) *If the court appoints more than one official liquidator, it must determine whether the duties mandated by or authorized under this Act shall be performed jointly by all the appointed liquidators or by one or more of them.*

(4) *The court may declare the acts of an official liquidator valid, even if it is later discovered that their appointment was flawed. However, any actions taken by the liquidator after the invalidity of their appointment becomes known shall not be considered valid.*

1. Qualifications of the Liquidator

As for the liquidator's qualifications, **Article (178/1)** of the Companies Act states:

"The official liquidator must possess appropriate qualifications and experience and shall be a certified accountant, auditor, or someone who has practiced law for no less than fifteen years, provided that the company's auditor may not be appointed as its liquidator."

(2) *The court may, for acceptable reasons recorded in the minutes, appoint a liquidator without being bound by the conditions set out in paragraph (1).*

2. Powers of the Official Liquidator

The powers of the official liquidator are outlined in **Article (180)** of the 2015 Companies Act as follows. The liquidator shall, with the permission of the court and under conditions it deems appropriate, have the authority to perform the following actions:

(a) File lawsuits and undertake legal proceedings—whether civil, criminal, or otherwise—and defend the company in such cases in its name and on its behalf.

(b) Continue to operate the company's business to the extent necessary for a fair and efficient liquidation that serves the company's interest.

(c) Sell the company's movable and immovable property through public auction or private sale, either wholly or in parts, and transfer ownership to any individual or company.

(d) Undertake all actions in the company's name and on its behalf.

(e) Engage with creditors and claim any receivables from the bankrupt estate of any contributory, and prove such claims. The liquidator may receive distributions from the bankrupt estate proportional to the company's debt, as if it were an independent, enforceable debt.

(f) Draw, accept, issue, and endorse promissory notes or cheques in the name and on behalf of the company.

(g) Arrange financing secured by the company's assets for the purposes of liquidation.

(h) Personally obtain orders to administer the estate of any deceased contributory and perform any actions necessary to recover the company's receivables from such estate. In such cases, the amounts are deemed due to the liquidator himself to enable him to obtain probate orders for the recovery of such funds. However, these powers do not infringe upon the rights, duties, or privileges of the official estate administrator.

(i) Carry out any other tasks necessary to wind up the company's affairs and distribute its assets.

Upon examining this article, the researcher notes that **all powers granted to the official liquidator are conditional on prior court approval**. Consequently, **any actions taken without such approval are considered null and void**. However, the liquidator may exercise these powers **without direct court intervention** if the court authorizes this in its orders, as confirmed by **Article (182)** of the 2015 Companies Act:

"The court may stipulate in any order it issues that the official liquidator is permitted to exercise any of the powers mentioned in Article (180) without seeking the court's permission or involvement. If the liquidator is appointed provisionally, the court may define and limit his powers in the appointment order."

As an official liquidator, he may perform all tasks necessary for the company's liquidation, including settling company expenses. Since liquidators often require liquidity to cover liquidation costs and settle debts, **they may need to sell company assets**, whether movable or immovable. Under Sudanese law, this authority depends on the **type of liquidation**:

- In **voluntary liquidation**, the liquidator may act without court permission.
- In **judicial liquidation**, court permission is required, as set out in **Article (180)** of the Companies Act (2015).

In contrast, the **Saudi legislator** has provided under **Article (220)** that, while observing all restrictions, **the liquidator must withhold sufficient funds to pay**

off future debts, in accordance with **Article (208)** of the Companies Law, which states:

1. The liquidator must pay off the company's due debts in order of priority, and reserve sufficient amounts for deferred or disputed debts.

2. Debts arising from the liquidation process have priority over other debts.

The **new Companies Law in Saudi Arabia**, issued by Royal Decree No. (M/3) dated 28/01/1437 AH, considers the liquidator the **legal representative of the company under liquidation**, whether the liquidation is judicial or voluntary. The liquidator must act within the powers granted by the appointment decision and may not exceed them.

In case of **multiple liquidators**, they are required to **cooperate and act collectively**, and their actions are only valid if made **unanimously**. **Article (206)** of the Companies Law provides:

"If there are multiple liquidators, they must act jointly. Their actions are not valid unless taken unanimously, unless the appointment decision or the appointing authority permits individual action. They are jointly liable for compensating any damage caused to the company, shareholders, or others as a result of exceeding their authority or due to errors made in the performance of their duties."

During the liquidation process, the liquidator may sell **movable or immovable assets** of the company via direct sale, public auction, or any method that ensures the **highest return**. However, they may not sell all of the company's assets as a whole or offer them as a share in another company unless **authorized by the appointing authority**.

Furthermore, under **Article (207)** of the Saudi Companies Law, the liquidator may not start new business activities **unless necessary to complete pre-liquidation obligations**. Therefore, they are **prohibited from initiating new operations**, even if profitable, unless such activities are necessary to fulfill prior commitments. For instance, if the company had previously agreed to supply goods, the liquidator may continue executing the contract to avoid legal liability. If the liquidator violates this rule and carries out unauthorized new operations, they are **personally liable** for any resulting obligations. In the case of multiple liquidators, **liability is individual**.

Any actions performed by the liquidator **within their authorized powers** are binding on the company, as long as they do not **exceed the limits defined in the liquidation resolution**.

In contrast, **the Jordanian legislator** adopted a **different approach**, strictly requiring **court authorization for the sale of the company's assets**, whether the liquidation is judicial or voluntary. This is confirmed by **Article (255) of the Jordanian Commercial Code**, which states:

"The court may authorize the liquidator to sell the assets of a public shareholding company under liquidation, whether voluntary or compulsory, if it deems it in the company's interest."

Based on the reviewed legislation, the researcher concludes that the **2015 Sudanese Companies Act** is **clearer and more detailed**. It specifies that court permission is required for judicial liquidation, while voluntary liquidation **only requires the general assembly's approval**, as decided under court supervision and with a pre-defined majority of the members.

Section fifteen: Powers of the Court to Dismiss the Official Liquidator

According to **Article (223/3)**, it states:

"The court may dismiss the liquidator it has appointed as previously mentioned or a liquidator who remains in office under a supervisory order. The court may also fill any vacancy resulting from dismissal, death, or resignation."

Thus, **the dismissal of a liquidator is carried out by the court** whenever the liquidator **commits a breach of duty** resulting in harm that justifies removal. According to **Article (786) of the Algerian Commercial Code**, the liquidator may be dismissed and replaced in accordance with the procedures used for their appointment. If the liquidator commits actions that conflict with his obligations toward the company, the persons who appointed him have the right to dismiss him. It is also permissible to resort to the judiciary to request the dismissal of the liquidator if there is a legitimate reason to do so.

Furthermore, **the liquidator may be dismissed either by the partners or by the judiciary**, and he also has the right to **resign from his position**, provided that such resignation occurs at an appropriate time and is **announced to the partners**. In all cases, **the liquidator may only be dismissed by the authority that appointed him**. If he was appointed by the partners, they alone have the right to remove him. If he was appointed by the court, the decision of dismissal is under the **jurisdiction and authority of the court**.

As for **resignation**, **Article (179/1)** stipulates:

"The official liquidator may resign from his position, and the resignation becomes effective from the date it is accepted. The court may also dismiss him, provided that the reasons justifying the dismissal are clarified."

Second Requirement: The Liquidation Petition

The company is liquidated through the court based on a petition submitted thereto. This petition is not considered a lawsuit in the legal sense but rather a mere request filed by an entitled party, upon which the liquidation procedures commence. According to the provisions of **Article (167) of the Sudanese Companies Law of 2015**, which states:

"A request for the liquidation of the company shall be submitted to the court by the company itself, or by any creditor, or by the liable party, or by a shareholder, or by any entity authorized by any law, or by all or any of these parties, jointly or separately. The petition shall include the names of the creditors, details of the company's assets and liabilities, and audited financial statements for the preceding three years, unless the court decides to exempt the petitioner from submitting some or all of the foregoing..."

In accordance with this provision, the liquidation petition may be submitted by the company itself, any of its creditors, the liable parties, or any combination thereof, whether jointly or individually. Additionally, the petition may be filed through the commercial registrar.

Consequently, liquidation under court supervision represents the second method of company liquidation, namely voluntary liquidation, as previously mentioned. This court supervision arises after the company has conducted voluntary liquidation outside the court's jurisdiction. Subsequently, any creditor or liable party may apply for court supervision over the liquidation, which is determined to be voluntary. The court then assumes this supervisory role.

Moreover, the company itself may submit a liquidation petition to the court; however, such a request must be founded upon a special resolution of the general assembly pursuant to **Article (202) of the Sudanese Companies Law of 2015**, which provides:

"Voluntary liquidation of the company may occur under the following circumstances:

(a) If the event specified in the company's articles of association triggering dissolution occurs and the company passes a general assembly resolution to liquidate voluntarily.

(b) If the company decides in a general assembly meeting, by a special resolution, to liquidate voluntarily."

Therefore, a liquidation petition submitted solely by the board of directors without a preceding special resolution of the general assembly cannot be accepted.

Any creditor from a group of creditors may submit a petition for liquidation, including those whose debts are secured against the partners, such as persons holding fixed mortgages. Although their rights are linked to the mortgaged assets, the law does not deprive them of exercising their rights as creditors. However, the court shall not consider a liquidation petition filed by a holder of a contingent or future debt unless the petitioner provides a security deemed reasonable by the court to cover the liquidation expenses, and only after the court is convinced of the existence of prima facie evidence justifying liquidation.

Where the petition is filed by a creditor, the debt must not be subject to a strong dispute. A substantial dispute over the debt renders the continuation of liquidation proceedings impossible. Similarly, if the debt is not established, it cannot serve as a basis for company liquidation. For instance, in the case of *Hashem Fadallah Mohamed v. Nile White Company for Marine Industries Ltd.*, the appellant filed for liquidation on the grounds that the company was insolvent and unable to repay its debts. However, the Supreme Court found that the appellant's debt was not proven and consequently rejected the liquidation request.

English law follows a similar principle. In the case of *Nile White Company for Marine Industries*, a creditor lodged a complaint alleging that the company had failed to repay its debt and requested the court to liquidate the company accordingly. The company denied the existence of the debt, arguing that the amount claimed was in exchange for shares in another company. The court held that the dispute over the debt was substantial and therefore the creditor did not have the right to file for liquidation.

The law also grants the liable parties the right to submit a liquidation petition. It defines the liable party as "any person obligated to pay money to the company's assets upon its liquidation and in all related procedures, including persons who must be considered liable and all procedures preceding their final appointment." This phrase encompasses any person claiming to be liable to pay.

Accordingly, the liable party has the right to submit a liquidation petition except in the two cases specified in **Article (167) of the Companies Law of 2015**, which provides:

"The liable party shall not have the right to submit a request for the liquidation of the company except in one of the following two cases:"

Exclusively, therefore, the founders or shareholders do not have the right to submit the petition. The Supreme Court has affirmed that this contradicts what it previously established in its rulings; however, it excused this on the grounds that an expansive interpretation of Article (167) granting others the right to request the liquidation of the company beyond those expressly enumerated by the legislator would undermine the legislator's intent and destabilize corporate operations. The dissenting opinion in this case leaned on prior Supreme Court rulings and recognized the right of a shareholder who is not liable to pay to request liquidation.

Finally, according to Article (145) of the Companies Law of 2015, the Commercial Registrar has the right to submit a liquidation petition to the court if it appears, based on reports submitted by inspectors, that it is in the public interest to liquidate the company concerned, provided that the court has not already ordered its liquidation based on considerations of justice and equity. This is reflected in the provision: "If the Registrar, through any facts appearing in an inspector's report, deems that liquidation of the company is necessary, he may file a petition with the court to liquidate it based on the principles of justice and equity."

Section sixteen: The Legal Personality of the Company Under Liquidation

As previously stated, a company is defined as an organization with an independent legal personality established on the agreement of a group of natural or juridical persons to operate and succeed in a specific business project pursuant to defined objectives. This legal entity manages its affairs and exercises its rights and obligations through specific bodies (the General Assembly, the Board of Directors, and Executive Management). Powers are distributed among these bodies pursuant to its founding documents and the provisions of the Companies

Law. The establishment of this legal entity is typically aimed at achieving material profit.

Once the company is registered in the commercial register, it acquires its legal personality, which it retains during the incorporation period pursuant to the provisions of the law, as stipulated in Article (14) of the Companies Law of 2015. The company maintains...

During the liquidation period, the company retains its legal personality to the extent necessary for the liquidation process, which is indicated by the clear addition of the phrase "Company Under Liquidation." The company maintains its corporate personality for the duration of the liquidation only to the extent required to carry out liquidation activities. The dissolution or winding up of the company creates a financial estate that must be liquidated by collecting its debts, fulfilling its obligations, selling its assets, and distributing its remaining property among the partners. This process may take a considerable amount of time, necessitating the continuation of the company's legal personality so that the aforementioned acts may be carried out in its name by the liquidators, who act on behalf of the partners.

Article (167) of the Companies Law grants the company, as a juridical person, the right to submit a liquidation petition through the court. To understand this provision in relation to the concept of the company, it must be recognized as a legal entity without physical existence but with a juridical personality.

From the foregoing and in accordance with the established principles in comparative jurisprudence of public law systems from which Sudan derived its legislation, the legal framework governing companies is based on four fundamental pillars around which all other provisions and principles revolve:

a) **Upon its proper establishment, the company becomes a legal person distinct and independent from its shareholders and board members.**

b) **The company, as a juridical person without physical existence, is managed through three bodies or organs, namely:**

- **The General Assembly of Shareholders**
- **The Board of Directors**
- **The Executive Management**

The powers and jurisdictions of these three bodies are determined according to a precise system of distribution of authorities, some of whose provisions are regulated by the Companies Law, while others are left to the company's internal regulations. The general rule is that the company's legal personality terminates upon its dissolution and liquidation; however, as is evident from the aforementioned article, the legislator permits the company to retain its legal personality during the liquidation period to the extent necessary for the liquidation process, and its bodies remain in place throughout the liquidation period, with their powers limited to liquidation activities that do not fall within the liquidators' jurisdiction.

The rationale requires that the company retains its legal personality because the consequences arising from the company's transactions cannot be liquidated instantaneously. It is in the interest of the shareholders and third parties to maintain the company's personality until the completion of the liquidation procedures, and only to the extent necessary for liquidation purposes. Accordingly, the company is not permitted to undertake new business activities; rather, its role is confined to liquidating prior business conducted before its dissolution, without engaging in new undertakings.

Commercial jurisprudence justifies the retention of the company's legal personality during the liquidation period on the grounds that: "The continuation of the company's personality is the limit consistent with respecting the acquired rights of the company's creditors who have dealt with a legal entity possessing an independent liability distinct from that of the shareholders." Hence, it can be stated that the company's retention of its legal personality during the liquidation period entails several consequences, including:

- The prohibition of initiating or continuing any civil proceedings against the company before any other court, except for criminal proceedings, pursuant to Article (170) of the Companies Law, which provides: "The court may initiate liquidation procedures upon the request of the company, one of its creditors, one of those liable to pay, or one of the shareholders, at any time after the submission of the liquidation request under the provisions of this law and before issuing an order for liquidation of the company, to stay any civil proceedings against the company or their continuation before any other court, except for criminal proceedings, provided that any arising civil rights be referred to the competent court handling the liquidation to adjudicate them."
- And as for Article (171), which concerns the suspension of lawsuits...

Civil Procedures Upon Issuance of the Liquidation Order: "Once an order for the liquidation of the company is issued, no lawsuit or any other legal proceeding may be initiated or continued against the company before any other court except with the permission of the liquidation court and under the conditions it prescribes. Criminal proceedings are exempted from this provision. Any civil claims arising shall be referred to the competent court handling the liquidation to adjudicate them."

- A joint-stock company retains its name, legal capacity, commercial address, domicile, and nationality, and the authority of the directors ends upon the dissolution of the company. Nevertheless, these directors remain in charge of managing the company and are considered liquidators until a liquidator is appointed.
- The company retains its independent financial liability separate from the shareholders' liabilities. Creditors who are not shareholders must first satisfy their claims from the company's assets. The company remains legally competent to litigate.
- During the liquidation period, the company's bankruptcy may be declared if it ceases payment of its debts, due to its retention of the status of a merchant.
- The company's registration in the commercial register shall not be canceled during the liquidation process except after its completion.

The reason the company retains its legal personality during the liquidation period is that if this personality were to cease, the company's assets would become a joint property among the shareholders, and the creditors of the individual shareholders could compete with the company's creditors to execute against its assets. This would hinder the completion of liquidation work, the collection of the company's rights, and the fulfillment of its debts, thereby protecting the rights of third parties.

The effects of the company's retention of legal personality during liquidation appear in its relations with third parties, as the company continues to have legal capacity to litigate. It remains liable to fulfill the debts owed by it. Third parties may therefore sue the company directly to recover debts, without the need to sue all shareholders collectively. Moreover, the liquidator has the authority to litigate against the company's debtors and represents the company in all claims filed by or against it, replacing the board of directors in exercising such litigation without the need to file new lawsuits.

Accordingly, and in applying this principle to the matter of submitting a liquidation petition, it is essential to determine who holds the authority to file such a petition. It is crucial to distinguish between two fundamentally different matters that are often confused: the mere physical submission of the petition to the court, and the decision or determination to initiate the filing of a liquidation petition before the court. These two matters are significantly different. The physical submission of a petition to the court is generally unproblematic and is considered a routine administrative act carried out by the company's management bodies—namely, the Board of Directors or the General Manager as the representative of the executive management. It is inconceivable that petitions would be submitted by the General Assembly. Thus, the physical act of submission itself is not the issue; rather, the question arises as to who is entitled to take the initiative and make the decision to liquidate the company through the court on behalf of the company's bodies.

This distinction is critical because if the decision to liquidate is made by the competent authority with legal standing, the subsequent submission of the petition is merely an execution of that authority's decision. Referring to the rules on the distribution of powers, the default position is that the Board of Directors exercises management powers as a proxy for the principal, which is the company, and represents the principal, namely, the General Assembly. The Board does not have the right to exercise any authority beyond ordinary management functions unless the company's bylaws provide otherwise. This matter is left, under Sudanese and English law, to the company's bylaws.

This principle was established in Rule (71) of Appendix A to the repealed Companies Act, which stated:

"The company's Board of Directors manages its affairs and may bear all expenses related to the company's incorporation and registration. It may exercise all the company's powers which do not require, by law, any other legislation in force or provisions of these bylaws, to be exercised in a general meeting. Nevertheless, the Board must adhere to the provisions of this law, these bylaws, and any regulations adopted by the company in a general meeting, provided they do not conflict with the provisions of this law and these bylaws. The adoption of any regulation by the company in a general meeting shall not invalidate any act undertaken by the Board prior to such adoption if that act was considered valid before the adoption of that regulation."

Accordingly, it has been well established in both doctrine and English jurisprudence, prior to the enactment of the Insolvency Law, and in interpreting provisions analogous to Article 167 of the Sudanese Companies Act, that the "company" referred to therein means the General Assembly of the company and not the management. The General Assembly alone is entitled to authorize the submission of a liquidation petition by a formal decision, unless the company's bylaws provide otherwise.

Chapter Eleven: Distribution of Assets Among the Parties and Types of Debts

Section One: Distribution of Assets

Upon the declaration of a company's bankruptcy, the partners become obligated to repay the debts incurred by the company—particularly in limited liability companies, where a partner's liability for the company's debts is limited to the value of their shares in the company's capital stock. The company's creditors do not have recourse to the partners personally to recover their debts if the company's capital is insufficient to cover such debts. Thus, a shareholder does not acquire the status of a merchant merely by joining the company, nor does the bankruptcy of the company automatically entail the bankruptcy of the shareholder.

Previously, we discussed the types of companies and the extent of partner liability in each type. For example, in a limited partnership, the limited partner is jointly liable with the general partners for the debts and obligations of the company; they bear personal, unlimited liability proportional to their share in the company, similar to the liability regime of partners in a general partnership.

When the debtor's assets are inventoried—whether the debtor is a merchant under the Bankruptcy Law or a company under the Companies Law—a creditors' body is established, represented by an agent and composed of ordinary creditors. This body is intended to ensure equality among creditors and prevent disputes during enforcement on the debtor's assets. Preferential creditors and secured creditors, whose rights are guaranteed by specific assets of the bankrupt debtor, do not participate in the creditors' body unless they waive their guarantees. Accordingly, they are only included in the creditors' body provisionally or as a notification, to preserve their rights as ordinary creditors with respect to the remaining portion of their debts.

Creditors whose debts arise after the issuance of the bankruptcy declaration are excluded from the creditors' body. Ordinary creditors include holders of general privileges. The fact that these rights are secured by such privileges does not affect their inclusion...

This guarantee covers all the debtor's assets, both movable and immovable. Upon the issuance of the bankruptcy declaration order, all individual

lawsuits and procedures are suspended. According to Article 22/3 of the Sudanese Bankruptcy Law:

"If the bankrupt person is imprisoned under the provisions of clause (2) of Article (16) or Article (19), they shall be released, and thereafter no creditor shall have any debt claim against the bankrupt, with respect to any debt that can be proven under the provisions of this law, nor any right against the bankrupt's property or person in relation to the debt except as provided in this law. No creditor may file any lawsuit or take any other legal action or continue any such action without the permission of the bankruptcy court and under the conditions it may impose."

Through the analysis of the legal provisions regulating the distribution of assets of bankrupt companies in Sudan, the researcher has extracted several key points:

1. **Balancing the Interests of Creditors and the Company:** Sudanese law seeks to achieve equality among ordinary creditors by establishing a creditors' committee, thereby preventing unfair competition in enforcing judgments against the company's assets. This aligns with comparative laws that adopt the concept of collective settlement of debts of the bankrupt debtor.
2. **Protection of Partners in Limited Liability Companies:** Granting partners in these companies immunity from personal liability for the company's debts is essential to attract investments and encourage entrepreneurship. However, this may also lead to some company owners exploiting this privilege to evade financial obligations, necessitating strengthened legal oversight mechanisms to prevent misuse of the system.
3. **Deficiency in Addressing Post-Bankruptcy Debts:** Sudanese law has not precisely addressed the status of debts incurred after the bankruptcy declaration, lacking clear mechanisms on how to handle them within the creditors' committee framework.
4. **Absence of Explicit Provisions on the Liability of Executive Directors:** In some legal systems, executive directors bear personal liability for certain company debts in cases of proven negligence or misconduct.
5. The management, which the Sudanese law has not explicitly addressed, may open the door to exploitation of legal loopholes.

   The researcher believes that the issue of distributing the assets of bankrupt companies represents a vital aspect of company and bankruptcy law, where the governing rules aim to balance protecting creditors' rights and enabling companies to operate without imposing undue burdens on the partners. Although Sudanese law adopts many internationally recognized principles in this field, there remain some aspects that require development to ensure fairness and effectiveness in handling bankruptcy cases.

Section Two: Types of Debts

It is clear from the legal text that when the liquidator begins to inventory the company's assets, they start by identifying and classifying debts in preparation for distribution according to priority: preferred debts, privileged debts, and then ordinary debts. After satisfying the debts, any remaining funds are distributed among the partners according to their respective shares, thereby concluding the liquidator's task, as mentioned previously.

Debts that have matured come before other debts since they are due and must be paid; some may be deferred for a legitimate reason. However, in terms of payment priority, preferred debts rank first. These debts confer upon the creditor a special real right that grants precedence in recovering their dues due to a special attribute or by statutory provision. Such preferred rights take precedence over other creditors either during liquidation or by operation of law. For example, under the Sudanese Transactions Law of 1984, Articles (816) and (817) recognize the vendor's privilege over sold immovable property to recover the purchase price, and the partners in the movable property also have a privilege to recover their rights from the immovable property if the distribution occurs in exchange for it. The law requires the registration of this privilege and the registration of land, with priority determined according to the registration date.

The legislator stipulated that: "Amounts due for wages, salaries, compensation, and bonuses of servants, clerks, laborers, and any other hired workers" are included, as well as what is stated in Article (813) regarding a privilege on wages for a maximum period of two years. Also, Article (814) of the Civil Transactions Law provides a privilege to the vendor of movable property for the price, unless it has passed to a bona fide third party.

2. First-Degree Debts:

The law expressly provides for first-degree debts, granting them priority of payment over all other debts due to their utmost preference, even over privileged debts. These debts include:

a. **Government Debts:** Non-commercial debts owed to the government or any government agency or authority empowered by the government to collect funds, including the liquidator's fees and court fees unpaid at the time.

b. **Salaries and Wages:** Provided that the amount does not exceed a specified limit during the six months preceding the date of the liquidation order or decision.

3. Ordinary Debts:

These are ordinary debts that have no statutory privilege, mortgage, or contractual priority.

Third: Classification of Debts by Payment Status

1. **Debts Due for Payment:**
   These are debts whose maturity date has already arrived, meaning they are due and payable at the date of issuance of the liquidation order or decision. Their payment depends on their type, whether privileged or ordinary.
2. **Debts with Deferred Payment:**
   These are debts whose maturity date has not yet arrived at the time the liquidation order is issued. The liquidator must settle these debts with the creditors, even though they do not become due immediately upon liquidation. The dissolution of the company does not extinguish the debt's maturity date, but it is in the interest of all parties that the liquidator negotiate settlement.

It is also permissible to reserve sufficient funds to settle deferred debts once the liquidation process concludes, as it is not necessary for the liquidation to continue until all deferred debts are paid.

3. Contingent (Social) Debts:

These are disputed debts, meaning those under contention—whether before courts or arbitrators—as well as debts that depend on the occurrence of a specific event, such as a promise of reward when the promisor is the company prior to liquidation. Entry into liquidation does not extinguish the promise, and the party who fulfills the conditions of the reward shall be entitled to the full amount, even if unaware of the existence of the reward.

The Sudanese legislator has permitted the proof of such contingent debts. Article (219) of the Companies Act of 2015 provides:

"All debts contingent on a possible event and all claims against the company, whether current, future, contingent, or notional, may be proved, and an estimate of the value of such contingent or otherwise unquantifiable debts or claims shall be made as far as possible."

The researcher holds that the current legal arrangement of debts reflects the principle of payment priority based on the nature of the debts and the rights of creditors. However, this structure may lead to several practical complications, most notably:

1. **Harm to Ordinary Creditors:**
   As all privileged and first-degree debts are settled prior to ordinary debts, this may result in some creditors not recovering their dues or receiving only a minimal portion after the company's assets are exhausted.
2. **Delays in the Liquidation Process Due to Disputed Debts:**
   Social or disputed debts may prolong the liquidation process, particularly in the absence of clear standards for prompt adjudication. This could adversely affect the rights of other creditors and shareholders.
3. **Challenges Related to Deferred Debts:**
   While the liquidator is obligated to settle such debts, the law does not provide a clear mechanism for dealing with them in the event of insufficient liquidity, potentially imposing additional constraints on the liquidation process.

4. Lack of Clear Standards for the Valuation of Contingent (Social) Debts: The law does not provide a precise methodology for assessing disputed or conditionally contingent debts, leaving their valuation to subjective judgment. This may significantly affect the distribution of the company's assets after liquidation.

Recommendations

To address these challenges, the researcher proposes the following:

1. **Allocate a Specific Percentage of Company Assets for Ordinary Debts:**

   The law could be amended to mandate the allocation of a specific percentage (e.g., 10–15%) of the remaining assets—after satisfying privileged and first-degree debts—for the benefit of ordinary creditors. This would help ensure their rights are not completely marginalized.

2. **Introduce a Mechanism to Resolve Contingent Debt Disputes Within a Specific Timeframe:**

   The legislation should include provisions requiring that disputes over contingent (social) debts be resolved within a set period (e.g., six months) to prevent undue delays in the liquidation process.

3. **Require the Liquidator to Establish a Payment Schedule for Deferred Debts:**

   Rather than merely settling deferred debts, the law should oblige the liquidator to prepare a clear repayment schedule based on available assets. This would help balance the fulfillment of creditors' rights with the smooth continuation of the liquidation process.

4. **Introduce Clear Standards for the Valuation of Contingent Debts:**

   The law should explicitly provide objective criteria for the valuation of contingent debts, such as relying on judicial precedents or the expertise of financial professionals. This would reduce delays resulting from imprecise estimations.

Section Three: Priority of Debts in Liquidation Distribution

Once the liquidator collects the company's receivables and entitlements from third parties, the process of discharging the company's debts and obligations begins. According to the provisions of **Article 239 of the Companies Act of 2015**, debts shall be settled in order of priority as follows:

(1) Company debts must be paid in the following order:

(a) *Judicial expenses, the liquidator's fees, and all reasonable expenses incurred in the course of the liquidation process.*

This includes payment of court fees, litigation costs, expenses related to judicial procedures, and liquidation expenses such as legal fees, stamps, petition charges, and other necessary costs for liquidation procedures, as well as the remuneration and compensation of the liquidator (or liquidators, in the event that more than one is appointed).

(2) *Non-commercial government dues,* provided they do not exceed **25%** of the remaining amount after satisfying the expenses outlined in paragraph (a).

Non-commercial debts owed to the government are placed high on the list of priorities. However, due to the proliferation and expansion of federal, state, and local governmental bodies—and the variety of non-commercial government entitlements such as taxes, zakat, fees, and other charges under various designations—holders of privileged debts, particularly banks, often receive only a minimal share in liquidation proceedings. This has contributed to the increase in non-performing debts and a decline in confidence in mortgages as an effective credit security mechanism, undermining the goal of equitable debt settlement.

It is important to note that non-commercial government debts enjoy a statutory lien over the company's assets and take precedence in payment—**except for judicial expenses**, which maintain **absolute priority** over all other claims on the company's estate.

(3) *All debts secured by mortgage (legal or contractual).*

(4) *All debts secured by possessory pledges or registered floating charges.*

(5) *Employee entitlements determined in accordance with labor laws,* provided such claims do not exceed **50,000 Sudanese Pounds.**

First-ranking debts that must be paid out of the total assets of the company collected by the liquidator shall include the following:

1. All amounts due to the lessor for the rent of houses and lands leased to the company for a period not exceeding six months prior to the date of the liquidation resolution, with respect to the houses and lands occupied by the company on that date.
2. All amounts not exceeding, in any individual case, the sum of fifty thousand pounds, due from the company by way of compensation under the provisions of any applicable workers' compensation laws, where liability arose prior to the date of liquidation.
3. Debts that are granted preferential status under the provisions of other laws.
4. Ordinary debts.
5. The rights of the company's members.

These first-ranking debts shall have equal priority and are to be satisfied in full from the company's assets, if possible. If the available assets are insufficient to cover all such debts, they shall be paid on a pro-rata basis according to the value of each debt as a percentage of the total available funds. This is the same principle as the *pari passu* distribution among creditors when there is a shortfall in the debtor's assets.

The costs and expenses of the liquidation are not subject to this distribution among creditors; rather, they must be paid in priority from the total assets of the company. These debts enjoy a special preferential right, even if a creditor has seized and sold the company's movables by way of execution. In such a case, these preferential debts must be paid first out of those movables or the proceeds thereof, in priority over the seizing creditor. However, that creditor retains the same priority rights with respect to any amount paid under a security or lien.

It may be observed that the precedence of first-ranking debts may render secured debts—those guaranteed by pledge or lien—ineffectual, in cases where such first-ranking debts exhaust all of the company's assets. In such cases, the secured debt may be rendered worthless despite the existence of the pledge or lien.

The Researcher's Opinion

An analysis of **Article 239 of the Companies Act of 2015** reveals that the prioritization of debt repayment in the event of company liquidation is based on clear principles intended to ensure fairness among various categories of creditors. However, the researcher identifies several practical issues within this hierarchy, the most prominent of which are:

1. Absolute Priority of Judicial Expenses and Liquidation Costs

Judicial expenses and the liquidator's fees are granted absolute priority in repayment. While this ensures the procedural integrity of liquidation, it may lead to the depletion of liquidation funds before any creditors receive their entitlements—particularly in cases where liquidation costs are high. This hierarchy opens the door for potential abuse by some liquidators or legal consultants, who may inflate expenses to the detriment of other creditors.

2. Disproportionate Allocation to Non-Commercial Government Debts

Although the law imposes a cap of **25%** on the portion of remaining funds allocated to settling **non-commercial government dues** (such as taxes, zakat, and municipal levies), this limit does not necessarily prevent such debts from consuming a substantial share of the distributable assets.

This situation negatively affects the interests of other creditors and may discourage potential investors or lenders from extending secured credit to companies, due to the limited prospects of recovering their funds upon liquidation.

3. Insufficient Legal Protection for Secured Creditors

Despite the fact that debts secured by **mortgages or possessory pledges** are given priority following judicial expenses and government debts, the existence of other senior preferential obligations may render such securities insufficient to fully protect the rights of secured creditors.

As a result, even those holding valid security interests may find themselves inadequately compensated during the distribution of liquidation proceeds.

If first-ranking debts consume all of the company's assets, secured loans become futile, potentially leading to a loss of confidence in the effectiveness of pledges or liens as means of securing debt.

4. Disparity in the Protection of Employees' Rights

The law sets a maximum cap on employee entitlements (50,000 pounds), which may be insufficient in many cases—particularly where a large number of employees are affected by the liquidation.

This limitation may result in unfair treatment of higher-paid workers or those with significant entitlements, thereby undermining their social protection.

5. Lack of Clarity Regarding the Fate of Ordinary Debts

Ordinary debts rank at the bottom of the priority scale, meaning there is a high likelihood that their holders will not receive any payment if the company's assets are depleted beforehand.

This arrangement may harm suppliers and business partners, negatively affecting the overall business environment.

Second: Proposals to Address These Issues

To address these challenges, the researcher proposes the following:

1. Setting a Cap on Liquidation Expenses and Court Costs

Clear legal standards should be established to determine the maximum allowable percentage for court expenses and liquidator fees—such as a limit of 10–15% of total assets. Judicial or administrative oversight may also be imposed on the estimation of such expenses to prevent potential abuse by the liquidator or legal representatives.

2. Reconsidering the Priority of Non-Commercial Government Debts:

Instead of the fixed 25% rate, a variable percentage may be adopted based on the company's total assets, in a manner that does not adversely affect the remaining creditors. Additionally, secured creditors could be granted a parallel priority alongside the government, thereby ensuring a balance between state entitlements and investor rights.

3. Strengthening Legal Protection for Secured Creditors:

The law should be amended to provide that creditors holding security interests—whether possessory or registered—are granted actual priority in recovering their funds before non-commercial government debts. This would restore confidence in the security framework, and a portion of the assets could be directly allocated to the repayment of secured debts prior to the general distribution of remaining assets.

4. Raising or Graduating the Cap on Employees' Entitlements:

The maximum limit for employee entitlements could be increased based on the number of years of service or the nature of the position, allowing employees with greater financial obligations to receive enhanced protection. A compensation fund could also be established to support workers adversely affected by corporate liquidation, thereby providing broader social protection.

5. Introducing a Fair Mechanism for the Distribution of Unsecured Debts:

A fixed percentage of the remaining assets (e.g., 10–20%) could be allocated to the repayment of unsecured debts, ensuring that all creditors receive at least a partial recovery instead of being entirely excluded. In the event of a surplus after settling preferential and secured debts, such surplus should be distributed equitably among the remaining creditors in proportion to their respective claims.

6. Based on the foregoing, the researcher has concluded that the current hierarchy of debt repayment in corporate liquidation suffers from several deficiencies that may hinder the realization of fairness among creditors—particularly due to inadequate protection for secured and unsecured debts. Therefore, amending the law to ensure a more balanced distribution of debts would contribute to enhancing confidence in the financial system and ensuring justice for all concerned parties.

Section four: Distribution Among Partners

Upon the completion of liquidation proceedings and the determination of the net assets of the company, these assets shall be divided among the partners either amicably or by a court decision. The distribution shall be carried out in accordance with the rules agreed upon by the partners in the company's memorandum of association or its articles of incorporation. In the absence of such agreed-upon rules, the provisions of the Companies Act or the Civil Code shall apply.

Consequently, the remaining assets shall be considered jointly owned property (undivided ownership) among the partners. The distribution may be carried out by the liquidator himself or by another person agreed upon by the partners, whether from among them or otherwise.

If the party responsible for distributing the company's assets among the partners after liquidation has not been designated, the matter shall be left to the partners. If the memorandum of association specifies who is to undertake the distribution, that designation shall be followed. Generally, this task is entrusted to the liquidator, as distribution is a natural extension of the liquidation process.

If the memorandum of association contains no such provision, the matter is left to the discretion of the partners, who may conduct the distribution themselves, appoint one or more partners, or delegate the task to the liquidator. In the event that the partners fail to reach an agreement, the court shall undertake the distribution at the request of one of the partners or one of the company's creditors, in order to enforce the creditor's right against the debtor partner's share.

Once the creditors have received their entitlements, the net remaining assets of the company shall be distributed among the partners, with each partner receiving a share of these assets proportionate to their share in the company.

The method of distributing the jointly owned funds among the partners shall involve allocating to each partner a portion equivalent to the value of their capital contribution. If any assets remain thereafter, such residual amount shall be treated as profits and distributed in accordance with the agreed-upon profit-sharing ratio. Conversely, if the company's assets are insufficient to cover the partners' capital contributions, the resulting shortfall shall be treated as a loss and allocated among the partners according to the agreed loss-sharing ratio.

This process can be detailed as follows:

1. **Distribution of the equivalent value of capital shares to the partners:**

Partner Rights and Distribution of Company Assets Upon Liquidation

1. Return of Partner Contributions

The liquidator shall begin by allocating to each partner, from the net assets of the company, an amount equivalent to the value of the capital contribution that partner had provided. If the value of each partner's share is specified in the company's articles of association, then the liquidator must assign to each partner an amount equal to that stated value.

However, where the values of the partners' contributions are **not specified** in the articles of association, the liquidator must **assess** the value of such contributions at the time they were delivered to the company. This evaluation must be based on the company's **documents, records, and books**, and may further require the opinion of **experts** or the testimony of **witnesses**, where necessary. If a partner disputes the value assigned to their share, they are entitled to **seek judicial recourse**.

A partner whose sole contribution to the company was **personal labor or service** shall **not participate** in the division of the remaining assets of the company. This is because **contributions of labor do not form part of the company's capital**. Such a partner merely regains their freedom to work elsewhere.

Likewise, a partner who contributed **usufruct rights** or provided **assets for temporary use** shall not partake in the division of the remaining company assets. Instead, that partner has the right to **recover** the usufruct or the contributed asset. If the asset has perished, then the partner is entitled to be compensated from the net assets of the company with the **value of the asset at the time of its loss**, before any distribution occurs.

2. Distribution of Profits Among Partners

Once each partner has been allocated the value of their respective contribution, any remaining net assets shall be treated as **company profits**, to be distributed among the partners according to the **profit-sharing ratio** stipulated in the partnership agreement.

If the company contract does **not specify** a profit-sharing ratio, profits shall be distributed in **proportion to each partner's contribution** to the company's capital. Accordingly, the remaining assets shall be divided among the partners based on the value of their capital shares.

3. Distribution of Losses Among Partners

If the net assets of the company are insufficient to cover the partners' shares, the shortfall in those shares shall be considered losses and distributed among the partners in the same proportion as losses are allocated. If a partner benefits from a certain percentage, the distribution shall be according to each partner's proportionate share in the capital.

From the foregoing, the researcher concludes that once each partner's share of the net assets and property of the company is determined, and the value of their capital contribution is allocated, their share of profits (if any) shall be added, or their share of losses (if any) shall be deducted. The remaining net assets of the company shall constitute joint ownership among the partners and shall be divided according to each partner's share in the capital, and in accordance with the company's articles of association and bylaws, applying the legal rules related to the partition of jointly owned property.

If the net assets of the company are converted into cash, each partner's share shall correspond to their proportion in the company's capital. If the partner's contribution was made in cash, they shall receive the same amount; if the contribution was made in kind and has a financial value specified in the founding contract, they shall receive an equivalent amount. Otherwise, the value of the contribution shall be appraised at the time it was made.

The net assets of the company may consist of specific tangible assets, whether movable or immovable, which may not be divisible without causing harm or significant diminution in value. In such cases, partners may sell their shares among themselves or request the court to order the sale. Until then, these assets remain held jointly by the partners. The dissolution of this joint ownership shall be governed by the applicable rules relating to the partition of jointly owned property.

Accordingly, if any partner is absent, legally incapacitated, or partially incapacitated, consensual division shall not be valid, and division must proceed through judicial means. In judicial partition, the absent or incapacitated partner shall be represented by a guardian or custodian. It is not permissible to revoke the division of assets among the partners once finalized, but all partners may, by mutual consent, rescind the division and restore the company's assets to joint ownership.

As it was prior to the distribution, if the division is consensual and one of the partners suffers from gross unfairness (ghubn fāḥish), he may request the court to annul the distribution and reorder the division of assets among the partners in an equitable manner.

The researcher observes that the order of priorities in distribution reflects legal rationality; however, it faces several practical challenges, most notably:

1. **Weakening of Credit Guarantees:** Due to the consumption of liquidation funds by preferential debts, secured debts—whether by mortgage or privilege—often become ineffective in many cases.
2. **Dominance of Government Debts in Distribution:** Government debts take precedence with a rate that may adversely affect the ability of banks and commercial lenders to recover their rights, thereby reducing the effectiveness of credit guarantees and undermining confidence in the credit market.
3. **Lack of Clarity in Distribution Procedures in Case of Disputes:** The matter is often left to the discretion of the parties or the court, which may lead to delays and complications in the division process.

Accordingly, the researcher recommends the following:

- **Reconsideration of the Priority Order** to ensure the protection of commercial creditors' rights, especially banks, in a more balanced manner without prejudice to the liquidator's rights or judicial expenses.

1. **Setting a Flexible Percentage for Non-Commercial Government Debts:** Rather than a fixed rate (25%), this percentage should vary depending on the company's condition, with a maximum cap to protect the rights of other creditors.
2. **Establishing a Swift Arbitration Mechanism:** This mechanism aims to resolve disputes regarding distribution among partners, avoiding recourse to courts, thereby reducing delays in concluding the liquidation.

3. **Enhancing Guarantees for Secured Debts:** Through legal mechanisms that ensure the value of the security is preserved during liquidation, thus increasing creditors' confidence in commercial transactions.

Chapter Twelve: Closure of Liquidation, Submission of the Final Account, Dissolution of the Company, and Removal from the Commercial Register

Section One: Preliminary Acts of Liquidation

If the court appoints an official liquidator or issues an order for liquidation, the liquidator shall be obligated to perform the necessary acts to liquidate the company. However, the liquidator shall not initiate any new management activities unless such actions are necessary to complete a prior undertaking. For example, if the company owns land that it sold prior to dissolution, and after dissolution a neighboring owner claims the right of pre-emption (shufa'a) over the land, the liquidator, as the company's representative, shall participate in the pre-emption proceedings.

The liquidator's primary duty is to prepare a report on the affairs of the company in the prescribed manner and submit it to the court, supported by an oath declaration, unless the court orders otherwise. This report must include detailed information regarding the company's assets, debts, liabilities, the names and domiciles of the creditors, the guarantees held by each creditor, the dates on which such guarantees were granted, and any other information that the court deems necessary or requests, or which the official liquidator may request as the case requires.

The report shall be submitted to the chairman of the board or the general manager, and in their absence, to any two members of the board or any persons designated by the official liquidator, taking into account the court's order. These individuals may include members of the board, company employees, former board members or employees, persons who participated in the company's establishment at any time within one year prior to the specified date, or persons who have served the company during the aforementioned year, provided the court deems them capable of providing the required information.

The report must be submitted within fifteen days from the specified date, or within any extended period determined by the official liquidator or the court for special reasons.

Article (216/2) provides that:

"If the liquidation of the company extends beyond one year, the liquidator shall convene a general meeting of the company at the end of the first year of liquidation and at the end of each subsequent year, or whenever possible."

(3) Any person who fails to comply with the provisions of this article without a valid excuse shall be deemed to have committed a violation of this article and shall be subject to penalties pursuant to the provisions of Article 257.

(4) Any person responsible for preparing the report and the sworn statement required under the provisions of this article, or any person assisting in their preparation, may request from the official liquidator reimbursement of the expenses and costs incurred in preparing the report and sworn statement, provided that the official liquidator considers such expenses reasonable. The official liquidator shall pay these amounts from the company's assets. The assessment of these expenses shall be subject to review before the liquidation court within a period not exceeding fifteen days.

(5) Any person claiming to be a creditor of the company or otherwise liable to pay may inspect the report submitted pursuant to the provisions of this article at all reasonable times, either personally or through an agent, upon payment of the prescribed fees. Such person may also obtain an official copy of the report.

(6) For the purposes of this article, the phrase "specified date" means the date of appointment of the official provisional liquidator if such appointment has been made; otherwise, it means the date of the liquidation order.

Pursuant to this article, the commencement of liquidation requires the submission of this initial report to the court, detailing the estimated authorized capital, subscribed capital, paid-up capital, the estimated value of the assets and liabilities, and the reasons leading to the liquidation. The report must include an investigation into the use of the company's funds and whether it is advisable to conduct further investigations concerning any matters related to the company's formation or management. The liquidator shall express an opinion on whether there was any fraud in the company's formation or whether any member of the board of directors or any other employee committed an act constituting fraud in the establishment of the company. The report should also include any other matters the liquidator deems important for the court's consideration in exercising its powers.

The researcher observes that the current procedures for company liquidation, despite being legally regulated, suffer from certain shortcomings that may affect the efficiency and speed of the liquidation process. This negatively impacts the rights of the concerned parties, especially the creditors. Among the most prominent challenges is the lengthy period required to prepare the liquidator's initial report, which causes a direct delay in the liquidation process. Additionally, there is an absence of an effective supervisory mechanism to ensure the accuracy and transparency of the information contained in the report. Moreover, limiting creditors' protection to merely reviewing the report—without providing them with legal mechanisms to intervene directly upon discovering any violations or negligence—may harm their financial rights.

Based on the foregoing, the researcher proposes the following amendments to the procedures applied in company liquidation:

1. **Reducing the timeframe granted to the liquidator to submit the initial report from fifteen (15) days to ten (10) days**, to expedite the liquidation process and reduce waiting periods that could worsen the financial condition of the debtor company.
2. **Establishing an independent supervisory committee composed of financial and legal experts** to review the liquidator's report prior to submission to the court, ensuring data accuracy and minimizing any manipulation or concealment of information that may affect procedural fairness.
3. **Enhancing the role of creditors in oversight by granting them the right to object to the contents of the report and request additional reviews where there is suspicion of financial or administrative irregularities**, along with the establishment of legal mechanisms allowing them to challenge the liquidator's decisions before the competent court.

These amendments would contribute to improving the efficiency of the liquidation process, protecting the rights of all concerned parties, and achieving a higher level of transparency and justice in managing the assets of companies undergoing liquidation.

Section Two: Submission of the Final Account and Convening the Partners

The closure of the liquidation signifies the completion of the liquidator's duties and marks the end of the company's legal personality after all liquidation tasks have been accomplished. This occurs once the liquidator submits the final accounts related to the liquidation process to the company's General Assembly, which then approves these final accounts, thereby officially closing the liquidation.

Subsection One: Submission of the Final Account

The liquidator must prepare the final liquidation account in accordance with the general principles of accounting and financial control, covering all revenues and expenses. This includes all cash received by the liquidator and all amounts disbursed to cover expenses. The liquidator shall then invite the partners at the conclusion of the liquidation to review the final account, grant discharge to the liquidator, conclude his duties, and approve his accounts within a specified timeframe, whether this period is determined by the partners or by the court that ordered the liquidation.

All partners have the right to inspect the liquidator's accounts prior to the date of the General Assembly meeting for the liquidation period. During the assembly, the partners are required to examine the liquidation and approve the final accounts. If the accounts are rejected, the liquidation cannot remain open indefinitely. Accordingly, the liquidator or any interested party may petition the competent court to order the closure of the liquidation. The account shall include all actions undertaken by the liquidator in liquidating the company, a statement of debts that have been recovered or settled, and the current net assets of the company available for distribution to the partners in preparation for division among them. If the balance is negative (i.e., a deficit), it defines the extent of the company's loss, which the partners may be required to bear according to the type of company.

Subsection Two: Convening the Company Assembly

Article (217) of the Sudanese Companies Act of 2015 provides for the final general meeting for the dissolution of the company, the consideration of the final account, the discharge of the liquidator's management, and the termination of his duties, in order to...

The liquidation shall be closed within the period specified for it, whether this period was determined by the partners or by the court that issued the liquidation order. The liquidator is obligated to convene the general assembly of the company. In the event that the general assembly refuses to approve the accounts, the liquidation process shall not remain unresolved indefinitely. The liquidator then has the right to file a petition to terminate the liquidation before the competent court, which shall proceed to close the liquidation. In such a case, the court acts in place of the partners to close the liquidation. This authority is granted to prevent undue prolongation of the liquidation without legitimate cause. The court also has the right to grant discharge (release from liability) to the liquidator and to relieve him from his mandate to liquidate the company.

If the court does not approve the liquidator's accounts, it cannot issue a judgment closing the liquidation. Instead, it shall return the accounts to the liquidator for revision and correction. The liquidator must then reorganize the final accounts in light of the court's observations.

Article (217) provides as follows:

1. bThe liquidator, upon the full completion of the company's liquidation activities, shall prepare an account showing the manner in which the liquidation was conducted and how the company's assets were disposed of. He must then call for a general meeting of the company to present the accounts and provide clarifications.
2. The notice for the meeting shall be made by way of an announcement specifying the time, place, and purpose of the meeting. Such announcement must be published at least one month prior to the meeting date and in the manner prescribed by this law.
3. The liquidator must submit to the registrar, within one week after the meeting, a full report on the meeting and its date, accompanied by a copy of the approved account statement referred to in paragraph (1). Failure to comply with this obligation constitutes a violation of this article and exposes the liquidator to penalties pursuant to Article (267).
4. Upon receiving the report, the registrar shall immediately register it. The company shall be considered dissolved after three months from the date of registration of the report. However, the court may, upon the request of the liquidator or any other person who demonstrates to the court a legitimate interest in the matter, issue an order postponing the effective date of dissolution to a date it deems appropriate.

(5) Any person who requested a stay from the court and obtained an order to that effect must, within twenty-one days from the date of issuance of the stay order, deposit a certified copy thereof with the Registrar. Failure to comply shall constitute a violation of this article, subjecting the offender to penalties pursuant to the provisions of Article 257.

According to Article (175/2) of the Companies Act of 2015, which provides: *"The official liquidator may, if deemed appropriate, prepare one or more additional reports stating..."*

The researcher considers that the submission of the final account and the calling of the partners to approve the liquidation represent a critical phase in terminating the company's legal personality. However, this phase faces legal and procedural challenges that affect the efficiency and transparency of the liquidation process. Among the most prominent challenges is the extended duration required for the approval of the final accounts, which may delay the closure of the liquidation and leave the company's obligations unresolved for prolonged periods. Additionally, the absence of a clear mechanism obligating the liquidator to submit detailed periodic reports on the liquidation process to the competent authorities may adversely affect the rights of the partners and creditors. This necessitates the development of a more stringent legal framework to ensure transparency and expedite these procedures.

Based on the foregoing, the researcher proposes amendments to the procedures regulating the submission of the final account and the calling of partners, as follows:

1. Setting a shorter deadline for preparing the final account, not exceeding thirty (30) days from the completion of the liquidation procedures, with clear sanctions imposed on the liquidator in case of unjustified delay.
2. Requiring the liquidator to submit periodic reports during the liquidation process, including detailed information on the financial and administrative operations carried out, to ensure procedural transparency and grant partners and creditors the opportunity to object or intervene if necessary.
3. Enhancing the role of the competent court in supervising the closure of the liquidation through a mandatory legal review mechanism of the final account, allowing partners and creditors to challenge any violations or irregularities prior to final approval.
4. **Developing the Mechanism for Convening the General Assembly** It is proposed that the final meeting be announced within a period of not less than fifteen (15) days and not exceeding thirty (30) days, with the imposition of legal penalties on the liquidator in case of non-compliance with the provisions of Article (217) of the Companies Law of 2015.
5. These amendments would accelerate the liquidation procedures, enhance the efficiency of legal oversight, and ensure the protection of the rights of all concerned parties. This would achieve a balance between the interests

of partners and creditors and reduce potential disputes related to the closure of the liquidation.

Section Three: Prescription of the Right of Recourse Against Partners and the Dissolution and Deletion of the Company from the Register

First Subsection: Recourse Claims Against Partners

The legislator has paid special attention to reducing the statute of limitations for commercial obligations due to merchants' need for liquidity and their keenness to collect debts and pursue debtors in order to obtain their funds. Furthermore, the legislator aims to place a timely limit on disputes arising from such obligations in a manner compatible with the nature of commercial transactions, which require speed in their conclusion and execution.

Therefore, most company laws worldwide stipulate a minimum period of ten years as the statute of limitations for commercial obligations in recourse claims against partners for debts arising from the company's operations after its dissolution and liquidation. The rationale behind shortening the limitation period for these debts and promptly settling the arising rights is to avoid prolonged durations that could cause significant harm to merchants and the overall economy and disrupt commercial activity and stability.

A company may dissolve and be liquidated, then after the liquidation and distribution of its net assets among partners, a creditor may claim payment of a debt due to the extinguishment of the company's legal personality upon completion of liquidation. The creditor has no recourse other than to demand payment from the partners, from the funds they received from the division of the company's assets or from their own assets if they are jointly liable partners, given their responsibility for the company's debts with all their personal assets. It is unjust for partners to be subjected to claims for their personal funds based on the debts of a dissolved company.

Given the long duration of limitation periods, this is intended to address economic considerations and to ensure that partners are protected from late or unexpected claims. It also encourages the establishment of companies without hesitation or fear of anticipated consequences. This limitation period benefits all types of companies, except for the **partnership in commendam (shirka al-muḥāṣa)**, which—as previously mentioned—exists only among the partners themselves and has no legal personality vis-à-vis third parties. The company's business is conducted by one of the partners in his own name according to the terms agreed upon in the partnership contract. Creditors of the company deal solely with the partner with whom they have contractual relations and, accordingly, the limitation of commercial or civil obligations applies to that partner's debt depending on whether the obligation is commercial or civil.

This limitation is only effective upon the dissolution of the company, whether such dissolution occurs by operation of law, by agreement of the partners, or by court order. The dissolution may pertain to all partners or to a specific partner, such as when a partner withdraws or is expelled by court order. In such cases, the limitation period applies to claims against the partner in respect of whom the company has dissolved. The limitation period similarly applies in cases of relative annulment that leave behind a de facto company. However, if the annulment is absolute, partners cannot benefit from the shortened limitation period, as its effect extends retroactively to the company's past and future.

Subsection Two: Dissolution of the Company

Article 200(1) of the Sudanese Companies Act of 2015 provides that: *"The court shall issue an order dissolving the company once the liquidation process is completed, and the company shall be deemed dissolved from the date of issuance of this order."*

The official liquidator is required to file the dissolution order with the Registrar within fifteen (15) days of its issuance. The Registrar must then file this order in the company's records. Failure by the official liquidator to comply constitutes a violation subject to penalties, pursuant to Article 200(2), which states: *"The official liquidator shall file the dissolution order with the Registrar within fifteen days from the date of issuance. The Registrar must file this order in the company's file. Failure by the official liquidator to comply shall be considered a violation of this article and render him subject to penalties in accordance with Article 257."*

Upon approval of the final accounts, the liquidation is closed and the liquidator's mandate comes to an end.

The liquidator shall cause the company to cease to exist as a legal entity entirely. Furthermore, the liquidator must request the cancellation of the company's registration in the commercial register within one month from the date of completion of the liquidation. Otherwise, the judge supervising the commercial register shall have the authority to initiate the cancellation of the registration ex officio.

Section Three: Publication of the Closure

After the liquidation is completed and the final accounts are submitted, the liquidator must deposit the company's books, papers, and documents with the court, unless the majority of the partners designate a person to receive them. These documents must remain preserved at a specified location from the date of deposit.

Article (184) provides that:

"The official liquidator of the company may maintain properly organized books in which all entries, minutes of meetings, and other decided matters are recorded, provided that the liquidator may seek assistance from auditors as appropriate, and submit a copy of these records to the court every six months. Any creditor or person liable to pay may inspect these books personally or through an agent, subject to the court's supervision."

Interested parties, their heirs, successors in rights, or other liquidators have the right to review and audit these documents.

Article (98) of the Companies Law of 2015 states:

"Subject to the provisions of the Market Law, the company may publish an announcement in daily newspapers regarding the closure of its register for a period or periods not exceeding thirty days in total within a year."

Section Four: Deregistration of the Company

The deregistration of a defunct company from the commercial register is an administrative procedure carried out by the commercial registrar to terminate the company's legal existence by removing its name from the companies' register. The Companies Law provides for two circumstances under which the company may be deregistered:

- If the company intended to be deregistered is not in liquidation.
- **If the Company to be Deleted is in Liquidation**
- **First Case: If the Company to be Deleted is Not in Liquidation**

The striking off of a company constitutes one of the general grounds for the dissolution of companies due to cessation of its activity for a specified period, or due to its adoption of a trade name that is registered under another company or so closely resembles the name of another company as to cause confusion or fraud. If the company is not in liquidation and the Registrar of Companies has reasonable grounds to believe that the company is not carrying on business or is not conducting any activity, the Registrar must send a registered letter to the company inquiring about the truth of this matter.

If no reply is received within one month of sending the letter, the Registrar, upon the expiry of that month, must send the company a second registered letter within twenty-four days by registered mail referring to the previous letter and stating that no response has been received. The second letter must warn the company that if no reply is received within one month from the date of the second letter, the Registrar intends to publish a notice in the Official Gazette indicating his intention to delete the company from the register.

Pursuant to the Companies Act of 2015, the Registrar is authorized to delete a company from the register if there is reasonable cause to believe that the company is no longer conducting its business, provided that the company has been contacted by a registered letter enquiring about its activity status. Should the company fail to reply within one month of the registered letter, the Registrar must send a second registered letter within three months referring to the first letter and indicating that no response was received. This second letter constitutes a warning that if no reply is received within one month from its date, a notice will be published in the Official Gazette and daily newspapers of wide circulation indicating the intention to delete the company's name from the register.

If no response is received within one month of sending the second letter, the Registrar may publish the notice in the Official Gazette and in the economic page of a widely circulated daily newspaper for three consecutive days. The Registrar must also send a notice by mail to the company informing it that its name will be deleted from the register after the expiry of three months from the date of publication unless a valid reason to the contrary is presented.

- The company shall be deleted based on this notice. However, if the company, any of its members, creditors, or any other interested party believes within two years from the date of deletion that they have been harmed by the deletion of the company's name from the register, the court may, upon request by the company, the member, creditor, or interested party, take appropriate measures.

- The court may order the company to resume its activities or, if justice so requires for other reasons, order the reinstatement of its name in the register. Upon issuance of such an order, the company shall be deemed to still exist and continue as if its name had never been removed from the register.
- If the registrar does not receive a response from the company stating that it has ceased operations or is no longer conducting its activities, or if the registrar does not receive a response to its second notice within one month of its dispatch, the registrar may publish an announcement in the Official Gazette and send the company a notification by mail indicating that its name will be removed from the register upon the expiration of three months from the date of the announcement, unless a valid reason to the contrary is presented. Based on this announcement, the company shall be dissolved and its legal existence shall terminate.
- The registrar shall send notices and announcements to the company at its registered address. If no registered address exists, the registrar shall send the correspondence to the address of one of the board members, directors, or any of its officers. If none of these individuals have a known address registered with the registrar, the correspondence shall be sent to each person who signed the articles of incorporation at the address listed therein.

- **Second: Removal of the Company from the Register in the Event of Liquidation**
- If the registrar has reasonable cause to believe that a company is no longer conducting its activities, he must send a letter by mail or by any other means to inquire about the actual status of the company. Upon expiration of the period specified in the notice, the registrar may remove the company from the register and publish a notice to that effect in the Official Gazette. Upon publication of this notice, the company shall be dissolved, unless the company submits a valid reason before the expiration of the period justifying the retention of its name.
- The removal of the company's name from the register does not affect the liability of the board members, and such liability may be enforced as if the company had not been dissolved. The legislator authorizes the registrar to reinstate the company's name in the register within two years if such removal causes harm to any member or creditor, or if justice requires its reinstatement. It is provided that:
- *"If the company or any of its members or any creditor believes they are harmed by the removal from the register, the court may, upon the request*

of the company, the member, or the creditor, order the reinstatement of the company's name in the register."

- If the court is satisfied that the company was conducting its business or activities at the time its name was removed from the register, or that justice requires otherwise for any reason, it may order the re-insertion of the company's name into the register. Upon issuance of such order, the company is deemed to have continued to exist and remain in existence as if its name had never been removed from the register. The court may also issue any other orders or rulings it deems just to restore the company and all other affected parties, as far as possible, to the position they occupied prior to the removal of the company's name from the register. By reinstating the company's name in the register, the company retroactively regains its legal existence, as if it had been continuously registered, even during the period its name was omitted from the register.
- The researcher notes that the legislator has set specific controls regarding the deletion of a foreign company's branch from the register. This occurs when the foreign entity declares its desire to terminate its operations in Sudan and must notify the Commercial Registrar in writing, confirming the fulfillment of all its obligations, supported by a notarized declaration. The Registrar is then required to publish this announcement in the economic section of two widely circulated daily newspapers for three consecutive days at the company's expense. After a one-month period from the date of publication, the Registrar shall delete the company's name from the register unless there is a claim from any interested party or any official authority.
- From the foregoing, the researcher concludes that the statute of limitations for claims for recourse against partners following the dissolution and liquidation of the company is a significant matter that modern legislations endeavor to regulate in a manner that preserves the rights of all parties and ensures the stability of commercial activity. The legislator has focused on shortening the limitation period for commercial claims purely for economic purposes, recognizing that prompt resolution of commercial disputes is essential to guarantee the stability of business operations and to protect partners and creditors from late claims that might affect economic efficiency.
- Legislation in various countries has emphasized the necessity of establishing a limitation period of no less than ten years for such claims, aiming to balance the protection of creditors' rights with the preservation of commercial stability. Nevertheless, the issue of the company's

dissolution and liquidation, as well as the deletion of its name from the register, remains a complex and delicate matter...

The commercial registry process poses a challenge to the partners, particularly in cases where creditors claim their rights after the prescribed period has elapsed.

From the analysis of these points, it can be concluded that a short and definite limitation period significantly contributes to achieving justice among the partners and limits legal complexities that may arise after the dissolution of the company. Furthermore, the attention given to the procedures for removing the company from the commercial register reflects the legislator's interest in regulating this aspect in a manner that enhances the stability of commercial activities.

Accordingly, the researcher recommends the following:

1. **Enhancing Flexibility of the Legal Limitation Period:** It is recommended to reconsider the determination of the limitation period for recourse claims against partners, especially in cases of companies that may experience delays in liquidation or in receiving due funds. Consideration may be given to reducing this period to between five and ten years, thereby providing affected parties sufficient opportunity to settle their claims without disrupting the economic cycle.
2. **Reconsideration of Grounds for Company Nullity:** It is essential to establish clear and specific mechanisms for dealing with companies declared null, particularly in cases of relative or conditional nullity. Specific criteria should be set to allow for the rapid restructuring or annulment of nullity to avoid unjust impacts on commercial operations.
3. **Focus on a Rapid Deregistration Mechanism:** It is recommended to activate a faster and more flexible procedure for removing companies that have ceased their operations from the commercial register, ensuring that companies are not left registered after the expiration of the liquidation period or prolonged inactivity, which could cause legal or economic confusion.
4. **Clear Legal Procedures for Challenging Deregistration:** There must be clear legal procedures enabling creditors or partners to challenge the deregistration and request the reinstatement of the company in the commercial register.
5. **Regulating Companies with Fragile Legal Personality:** It is recommended to apply specific laws or regulations that govern companies with fragile legal personality (such as joint ventures) that do not have an

independent legal personality separate from their partners. This may require specifying a statute of limitations period or determining the types of claims that can be filed against partners in case of liquidation of these companies. Through these proposals, a legal balance can be achieved that ensures the stability of companies on one hand and protects the rights of creditors and partners on the other, thereby contributing to facilitating the business environment in the country.

Conclusion:

Praise be to Allah, by whose grace good deeds are completed. Praise be to Allah who taught us what we did not know and made our knowledge a means of goodness and benefit. I ask Allah Almighty to make this research in the balance of our good deeds and to guide us all to what is good for business interests.

At the end of this study, I ask Allah to make it a continuing charity and that it has contributed to shedding light on the legal issues facing bankruptcy and company laws in Sudan. The study attempted to provide a critical analysis of these laws, assessing their suitability for the economic and commercial reality, revealing shortcomings affecting the rights of creditors and bankrupts, and addressing necessary reforms to ensure a stable and fair investment environment.

First: Results:

The research reached a set of important conclusions confirming the need for fundamental amendments to Sudanese legislation related to bankruptcy and companies. The most prominent of these results are as follows:

1. The Sudanese Companies Law of 1925 was not compatible with Islamic Sharia, allowing the introduction of usurious interest on shares and bonds.
2. The Sudanese Companies Law did not reflect Sudan's economic and social needs, nor did it consider the Islamic nature of the economy or ensure fair mechanisms for protecting investors and creditors.
3. The law focused on protecting large companies and major shareholders without providing sufficient guarantees for small investors, leading to widespread exploitation.
4. Although the new law attempted to address some issues, it did not resolve conflicts in judicial rulings regarding shareholders' rights to file company liquidation claims.
5. The new law lacks adequate safeguards to prevent some companies from abusing the bankruptcy system to evade financial responsibilities.
6. There are no clear mechanisms to facilitate dispute settlement between shareholders and creditors, resulting in ongoing ambiguity in some rulings.
7. The 1929 Companies Law did not include provisions preventing bankrupt individuals from leaving Sudan before settling their financial obligations, allowing some businessmen to evade responsibility after bankruptcy declaration.
8. The absence of explicit provisions to distinguish bankruptcy caused by force majeure from fraudulent bankruptcy led to unclear legal standards in differentiating these cases.
9. These gaps have created an unstable legal environment, making it difficult for creditors to recover their rights after company bankruptcy declarations.
10. Current bankruptcy procedures are slow and bureaucratically complex, negatively impacting market stability and reducing investor confidence in the Sudanese legal system.
11. The lack of flexible legal mechanisms for restructuring troubled companies reduces opportunities to rescue companies facing temporary financial difficulties.
12. The unclear legal procedures complicate the uniform application of laws, resulting in inconsistent judicial rulings.

13. Confusing these two concepts causes legal uncertainty, adversely affecting the rights of creditors and bankrupt companies, making it difficult to define legal responsibilities in bankruptcy cases.

Second: Recommendations:

1. The study recommends that the legislature amend the Sudanese Bankruptcy Law of 1929 to keep pace with modern developments and reflect contemporary economic and legal changes
2. The concept of "preventive restructuring" should be introduced, allowing distressed companies a chance to repair their financial situation before complete bankruptcy.
3. Cases of fraudulent bankruptcy should be clearly defined, and penalties tightened on companies exploiting legal loopholes to evade financial obligations, ensuring justice and protecting creditors' rights.
4. Legal provisions should be introduced to prevent bankrupt individuals from leaving Sudan before settling their financial obligations, preventing abuse of the system to evade debts.
5. A national registry for bankrupts should be established, including names of individuals and companies declared bankrupt, enhancing transparency and allowing careful monitoring.
6. Simplified legal mechanisms should be developed to allow rapid and efficient completion of bankruptcy procedures, contributing to market stability and protecting creditors' rights.
7. Adoption of a bankruptcy-protective settlement model allowing distressed companies to reschedule debts through agreements with creditors, helping avoid complete bankruptcy and enabling company rehabilitation.
8. Legal oversight should be strengthened to prevent misuse of bankruptcy by establishing a specialized regulatory authority to monitor bankruptcy cases and ensure no manipulation or unlawful exploitation.
9. The state should impose strict supervision over asset liquidation and direct available funds in liquidation to debt settlement, preventing asset flight before bankruptcy declaration.
10. Clear laws defining bankruptcy-related legal concepts precisely should be adopted to avoid ambiguity or legal confusion that may lead to prolonged legal disputes.
11. The law should include mechanisms to guarantee creditors' recovery of their rights while providing bankrupt individuals with opportunities to reintegrate economically after settling obligations.
12. Policies for the financial rehabilitation of bankrupts should be adopted, such as granting them opportunities to restart after debt settlement, thus positively reintegrating them into economic activities.

References and Sources:

References:

- The Holy Quran and Hadith.

A. Arabic Language Dictionaries:

1. Ibn Manzur, Abu Al-Fadl Jamal Al-Din Muhammad Ibn Makram Ibn Manzur Al-Afriqi, *Lisan Al-Arab*, Dar Sadir, Beirut, 6th Edition, 1417 AH / 1997 CE.
2. Al-Razi, Muhammad Ibn Abi Bakr Ibn Abd Al-Qadir Al-Razi, *Mukhtar Al-Sihah*, Maktabat Al-Ma'arif, Beirut, 1998 CE.

B. Jurisprudence Books:

1. *Fiqh According to the Four Schools* (Abdul Rahman Al-Jaziri).
2. Ibn Juzayy, Muhammad Ahmad Ibn Juzayy Al-Qurbati, Maliki, *Qawanin Al-Ahkam Al-Shar'iyya wa Masa'il Al-Furu' Al-Fiqhiyya*, Dar Al-Ilm Lil-Malayin, Beirut.
3. Al-Dardiri, Ahmad Al-Dardiri, *Al-Sharh Al-Saghir*, Maktub Ma' Bighlat Al-Salik, Dar Al-Kutub Al-Ilmiyya, Beirut.
4. Al-Shanqeeti, Muhammad Al-Shaybani Ibn Muhammad Ibn Ahmad Al-Shanqeeti, *Tabyin Al-Masalik Sharh Tadrib Al-Masalik*, Dar Al-Arab Al-Islami, Beirut, 2nd Edition, 1995 CE.
5. Al-Qarafi, Shihab Al-Din Ahmad Ibn Idris Al-Qarafi, *Al-Dhakira*, Dar Al-Gharb Al-Islami, Beirut, 1st Edition, 1994 CE.
6. Al-Sawi, Ahmad, *Bighlat Al-Salik Li-Aqrab Al-Masalik*, Dar Al-Kutub Al-Ilmiyya, 1st Edition, 1415 AH / 1995 CE.

C. Shafi'i Jurisprudence:

1. Al-Mawardi, Abu Al-Hasan Ali Ibn Muhammad Ibn Habib Al-Basri Al-Baghdadi Al-Mawardi, *Al-Ahkam Al-Sultaniyya*, 1st Edition, 1327 AH / 1990 CE.
2. Al-Muhalli, Jalal Al-Din Muhammad Ibn Ahmad Al-Muhalli, *Sharh Jalal Al-Din Al-Muhalli 'Ala Minhaj Al-Talibin*, Dar Al-Fikr, Beirut.

3. Al-Jamal, Sulayman Ibn Omar Ibn Mansour Al-Masri Al-Shafi'i Al-Ma'ruf Bil-Jamal, *Hashiyat Al-Jamal 'Ala Minhaj Al-Tullab*, Dar Al-Kutub Al-Ilmiyya, Beirut, 1st Edition, 1417 AH / 1996 CE.
4. Ibn Abi Al-Damm, Shihab Al-Din Abu Ishaq Ibrahim Ibn Abdullah Al-Hamdani Al-Hamawi, *Adab Al-Qada'*, Edited by Muhyi Hilal Al-Sarhan, Al-Irshad Press, Baghdad, 1st Edition, 1404 AH / 1984 CE.
5. Al-Shafi'i, Abu Abdullah Muhammad Ibn Idris (*Kitab Al-Umm*), Dar Al-Fikr, Beirut, 1413 AH / 1983 CE.
6. Al-Haythami, Shihab Al-Din Ahmad Ibn Hajar Al-Haythami, *Tuhfat Al-Muhtaj Bisharh Al-Minhaj*, with marginal notes by Al-Sharwani and Ibn Al-Qasim, Dar Sadir, Beirut.

Hanbali Jurisprudence:

1. Ibn Qudamah, Abu Muhammad Muwaffaq Al-Din Abdullah Ibn Qudamah Al-Maqdisi, *Al-Mughni*, Dar Al-Kitab Al-Arabi, Beirut, 1392 AH / 1972 CE.
2. Ibn Al-Qayyim, Shams Al-Din Muhammad Ibn Abi Bakr Ibn Qayyim Al-Jawziyya, *A'lam Al-Muwaqqi'in 'Inda Rabb Al-'Alamin*, Dar Al-Jeel, Beirut, 1973 CE.
3. Al-Zarkashi, Shams Al-Din Muhammad Ibn Abdullah Al-Zarkashi, *Sharh Al-Zarkashi 'Ala Mukhtasar Al-Kharafi*, Maktabat Al-'Ubikan, Saudi Arabia, 1st Edition, 1993 CE.
4. Al-Farra', Abu Ya'la Muhammad Ibn Al-Husayn Al-Farra', *Al-Ahkam Al-Sultaniyya*, Ahmad Bin Sa'id Library Company, Dar Al-Fikr, Beirut, 1394 AH / 1974 CE.

Hanafi Jurisprudence:

1. Ibn Abidin, Muhammad Amin Al-Shahir Bil-Ibn Abidin, *Al-'Uqud Al-Durriyya Taniqih Al-Fatawa Al-Hamidiyya*, Al-Matba'a Al-Amiriya Bi Bulak, Egypt, 1300 AH.
2. Ibn Al-Bazzaz, Hafiz Al-Din Muhammad Ibn Muhammad Ibn Shihab, known as Ibn Al-Bazzar Al-Kurdi Al-Hanafi, *Al-Fatawa Al-Bazzaziyya*, published with margin notes on *Al-Fatawa Al-Hindiya*, Dar Al-Fikr, Beirut, 2nd Edition, 1411 AH / 1991 CE.
3. Al-Zil'i, Fakhr Al-Din Uthman Ibn Ali Al-Zil'i, *Tabyin Al-Haqa'iq Sharh Kanz Al-Daqa'iq*, Dar Al-Kitab Al-Islami, Cairo, 2nd Edition.
4. Al-Sarakhsi, Shams Al-A'immah Al-Radi, *Al-Mabsut*, Dar Al-Ma'rifa, Beirut, 3rd Edition.

5. Al-Kasani, 'Ala' Al-Din Abu Bakr Mas'ud Al-Kasani, *Bada'i' Al-Sana'i' Fi Tartib Al-Shara'i'*, Dar Al-Kutub Al-Ilmiyya, Beirut, 2nd Edition, 1406 AH / 1986 CE.

Usul Al-Fiqh Books:

1. Al-Ghazali, Abu Hamid Muhammad Ibn Muhammad Al-Ghazali, *Al-Mustasfa Min 'Ilm Al-Usul*, Dar Sadir, Beirut.
2. Al-Shatibi, Abu Ishaq Ibrahim Ibn Musa Al-Lakhmi Al-Gharnati, *Al-Muwafaqat Fi Usul Al-Sharia*, Dar Al-Kutub Al-Ilmiyya, Beirut.
3. Abu Zahra, Muhammad Abu Zahra, *Usul Al-Fiqh*, Dar Al-Fikr Al-Arabi, Egypt.

Terminology Books:

1. Union of Arabic Scientific Academies, *Legal Terminologies*.
2. Sulayman, Al-Harthi, *Legal Dictionary*.
3. Girgis, Girgis Girgis, *Legal Dictionary*.

Legal Books:

- Al-Husseini, Medhat, *Bankruptcy*, Dar Al-Matbou'at Al-Jam'iyya, Alexandria, 1993.
- Al-Sanhouri, Abdul Razzaq, *Al-Wasit Fi Sharh Al-Qanun Al-Madani*, Dar Ihya Al-Turath Al-Arabi, Beirut.
- Ahmed, Nafei, *Al-Iqta'a Al-Shar'i Fi Al-Shar', Al-Qanun, Wa Al-Fiqh*, Dar Al-Ma'rifa, Cairo, 2006.
- Tawfiq, Al-Bayoumi, *Al-Qanun Al-Madani Al-Jadid*, Dar Al-Fikr, Cairo, 1984.
- Bassiouni, M. Cherif, *International Criminal Law*, Martinus Nijhoff Publishers, 1999.
- Rawlinson, Alan, *Bankruptcy Law*, Sweet & Maxwell, 2003.
- Johnson, Herbert A., *Company Law*, Oxford University Press, 2005.
- Al-Gharbawi, Kamal, *The Legal Regulation of Companies*, Al-Nahda Al-Arabiya Library, Cairo, 1992.

Legislation:

- Sudanese Companies Bankruptcy Law of 1929.
- Sudanese Companies Law No. 24 of 1925, amended in 2015.

- Civil Transactions Law of 1984.
- Commercial Law.
- Sudanese Labor Law.
- Sudanese Criminal Law.
- Law of Evidence in Civil and Commercial Transactions.
- Sudanese Constitution (various versions).

Theses and Dissertations:

- Hassan, Ayman Mohamed, *The Regulation of Corporate Insolvency in Sudan*, PhD thesis, University of Khartoum, 2017.
- Abdallah, Noor Hassan, *The Impact of Bankruptcy Law on Investment Environment*, Master's thesis, University of Khartoum, 2019.
- Al-Tayeb, Fatima Ahmed, *Legal Challenges of Company Liquidation in Sudan*, Master's thesis, University of Khartoum, 2021.

Academic Research and Articles:

- Ahmed, Salih, "The Role of Bankruptcy Law in Economic Stability," *Sudanese Law Journal*, Vol. 12, Issue 3, 2018.
- Mohamed, Eman, "Fraudulent Bankruptcy and Its Legal Consequences," *Journal of Commercial Law*, 2020.
- Ali, Hassan, "Legal Mechanisms for Restructuring Companies in Sudan," *University of Khartoum Law Review*, 2022.

www.ingramcontent.com/pod-product-compliance
Lightning Source LLC
LaVergne TN
LVHW052254200926
848481LV00002B/363
* 9 7 9 8 8 9 9 6 6 4 8 7 8 *